New Frontiers in Regional Science: Asian Perspectives

Volume 28

New Frontiers in Regional Science: Asian Perspectives

This series is a constellation of works by scholars in the field of regional science and in related disciplines specifically focusing on dynamism in Asia.

Asia is the most dynamic part of the world. Japan, Korea, Taiwan, and Singapore experienced rapid and miracle economic growth in the 1970s. Malaysia, Indonesia, and Thailand followed in the 1980s. China, India, and Vietnam are now rising countries in Asia and are even leading the world economy. Due to their rapid economic development and growth, Asian countries continue to face a variety of urgent issues including regional and institutional unbalanced growth, environmental problems, poverty amidst prosperity, an ageing society, the collapse of the bubble economy, and deflation, among others.

Asian countries are diversified as they have their own cultural, historical, and geographical as well as political conditions. Due to this fact, scholars specializing in regional science as an inter- and multi-discipline have taken leading roles in providing mitigating policy proposals based on robust interdisciplinary analysis of multifaceted regional issues and subjects in Asia. This series not only will present unique research results from Asia that are unfamiliar in other parts of the world because of language barriers, but also will publish advanced research results from those regions that have focused on regional and urban issues in Asia from different perspectives.

The series aims to expand the frontiers of regional science through diffusion of intrinsically developed and advanced modern regional science methodologies in Asia and other areas of the world. Readers will be inspired to realize that regional and urban issues in the world are so vast that their established methodologies still have space for development and refinement, and to understand the importance of the interdisciplinary and multidisciplinary approach that is inherent in regional science for analyzing and resolving urgent regional and urban issues in Asia.

Topics under consideration in this series include the theory of social cost and benefit analysis and criteria of public investments, socio-economic vulnerability against disasters, food security and policy, agro-food systems in China, industrial clustering in Asia, comprehensive management of water environment and resources in a river basin, the international trade bloc and food security, migration and labor market in Asia, land policy and local property tax, Information and Communication Technology planning, consumer "shop-around" movements, and regeneration of downtowns, among others.

Researchers who are interested in publishing their books in this Series should obtain a proposal form from Yoshiro Higano (Editor in Chief, higano@jsrsai.jp) and return the completed form to him.

More information about this series at http://www.springer.com/series/13039

João Romão

Tourism, Territory and Sustainable Development

Theoretical Foundations and Empirical
Applications in Japan and Europe

 Springer

João Romão
Centre for Advanced Studies in Management and Economics
University of Algarve
Faro, Portugal

Regional Economics and Business Network
Hokkaido University
Sapporo, Japan

ISSN 2199-5974   ISSN 2199-5982   (electronic)
New Frontiers in Regional Science: Asian Perspectives
ISBN 978-981-13-0425-5   ISBN 978-981-13-0426-2   (eBook)
https://doi.org/10.1007/978-981-13-0426-2

Library of Congress Control Number: 2018940531

Printed on acid-free paper

This Springer imprint is published by the registered company Springer Nature Singapore Pte Ltd.
The registered company address is: 152 Beach Road, #21-01/04 Gateway East, Singapore 189721,
Singapore

Preface

This book is the result of an extensive and diversified research work undertaken since the completion of my Ph.D. (2012), covering a large set of topics on the spatial-economic aspects of tourism, with different territorial levels in different countries. Most of these works are briefly summarized along the book, comprising 15 case studies complementing the theoretical and conceptual analysis presented.

During these 6 years, I had the privilege to cooperate with a diversified group of researchers, with different nationalities and working in different parts of the world. The diversity of these working experiences in different countries and cultural contexts clearly contributed to enrich my knowledge, while opening the opportunity to develop the comprehensive analysis of contemporary tourism dynamics offered in this book. I am extremely grateful to all of them.

In particular, Peter Nijkamp (Tinbergen Institute, the Netherlands) has been a permanent source of support and inspiration for my career. His continuous proposals to develop new research topics, his critical observations, suggestions and remarks, and his motivation to participate actively in a large part of my empirical studies were crucial to all my academic work. This close collaboration is clearly expressed through Peter's participation in 10 of the case studies presented in the book (2.1, 2.3, 3.3, 3.4, 4.1, 4.2, 4.3, 4.4, 5.3, and 5.4).

Another long, regular, and enriching collaboration I had the opportunity to develop was with Bart Neuts (Auckland University of Technology, New Zealand), who complements his interest in the tourism sector with a deep knowledge on advanced econometric methods. Bart was involved in 7 of the case studies presented (2.1, 3.3, 3.4, 4.1, 4.2, 4.4, and 5.2), developing the sophisticated and useful econometric models applied in all of them.

I am also grateful to *Fundação para a Ciência e Tecnologia* (FCT, Portugal) for supporting a significant part of the research conducting to the publication of this book through a post-doctoral research grant (BPD/98938/2013), under supervision of João Guerreiro (University of Algarve, Portugal) and Paulo MM Rodrigues (Nova School of Business and Economics, Portugal). They also contributed actively for the articles presented as case studies 2.2 (whose econometric model was developed by Rodrigues) and 3.2.

With less regular collaborations, I would like to thank all the other co-authors who have participated in the production of the case studies presented along the book. Asami Shikida, from Japan Advanced Institute of Science and Technology, Japan (2.1, 3.3, and 4.1); Eveline van Leeuwen, from Wageningen University, the Netherlands (3.4 and 4.2); Kazuo Machino, from Hokkaido University, Japan (5.3 and 5.4); Karima Kourtit, from Jheronimus Academy of Data Science, the Netherlands (4.4); and Hisamitsu Saito, from Hokkaido University, Japan (5.1).

The collaboration with different Japanese researchers and the study of diverse aspects of tourism in Japan would not have been possible without the invitation from Hokkaido University to work as a Special Appointed Lecturer. I am deeply honored for having this opportunity.

Finally, I would like to thank all my family in Portugal for their permanent personal support during very long stays in Japan over the last 3 years. And I would like to dedicate this book to my wife, who made my life in Japan, not only possible and productive, but also extremely beautiful:

to Maki, with love!

Sapporo, Japan   João Romão

Contents

Chapter 1
Introduction

Contents

Abstract This book offers a comprehensive, systematic, and critical conceptual overview of the spatial-economic aspects of contemporary tourism dynamics, establishing connections with other disciplines with relevancy for tourism studies, such as geography, environmental sciences, management, marketing, anthropology, or urban studies. This conceptual analysis is complemented with practical examples related to empirical applications recently undertaken by the author. Although the work does not focus on quantitative methods of analysis, appropriate references for related quantitative approaches are presented for each of the topics under analysis.

By combining an extensive literature review on the abundant existing research for each topic discussed along the book with institutional analyses and guidelines defined by different organizations with relevant work in the field of tourism (United Nations World Tourism Organization, World Economic Forum, UNESCO, ICOMOS, OECD, or European Commission), this work offers a policy- and managerial-oriented perspective on the spatial aspects of tourism, including resource management, innovation dynamics, marketing issues, economic impacts, or the relation with processes of sustainable development.

The study of tourism as an economic activity has recently gained renewed attention, as tourism assumes a larger importance in the global economy. According to recent data, more than 1 billion international arrivals were registered for the first time in 2012, and this number has continuously increased since then, reaching 1,322 billion in 2017 (UNWTO 2018). Currently, estimates suggest that 10% of the world GDP, 7% of the international exports, and 30% of the global exports of services are related to the tourism sector, which employs 10% of global workforce. As it will be discussed, although these estimations may raise different questions related to

© Springer Nature Singapore Pte Ltd. 2018
J. Romão, *Tourism, Territory and Sustainable Development*, New Frontiers in Regional Science: Asian Perspectives 28,
https://doi.org/10.1007/978-981-13-0426-2_1

methodological problems, it is noteworthy that tourism is today a major economic activity at the international level.

Developments in transportation services, networks, and infrastructures, increase in discretionary income, larger holiday periods, and higher importance of leisure time in contemporary lifestyles clearly contributed to this development of tourism. The example of China, becoming the third largest issuing country in the world in 2016, clearly shows the importance of a strong economic dynamics and the increase in personal revenues to boost tourism activities. At the same time, tourism is reaching new areas and destinations: the global market share of the emerging economies in 2016 was 45% (26% in 1995), while the Asia-Pacific region registered 25% (16% in 1995), and Africa and the Middle East reached 9% (6% in 1995). Focusing on national destinations, the highest annual growth rates in 2016 were observed in Iceland (39%), South Korea (30%), Vietnam (26%), Chile (26%), or Japan (22%).

Despite this impressive contemporary dynamics, travelling and tourism are very ancient activities, as observed in detail by Butler (2015). Similarly, the study of temporary human flows with recreational or educational motivations and the corresponding choice of locations are documented for more than 2,000 years, involving different disciplines, like literature, anthropology, sociology, geography, environmental sciences, economy, or marketing. The close link between travel motivations and the specific characteristics of each place has been for long time an object of fascination and a motive for research. In contemporary societies, it is not surprising that regional economics or other spatial-oriented scientific approaches also give particular attention to the tourism sector.

In particular for the field of economics – including its spatial approaches, like regional economics or economic geography – the attention to tourism activities increased as tourism has become a more important economic activity. This importance can be now clearly observed at the global level, but it was already acknowledged in places where tourism plays a relevant role within the local or regional economic structures. Thus, different methods have been developed along the last decades in order to estimate the importance and impacts of tourism (Dwyer et al. 2004), both at the macro-level of the sectorial relations within the overall economic structure (*tourism satellite accounts*, *input-output* methods, or *computable general equilibrium* and *social account models*) and at the micro-level of the value of specific assets, infrastructures, or events (*hedonic prices* or *contingent valuation*). A discussion on the utilizations and limitations of these methodologies will constitute the starting point of Chap. 2.

A more specific discussion on the contribution of tourism for economic growth and the so-called *tourism-led growth* hypothesis (Adamou and Clerides 2010) will follow. Although this hypothesis appeared to be consensually accepted in the literature, recent works, taking advantage of the availability of longer series of data, have found ambiguous relations between tourism dynamics and economic growth, or even negative long-term impacts of tourism on regional growth, as a result of structural transformations within regional economic structures induced by tourism development. These variations along time on the economic impacts of tourism on the local and regional economic performances also emphasize the importance of taking into account the *tourism area life cycle* (Butler 1980) and its evolutionary aspects in each destination.

By combining the importance of place for the development of tourism activities with the importance of time (and history) for the analysis of its impacts on the destinations, different authors have recently pointed out the relevancy of the analytical contributions related to the *evolutionary economic geography* (Boschma and Martin 2010) to tourism studies (Brouder and Eriksson 2013). In particular, the concepts of *path dependence* (Martin 2014), defining how the current situation shapes and constrains future developments, and *relatedness* or *related variety* (Neffke et al. 2009; Boschma et al. 2016), discussing how the relations between different sectors can contribute for their reinforcement, can be particularly useful for the analysis of the role of tourism within regional economic structures.

The importance of the specific characteristics of each place influencing and shaping tourism dynamics will be discussed in Chap. 3. The role of natural resources is especially relevant in this case, as the ecological characteristics of destinations are – and they always have been – major determinants for the attractiveness of a destination. As these are very sensitive resources, whose utilization in the context of tourism requires their integration into products and services, problems of degradation or even destruction may arise. As observed by Williams and Ponsford (2009), tourism based on natural assets implies an *environmental paradox*, as it relies on the utilization of resources that, at the same time, must be preserved.

Similarly, cultural resources and heritage are also major aspects shaping the uniqueness of a destination while constituting a source for the supply of an *authentic* and differentiated tourism *experience* (Tussyadiah 2014). Nevertheless, as Cohen (1988) observes, their integration into tourism products and services is generally based on a simplified version of *authenticity*, adapted to the requirements of marketing strategies. Moreover, the perception of *authenticity* and local *identity* normally varies, not only among the visitors (with their different characteristics, cultural backgrounds, and motivations) but also within local communities (where residents may have different and eventually conflictual views on their own *identity*). Thus, the utilization of cultural heritage for tourism purposes – or in broader terms, for a process of regional development (Fusco-Girard and Nijkamp 2009) – implies a process of permanent *negotiation*, as it will be discussed.

In this context, the process of destination differentiation based on the uniqueness of its resources (which cannot be replicated elsewhere) implies the provision of interpretation tools for their utilization by different types of visitors, as pointed out by ICOMOS (2008). This aspect is emphasized by the importance of the immaterial aspects of cultural heritage, which appear as crucial elements of contemporary tourism experiences (UNESCO 2003; UNWTO 2003). Those interpretation tools are critical elements for the match between the processes of strategic differentiation and market segmentation, by contributing to the supply of adequate services for each market segment.

Chapter 4 will analyze the developments in information and communication technologies (ICT) observed in the last decades, with deep implications on the tourism sector (Buhalis and Law 2008) and in particular on the matching process between differentiation of destinations and market segmentation, contributing to the emergence of the concept of *co-creation* of experiences (Binkhorst and Dekker 2009). Through interactive processes based on the utilization of digital technologies, the supply of tourism services can be adapted to the specific needs of individual travellers, as it is also observed in other creative contemporary economic activities (OECD 2014; Scott 2017). Moreover, as pointed out by Sigala (2012), the generalization of the utilization of social networks (Web 2.0), increasingly based on mobile devices (Web 3.0), along with the easy access to multimedia tools, contributes to mediatization of tourism, as tourists become active elements shaping the image of destinations, based on their own perceptions (Mansson 2011).

Being noteworthy that tourism destinations comprise a large number of small and medium enterprises (SME), tourism services are provided by a large variety of different and independent companies comprising a decentralized value chain, while tourists constitute a multifaceted market, with different characteristics, perceptions, motivations, and needs. The interactive processes emerging between suppliers and consumers make the destination a repository of decentralized information, which may be used for innovative practices. Nevertheless, in general terms, SME do not have well-structured learning process to codify and to embed this information into new practices and services. Thus, *coopetition* processes (cooperation between rival companies) may emerge as potential useful tools to improve innovation capabilities at the destination level, as discussed by Boes et al. (2016), when proposing the concept of *smart tourism*.

In the context of the contemporary transformations in consumption and production systems, with the emergence of a *creative economy* (OECD 2014), where products tend to integrate cultural values and symbols and culture is increasingly commodified (Scott 2017), tourism appears to have high potential to reinforce solid connections with other sectors, not only those related to ICT but also to other creative activities, which may reinforce the unique cultural aspects of the destinations. Despite this potential, the relation between tourism dynamics and regional innovation capabilities seems to be weak, even in the context of the most advanced economies, as observed by Romão and Nijkamp (2017) in a recent study involving a large number of European regions.

Moreover, the increasing importance of urban tourism and the massive presence of tourists in cities are raising new problems, both regarding the shared use of spaces, facilities, and infrastructures, and related to the impacts on local markets (and particularly on the housing market). As a consequence, several recent studies apply to urban destinations theoretical approaches that had been previously used to address the impacts of tourism in coastal areas, when *sun and sea* tourism became massified. The *Irridex* (index of irritation) proposed by Doxey (1975) constitutes an early attempt to analyze this problematic relation between *hosts and guests*. Current approaches to address these problems include the analysis of different forms of community organization in face of excessive tourism development (Colomb and Navy 2017) or the implementation of participatory planning process at the local level (Barcelona City Council 2017), concluding the fourth chapter of this book.

Decision-making participatory processes are also at the core of the principles for sustainable development, a concept that received generalized recognition after the publication of *Our Common Future* (World Commission on Environment and Development 1987), being quickly adopted in tourism studies (Sharpley 2009), as discussed in Chap. 6. Initially linked to the idea of small-scale forms of tourism and focusing on the preservation of sensitive natural resources, it contributed for the emergence of new forms of tourism, like ecotourism, responsible tourism, cultural tourism, or, more recently, *wellness tourism* (Yeung and Johnston 2015), which receives particular attention in this book, due to its novelty. Nevertheless, Butler (1999) would emphasize the human aspects of sustainability and the importance of taking into consideration the socio-economic aspects of tourism development, thus addressing the three pillars of sustainable development (environmental, social, and economic). In a similar way, Jafari (2001) would claim that the principles of sustainability should underlie the analysis and planning of all types of tourism destination, including the areas where *mass tourism* prevails.

A comprehensive framework for the definition and implementation of policies and governance methods for sustainable tourism is proposed by David (2016), while different organizations have also addressed this question in the last decades. UNESCO (2000, 2005) has focused on the role of cultural heritage for sustainable tourism development, while broader perspectives on sustainable tourism were proposed by UNWTO (2013, 2015, 2017), also including an analysis of the specific potential impacts of tourism on the *Millennium Goals* proposed by the United Nations (2015), the definition of a framework for a quantitative assessment of sustainability in tourism, or even the creation of the International Year of Sustainable Tourism, in 2017. Despite these concerns, Mullis (2017) questions whether tourism can ever be sustainable, considering the large environmental impacts of air travel (5% of the global CO_2 emission, according to UNWTO 2013) or the necessary commodification of territorial resources.

Similarly to the idea of sustainability, the concept of competitiveness also emerged in the economic literature during the 1980s (Porter 1985), being adopted by tourism researchers and institutions during the 1990s. Again, competitiveness was initially linked to the idea of development of niche forms of tourism, with low-scale, high-value-added, and limited environmental impacts. Nevertheless, Ritchie and Crouch (2003) would later on claim that the concepts of competitiveness and sustainability are necessarily linked when observing tourism dynamics with a long-term perspective while defining a systematic framework for the analysis of the structural conditions affecting the competitiveness of destinations. Similarly, the European Commission (2007) would also propose guidelines for a sustainable and competitive tourism sector.

Difficulties in implementing appropriate methods for the comparison of the competitiveness of tourism destinations (mostly related to the absence of comparable data at the international level) imply that most of the studies focus on the national level (World Economic Forum 2017). Nevertheless, when adopting an explanatory perspective (Mazanek et al. 2007), by linking input indicators related to tourism resources to output indicators related to the performance of the sector, it is possible to analyze other territorial scales, like the region (Cracolici and Nijkamp 2008; Romão and Nijkamp 2017; Romão and Saito 2017), even if the generalization to regions with different methodologies for data collection and available indicators remains problematic.

It also noteworthy the many resources attracting tourists to a destination (nature, landscapes, cultural heritage, lifestyles, etc.) can be framed within the *common pool resources* approach, as observed by Briassoulis (2002). Thus, although the economic benefits of tourism are subject to private appropriation (to a large extent, within the transportation and accommodation sectors), most of the resources determining the attractiveness of a destination are commonly produced or used by a local community. As noted by Olstrom (2011), this unequal share of benefits (appropriation problem) is a general problematic characteristic of the commons. Other problems relate to the *free-ride* (leading to overuse) or the lack of incentives for preservation (leading to degradation) of communal resources. These aspects, which did not receive much attention within the economic literature (Scott 2017), reinforce the importance of community involvement into strategic planning processes for tourism development and resource management.

The concluding chapter of this book is based on the identification of several problems in the contemporary dynamics of tourism activities, observed through five empirical studies comprising a large number of European regions (237, at least), with different levels of economic development, innovation capabilities, natural endowment, or tourism specialization patterns. As four of these studies are based on spatial econometric methods, it is also possible to identify different spatial patterns, agglomeration processes, or spatial heterogeneity along the regions under analysis. These studies focus on the relation between the material regional resources (natural or cultural) and tourism performance (Romão 2015; Romão et al. 2017); the impacts of immaterial resources on regional tourism competitiveness (Romão and Nijkamp 2017); the relation between territorial capital, tourism dynamics, and regional economic performance (Romão and Nijkamp Forthcoming); and finally an enlargement of the later analysis to the impacts on the three pillars of sustainable development (Romão and Neuts 2017), in this case by using a structural equations model. These five studies are also briefly presented as case studies along this book. As they are based on a broad set of very diverse European regions, the results can be generalized to other parts of the world.

By combining the theoretical formulations discussed along the book with the results obtained in these empirical studies, a conceptual framework is proposed in order to address the main problems identified. This framework is based on the concepts of *authenticity, significance*, the *environmental paradox, smart tourism, co-creation* of destinations and experiences, the role of information for the segmentation of markets and differentiation of supply, the *life cycle of tourism destinations, path dependence* processes, and the importance of history, variety, specialization, or *integrative diversification* of tourism products. Finally, a set of challenges for the future of tourism – to be addressed at policy and managerial levels – is discussed, based on the conceptual framework proposed. These challenges relate to the provision of memorable trips oriented to personalized and significant experiences based on a sustainable use of territorial resources, the promotion of diverse and balanced regional economies by reinforcing the interrelations between the tourism sector and the overall creative economy, and the implementation of effective processes of participatory governance for the definition of sustainable development strategies.

Based on a comprehensive theoretical approach combined with relevant empirical studies for all the questions under analysis, this book offers a systematic overview of contemporary tourism dynamics, which can be used by students, researchers, and teachers with interest in tourism studies or regional science. Moreover, by linking academic research with policy and managerial guidelines defined by the most relevant international institutions operating in the tourism sector, the book also offers relevant insights for tourism managers and planners, both at the private and the public sectors. Despite the focus on the economic aspects of tourism and the advanced methods and conceptual frameworks presented, all the analyses and discussions are supported by clear explanations of the technical concepts involved, not requiring previous specialized knowledge in economics or tourism, while establishing clear connections with other disciplines and opening new questions for further research. Thus, the book aims at offering advanced analytical tools for all those interested in tourism dynamics in the context of contemporary regional socio-economic structures and innovation systems. Figure 1.1 offers a general overview of the structure of the book.

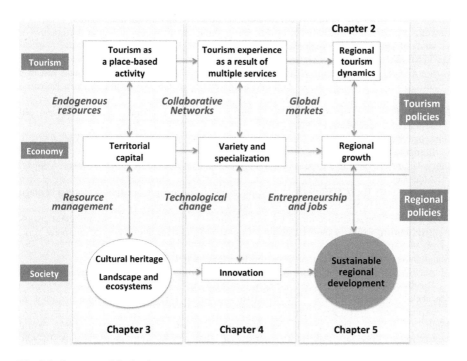

Fig. 1.1 Structure of the book

References

Adamou A, Clerides S (2010) Prospects and limits of tourism-led growth: the international evidence. Rev Econ Anal 3:287–303

Barcelona City Council (2017) Barcelona tourism for 2020 a collective strategy for sustainable tourism. Ajuntament de Barcelona, Barcelona

Binkhorst E, Dekker T (2009) Towards the co-creation tourism experience? Journal of Hospitality Marketing and Management 18(2–3):311–327

Boes K, Buhalis D, Inversini A (2016) Smart tourism destinations: ecosystems for tourism destination competitiveness. Int J Tour Cities 2(2):108–124

Boschma R, Martin R (2010) The aims and scope of evolutionary economic geography. In: Boschma R, Martin R (eds) The handbook of evolutionary economic geography. Edward Elgar, Cheltenham, pp 3–39

Boschma R, Coenen L, Frenken K, Truffer B (2016) Towards a theory of regional diversification. Papers in Evolutionary Economic Geography 16:17

Briassoulis H (2002) Sustainable tourism and the question of commons. Ann Tour Res 29(4):1065–1085

Brouder P, Eriksson R (2013) Tourism evolution: on the synergies of tourism studies and evolutionary economic geography. Ann Tour Res 43:370–389

Buhalis D, Law R (2008) Progress in information technology and tourism management. Tour Manage 29:609–623

Butler R (1980) The concept of a tourism area life cycle of evolution: implications for management of resources. Can Geogr 24(1):5–12

Butler R (1999) Sustainable tourism: a state-of-the-art review. Tour Geogr 1(1):7–25

Butler R (2015) The evolution of tourism and tourism research. Tour Recreat Res 40(1):16–27

Cohen E (1988) Authenticity and commoditization in tourism. Ann Tour Res 15:371–386

Colomb C, Navy J (2017) Protest and resistance in the tourist city. Routledge, London

Cracolici M, Nijkamp P (2008) The attractiveness and competitiveness of tourist destinations: a study of southern Italian regions. Tour Manage 30:336–344

David LE (2016) Managing sustainable tourism, 2nd edn. Routledge, New York

Doxey G (1975) A causation theory of visitor-resident irritants: methodology and research inferences. Proceedings of the 6th annual conference of the Travel and Tourism Research Association. Travel and Tourism Research Association, San Diego

Dwyer L, Forsyth P, Spurr R (2004) Evaluating tourism's economic effects: new and old approaches. Tour Manage 25:307–317

European Commission (2007) Agenda for a sustainable and competitive European tourism. European Commission, Luxembourg

Fusco-Girard L, Nijkamp P (2009) Cultural tourism and sustainable local development. Ashgate, Aldershot

ICOMOS (2008) The ICOMOS charter for the interpretation and presentation of cultural heritage sites. Ratified by the 16th General Assembly of ICOMOS, Québec

Jafari J (2001) The scientification of tourism. In: Smith V, Brent M (eds) Hosts and guests revisited: tourism issues of the 21st century. Cognizant Communication Corporation, New York, pp 28–41

Mansson M (2011) Mediatized tourism. Ann Tour Res 38(4):1634–1652

Martin R (2014) Path dependence and the spatial economy. In: Fischer M, Nijkamp P (eds) Handbook of regional sciences. Springer, New York, pp 609–629

Mazanek J, Wober K, Zins A (2007) Tourism destination competitiveness: from definition to explanation? J Travel Res 46:86–95

Mullis B (2017) The growth paradox: can tourism ever be sustainable?. World Economic Forum. Available online at https://www.weforum.org/agenda/2017/08/the-growth-paradox-can-tourism-ever-be-sustainable/

Neffke F, Henning M, Boschma R (2009) How do regions diversify over time? Industry relatedness and the development of new growth paths in regions. Econ Geogr 87(3):237–265

OECD (2014) Tourism and the creative economy. OECD, Paris

Olstrom E (2011) Background on the institutional analysis and development framework. Policy Stud J 39(1):7–27

Porter M (1985) Competitive advantage – creating and sustaining superior performance. The Free Press, New York

Ritchie J, Crouch G (2003) The competitive destination: a sustainable tourism perspective. CABI International, Oxfordshire

Romão J (2015) Culture or nature: a space-time analysis on the determinants of tourism demand in European regions. Discussion Papers Spatial and Organizational Dynamics 14

Romão J, Neuts B (2017) Smart tourism, territorial capital, and sustainable regional development: experiences from Europe. Habitat Int 68:64–74

Romão J, Nijkamp P (2017) A spatial econometric analysis of impacts of innovation, productivity and agglomeration on tourism competitiveness. Curr Issues Tour. https://doi.org/10.1080/136 83500.2017.1366434

Romão J, Nijkamp P (Forthcoming) Spatial impacts assessment of tourism and territorial capital: a modelling study on regional development in Europe

Romão J, Saito H (2017) A spatial econometric analysis on the determinants of tourism. Competitiveness in Japanese prefectures. Asia Pac J Reg Sci 1(1):243–264

Romão J, Guerreiro J, Rodrigues PMM (2017) Territory and sustainable tourism development: a space-time analysis on European regions. Region 4(3):1–17

Scott AJ (2017) The constitution of the city. Palgrave Macmillan, Cham

Sharpley R (2009) Tourism development and the environment: beyond sustainability? Earthscan, London

Sigala M (2012) Exploiting web 2.0 for new service development: findings and implications from the Greek tourism industry. Int J Tour Res 14:551–566

Tussyadiah IP (2014) Toward a theoretical foundation for experience design in tourism. J Travel Res 53(5):543–564

UNESCO (2000) Sustainable tourism and the environment. UNESCO, Paris

UNESCO (2003) Convention for the safeguarding of the intangible cultural heritage. UNESCO, Paris

UNESCO (2005) World Heritage Centre – sustainable tourism programme. UNESCO, Paris

United Nations (2015) Transforming our world: the 2030 agenda for sustainable development. A/RES/70/1, resolution adopted by the general assembly on 25 September 2015 (New York)

UNWTO (2003) Study on tourism and intangible cultural heritage. UNWTO, Madrid

UNWTO (2013) Sustainable tourism for development guidebook. UNWTO, Madrid

UNWTO (2015) Tourism and the sustainable development goals. UNWTO, Madrid

UNWTO (2017) Measuring sustainable tourism. UNWTO, Madrid

UNWTO (2018) World tourism barometer. UNWTO, Madrid

Williams P, Ponsford I (2009) Confronting tourism's environmental paradox: transitioning for sustainable tourism. Futures 41:396–404

World Commission on Environment and Development (1987) Our common future. Oxford University Press, Oxford

World Economic Forum (2017) The travel & tourism competitiveness report 2017. World Economic Forum, Geneva

Yeung O, Johnston K (2015) The global wellness tourism economy report 2013 and 2014. Global Wellness Institute, Miami

Chapter 2
Tourism Economic Impacts

Contents

Abstract Tourism is following a path of sustained growth at the global level, with important socio-economic impacts all over the world, justifying a critical discussion on the existing methods (and limitations) for their estimation (*tourism satellite accounts*, *input-output* methods, or *computable general equilibrium* and *social account models*), along with an overview and analysis of different techniques to assess the economic value of nonmarketable tourism-related assets, like nature or cultural heritage (*hedonic prices* or *contingent valuation*) or immaterial valuable aspects (like the *loyalty* of visitors). The communal character of many tourism resources, with the consequent appropriation and provision problems characterizing the *common pool resources*, is also discussed. A more specific discussion on the contribution of tourism for economic growth (*tourism-led growth* hypothesis) and

---

Case study 2.1: Market Segmentation and Tourism Economic Impacts
Neuts B, Romão J, Nijkamp P, Shikida A (2016) Market segmentation and their economic impacts in an ecotourism destination: An applied modelling study on Hokkaido, Japan. Tourism Economics 22(4):793-808
Case study 2.2: Tourism and Regional Resilience
Romão J, Guerreiro J, Rodrigues P (2016) Tourism Growth and Regional Resilience: the "Beach Disease" and the Consequences of the Global Crisis of 2007. Tourism Economics 22(4):699-714
Case study 2.3: Tourism and Regional Growth
Romão J, Nijkamp P (forthcoming) Spatial Impacts Assessment of Tourism and Territorial Capital: A Modelling Study on Regional Development in Europe

© Springer Nature Singapore Pte Ltd. 2018   11
J. Romão, *Tourism, Territory and Sustainable Development*, New Frontiers
in Regional Science: Asian Perspectives 28,
https://doi.org/10.1007/978-981-13-0426-2_2

its limitations in the long run is framed within the consideration of the historical dimension of tourism development, through the analysis of the evolutionary aspects of the life cycle of tourism destinations, including potential negative long-term consequences of specialization in tourism. In this context, the analytic contributions related to the *evolutionary economic geography*, emphasizing the roles of place and time, emerge as useful tools for the study of the economic dynamics of tourism in contemporary societies, mostly when discussing the role of tourism within the context of a regional economy and its relations with other sectors, activities, and innovation dynamics.

Keywords Tourism economic impacts · Economic growth · Resilience · Tourism Area Life Cycle · Evolutionary economic geography · Path dependence

2.1 Introduction

For the first time in human history, more than 1 billion international arrivals were globally registered in 2012. Since then, this number continued to grow continuously, clearly revealing the increasing importance of tourism and leisure in contemporary societies and economies. According to UNWTO (2018), 1.322 billion international tourist arrivals were registered in the world in 2017, a figure that is expected to reach 1.8 billion until 2030.

The importance of tourism is clearly linked to the development of transportation services, networks, and infrastructures but also to the relevant increase in the discretionary income of families observed since the second part of the twentieth century, along with an increase of the holiday periods and leisure time. It is noteworthy that China became the third largest issuing country in the world in 2016, clearly reflecting the recent economic dynamics of the country, with its positive impacts on wages, well-being, and willingness to travel. In fact, tourism consumption tends to reveal a very high elasticity, with strong reactions to variations in price (due to the high competition between destinations at the global level) and in the revenues (as tourism is not a primary need, as it would be housing, food, or health care).

Along with this rising importance, tourism is also reaching new territories and destinations, with the emerging economies receiving 45% of the international air travellers in 2016 (36% in 1995). In particular, the Asia-Pacific region (growing from 16% to 25% during the same period) and Africa and the Middle East (6–9%) conquered important shares of the global tourism market to the American (21–16%) and the European (58–50%) continents. Moreover, at the national level, the destinations where the highest growth rates were observed in 2016 were Iceland (39%), South Korea (30%), Vietnam (26%), Chile (26%), and Japan (22%) – clearly not the main national tourism destinations in the world.

This continuous growth has also important impacts on the global economy. The estimates offered by UNWTO (2018) for 2017 suggest that 10% of the world GDP, 7% of the international exports, and 30% of the global exports of services are related to tourism activities, while this sector employs 10% of the workers in the world. Even if these estimations are often questioned – in fact, there is no precise definition of the tourism sector within the national economic accounts – it seems clear that tourism plays a major role within contemporary economies and societies.

Tourism destinations comprise a wide range of activities, which include accommodation, transportation, and food services but also retail, entertainment, educational, cultural, or environmental services. Clearly, most of the times these products and services – and also the related facilities and infrastructures – are used and consumed both by residents and tourists in each particular destination. This represents a potential source of conflicts (as it will be discussed in Chaps. 4 and 5), while also imposing relevant difficulties in order to measure with precision what are the effective economic impacts of tourism.

Even the most conventional tourism services, like those related to accommodation, are today commonly shared with local residents in many tourism destinations. The emergence, development, and expansion of online platforms for house sharing significantly enlarged the scope of tourism accommodation, with a large supply of housing solutions being offered beyond the conventional hotel services. While creating new opportunities and solutions for travellers, along with new opportunities for an increased revenue to house owners, these services have also revealed different types of problems, related to local inflationary processes in housing costs or house scarcity for local residents. Moreover, the difficulties to control and to measure the revenues generated by these new and emergent market segments increase the difficulties to estimate the economic benefits and impacts related to tourism, even within the most conventional services offered by this sector.

Similar difficulties are observed in transportation services within tourism destinations, as these are also – most of the times – shared with the local population. Despite the possible existence of different means of transportation specially oriented to tourists (like sightseeing buses or touristic trains), the utilization of public transport networks by tourists is also a common practice. This also implies some potential conflicts with the daily utilization by residents (as the movements of tourists are less regular and predictable) and introduces a new difficulty when estimating the effective impact of tourism dynamics on local economies.

Even more problematic is the estimation of tourism impacts on the regular activity of restaurants, retail shops, museums, cultural events and festivals, natural parks or other open-air activities, and nightlife or other entertainment services. Additionally, it is normally observed that the presence of tourists is not homogeneously distributed along the year, and it tends to concentrate in some parts of the cities or towns. Moreover, when analyzing the economic impacts of tourism at the national level, it must be considered that each city, town, or rural area has a different pattern of tourism dynamics. Thus, the estimation of the impacts and value of the

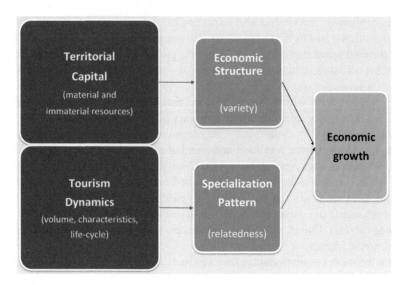

Fig. 2.1 Tourism, regional economic structures, and economic growth

tourism sector generally relies on methodologies and assumptions that require a very careful interpretation of results, mostly when comparing different countries.

This chapter will offer an overview of the methods and techniques currently used to evaluate different types of economic impacts of tourism (Sect. 2.2). Assuming that the impacts of tourism tend be different along the historical evolution of a tourism destination, Sect. 2.3 will focus on the concept of *Tourism Area Life Cycle* (as defined by Butler 1980). These variations along the life cycle of destinations will be taken into consideration in Sect. 2.4, when focusing the attention on the relations between tourism dynamics and economic growth. Finally – and considering the interconnections between the tourism sector and other economic activities – Sect. 2.5 will explore the potential contributions of evolutionary economic geography, with its emphasis on the role of history and geography. The main ideas presented and discussed along this chapter will be summarized in Sect. 2.6, and three case studies will be presented in order to illustrate some of the concepts presented and discussed. The diagram in Fig. 2.1 represents the impacts of tourism on economic growth, mediated by its role within the regional economic structures. As it will be discussed, this mediation – and its evolution along time – is a crucial aspect for the achievement of relevant economic benefits in tourism destinations.

2.2 Measuring Economic Impacts of Tourism

Despite the problems and limitations mentioned before, especially when related to international studies and comparisons, it is noteworthy that the awareness of national and international tourism-related institutions for the importance of a precise estimation of the economic impacts of tourism is generally increasing, along with the necessary resources required for this kind of analysis. Moreover, the methodologies for data collection and analysis are also becoming more sophisticated and precise. In fact, a correct evaluation of the impacts of tourism for local, regional, and national economies is an important tool, not only for tourism policies (marketing, infrastructures, or investment plans) but also within the broader context of development plans, where tourism can play a relevant role, in interconnection with other economic sectors.

In order to overcome some of these problems, many countries implemented *tourism satellite accounts,* which aim at identifying, for each economic sector in a national or regional economy, the importance of tourism activities. This is normally done by using surveys in each destination, in order to distinguish the consumption from residents and nonresidents, implying that not all the countries apply the same methodologies or devote similar resources for the implementation of such a tool. In fact, many countries did not even implement these satellite accounts. Thus, any international estimation or comparison of the economic impacts of tourism always relies on questionable methodologies and assumptions.

In this context, different methodologies have been used along the last decades to estimate the economic impacts of tourism within a local, regional, or national economy. One of these methods relies on the utilization of input-output tables, where the relations of consumption and production between the different sectors are defined through a set of fixed parameters (the technical coefficients, which define the amount of a given product required for the production of another product), which allow the estimation of the impact of an increase (decrease) of the production in one sector on the interrelated sectors. These input-output methods allow the consideration of direct effects (consumption of tourism products and services), indirect effects (inputs required to other services for the supply of tourism products and services), and induced effects (consumption made by the workers employed in the tourism sector). Implicit to this analysis is the idea that tourism consumption has a multiplier effect on the local economies (related to the indirect and induced impacts), which depends on the type of relations created between the tourism sector and the overall economic structure, as observed by Crompton et al. (2016).

The estimation of this kind of table implies high costs (including time), and often they are not available at the regional or local levels. Moreover, even if they are available, they are normally not updated in a yearly basis, which implies possible errors in the technical coefficients, once technological or organizational developments with impacts on productivity normally imply changes in those coefficients. Other limitations of this model (like the restrictions of mobility of products and production factors between sectors, demand constrains, or feedback effects) have been addressed in the recent years, improving its reliability. Polo and Valle (2012) offer a detailed overview of these methods.

Input-output tables can also be embedded into social account models (SAM) and/ or computable general equilibrium (CGE) optimization models, which provide estimations for the optimal solutions within an economic system when facing an external shock (like an increase in tourism demand). Although the estimation methods are different, the critical remarks about the temporal stability of the technical coefficients of the input-output tables still remain. A critical review of these methods can be found in Dwyer, Forsyth, and Spurr (2004).

These methods (input-output, SAM, or CGE) can also be used to estimate the economic impact of a specific event or a new facility, in order to support decision-making processes related to investments in tourism. Other types of economic evaluation of tourism assets relate to natural parks, landscapes, or monuments, which are (normally) not object of market transactions. In these cases, it is especially important to estimate, not only the use value of those assets (the expected value each user assigns to the asset) but also the non-use values (like the ecological or cultural importance of the resources), as pointed out, among others, by Andersson, Armbrecht, and Lundberg (2012).

These values are object of different classifications in the literature, as noted by Lee and Han (2002) or Choi et al. (2015), who propose to distinguish three different types of perceived values: functional value (related to the difference between estimated costs and benefits), emotional value (related to the affective relation with the asset), and reputational value (related to the reputation of the site or event). It is noteworthy that both the use and non-use values are subjective and depending on the characteristics, motivations, or perceptions of different users, requiring exhaustive surveys, involving different types of stakeholders. As an example, Saayman and Saayman (2014) point out income, education, age, nationality, marital status, children, revenues, or professional situation as factors influencing the subjectivity of perceived value for different users.

Generally originating from environmental studies but currently also applied in the urban context, in particular for the economic assessment of cultural heritage, the most popular methods for evaluation of perceived value are presented in detail by Loomis (2014) or Weaver and Lawton (2007), with a more clear focus on the applications in tourism studies. With a wide utilization in this field, the *hedonic travel cost method* (Brown and Mendelsohn, 1984) considers the travel cost to a particular destination (as a form of revealed preference) in order to estimate the value of a particular asset. Despite its popularity, this method is not always easy to apply, once tourists are normally motivated by more than one attraction in a destination.

Other types of popular models are based on stated preferences, like the *contingent valuation method* (Wright and Eppink 2016), which is based on surveys aiming at identifying the willingness to pay for the visit to a particular place (normally with free access). By aggregating individual preferences, this method requires a large number of interviews to different types of users, once it is normal to observe large differences between individual stated preferences. Moreover, the stated willingness to pay is not necessarily the same as the effective payment that the visitor would make in case a real fee would be applied. On the other hand, different characteristics (education, income, age, etc.), perceptions, or motivations (quality or importance of the asset according to each person) clearly influence the individual stated preferences.

Despite their limitations, both methods (hedonic prices and stated preferences) are frequently used, mostly when decision about investment projects; creation of new services, facilities, or events; or introduction of entrance fees are being evaluated. These tools can help to identify the potential economic benefits to be expected from different types of tourism-oriented projects in order to support decision-making processes by public or private institutions or to identify and estimate the potential *willingness-to-pay* of users for services or infrastructures. Other type of methods, which can offer useful insights for this purpose, are *benchmarking* (through comparison of similar assets in different places), cost evaluation of the provision of services (including maintenance costs), or *multi-criteria analysis* (assuming that different stakeholders can reveal different valuations, based on different criteria, not directly comparable). Additionally, limits to the carrying capacity of sensitive sites (both natural and cultural) must be taken into account, while price discrimination between local users and tourists is a practice that tends to be more used as tourism fluxes tend to increase.

The study briefly presented in Case Study 2.1 (Neuts et al. 2016) emphasizes the heterogeneity of tourists, by analyzing the relation between the characteristics of visitors, their satisfaction with different aspects of the trip, and the impacts on loyalty. This type of segmentation is relevant, in particular for a sensitive ecological site, once it allows to identify the visitors which are more aware of the characteristics of the place, achieve higher satisfaction, and, thus, decide to revisit or to recommend the visit to their families and friends. Although the economic importance of loyalty is not easy to quantify with precision, surely it constitutes an important asset for the region, as it allows to focus on the attraction of the most satisfied types of visitors, who will actively promote the destination within their social circles, an aspect whose importance is emphasized by the generalization of the utilization of social media, as will discussed with more detail in Chap. 4.

Another problem arising when estimating the economic value of tourism assets and the economic impacts of tourism activities relates to the communal character of many (tangible and intangible) resources, which are determinant for the attractiveness of a tourism destination, as it will be discussed in detail in Chap. 5. In fact, as observed by Briassoulis (2002), not only natural resources and landscapes but also cultural heritage, traditions, lifestyles, or the urban atmosphere can be described as *common pool resources*. These types of resources are normally beyond market regulation and private property, and they do not necessarily fit the conditions to be analyzed within the public economy approach. Thus, economic theory normally deals with these resources as *market failures*, not offering sufficient tools for its analysis and management.

Common pool resources are normally characterized by subtractability and non-excludability, implying that their exploitation by one user reduces the amount available for others, but the exclusion of additional users is difficult or impossible (Ostrom 2010). These assets, cumulatively used while shared by local residents and tourists in a destination (with different motivations and values), generate externalities (related to education, culture, enjoyment, safety, security, or others), which can have positive impacts on tourism attractiveness. Nevertheless, despite their collective production, the appropriation of the resulting benefits, within the context of tourism, is private (and difficult – or impossible – to measure).

Other potential impacts of tourism dynamics not easy to measure are those related to the agglomeration economies arising from the attraction of tourists, contributing to the development of new local markets, which may open the opportunity for innovative practices and the emergence of new products and services, not necessarily strictly oriented to the tourism sector, as observed by Liu, Nijkamp, and Lin (2017). As it will be discussed with more detail in Chap. 4, these new products and services are more likely to be related to information and communication technologies or to creative activities, but they may also include other sectors, like transportation and mobility or energy consumption and production. Moreover, this impact can be especially important in rural areas, where the small scale of local markets may impose difficulties to the emergence and development of innovative products and services.

2.3   The Tourism Area Life Cycle Model

It is noteworthy that the impacts of tourism on local communities and the related socio-economic or environmental aspects are not stable over time. In fact, very large variations can be observed for those impacts when observing the historical evolution of tourism in a certain territory. In that sense, the theoretical formulation proposed by Butler (1980) for the life cycle of tourism destinations helps to understand and to frame those variations, with their implications for tourism policies and territorial management.

By applying to tourism destinations a similar approach to the one developed in marketing studies for the life cycle of products, the *Tourism Area Life Cycle* (TALC) model (Butler 1980) defines a unique and linear standard for the evolution of tourism destinations, at least in the first stages. Despite this limitation, the model clearly contributes to understand the dynamic and evolving character of tourism destinations. Although it does not take into account different internal and external influences affecting each particular destination (as early observed by Agarwal 1997), the model can be seen as an ideal of evolution (Weaver 2006), against which each concrete example can be compared.

According to this model, the historical evolution of a tourism area can be divided into five stages (involvement, exploration, development, consolidation, and stagnation), with different growth dynamics, types of tourists, infrastructures for tourism, socio-economic impacts or impacts in local ecosystems, cultural resources, and daily life of the resident communities. These differences imply adaptive strategic approaches, from the point of view of tourism policies and plans and also from the point of view of regional development strategies.

Nevertheless, this general evolutionary trend of tourism destinations is not universal, and it cannot be equally observed in all places. Obvious examples of places that do not fit this standard evolution are the *ready-made* destinations, which, through large-scale international promotional campaigns and massive investments in infrastructures, facilities, and organized travels, reach directly the *development* stage, without passing the two initial stages defined in this model. Moreover, the duration of each stage is not necessarily the same in all destinations, also implying that the overall duration of a cycle can be different and difficult to estimate.

It is also noticeable that the lack or absence of relevant statistical information implies that the measurability of these stages is not always clear or possible, mostly during the first stages, when the tourism sector is not adequately structured and organized. Additionally, Lagiewsky (2006) noted that characteristics of different stages can coexist in a destination at the same moment. It is also important to notice that the precise boundaries of a tourism area are not always easy – or even possible – to define (except for small islands, without adjacent territories).

According to this theoretical framework, the first stage of evolution of a tourism area is *involvement*, when occasional travellers find reasons to visit it, even without organized travels, tourism-oriented infrastructures, or even accommodation facilities. Following the classification of travellers proposed by Plog (1972), these travellers can be considered as *allocentric*, looking for non-commodified experiences and for interaction with local communities while avoiding the presence of other tourists. In a similar sense, Cohen (1972) defines these visitors as *explorers* or *non-institutionalized*. It is noteworthy that the socio-economic impacts of tourism activities are very low.

When the number of visitors tends to increase, even with a low growth rate, these areas can enter the phase of *exploration*, when local entrepreneurial initiatives start to be implemented, normally related to small accommodation facilities or other small-scale tourism-oriented services. In spite of a relatively low level of organization of the tourism sector, large numbers of visitors can reach a destination (*individual mass tourism*, as defined by Cohen 1972), while the socio-economic impacts become more relevant, and tourism-oriented activities start to be perceived as an opportunity, both at the local level and also for external entrepreneurs.

If the destination keeps attracting larger numbers of visitors, the third stage of the model – *development* – can be reached. During this phase, a large variety of tourism-related services are implemented, often by nonlocal entrepreneurs (including large international hotel chains). As the travels tend to be more organized and oriented to the motivations and characteristics of tourists, *explorer* tourists tend to be replaced by *drifters* and travels tend to be more organized and *institutionalized*, leading to a form of *organized mass tourism* (Cohen 1972). In a similar sense, Plog (1972) defines the tourists preferring this type of destination as *allocentric* (oriented to well-known and organized places, rather than unexploited areas), replacing the *psychocentric* visitors prevailing in the previous stages.

As tourism demand tends to increase at high rates during this stage, the expectations about high returns on investment and short payback periods also tend to increase. As a result, investments in new tourism products and services tend to be very high, both at private and public levels (normally including large infrastructures related to transportation, thematic parks or built recreation, and entertainment facilities). It is also possible that other sectors (normally related to the primary sector or manufacturing industries) tend to lose importance within the regional economy, while tourism achieves a more prominent role, as it was observed in the analysis presented in Case

Study 2.2 (Romão, Guerreiro and Rodrigues 2016), focused on a region within the *development* stage of evolution as a tourism area.

Questions related to sustainability also become more relevant during this stage, as the number of visitors increases and the impacts are larger, not only from the point of view of the socio-economic aspects (more jobs and revenues in the tourism sector) but also from the point of view of the environment (higher pressure on local ecosystems), cultural elements (commodification of cultural traditions, with possible loss of authenticity, while adapting to the preferences of tourists), and daily life (cumulative use of shared public spaces and transportation networks or inflationary processes in some parts of the cities and towns, including in the housing markets). These different aspects will be discussed in Chaps. 3, 4, and 5.

In this context, an adequate management of tourism fluxes and the introduction of limits to the utilization of local resources, facilities, and infrastructures may be required in order to preserve the integrity of the local resources and the livability of residents. Moreover, large investments in tourism-oriented infrastructures (like airports) must be carefully considered, as tourism flows are extremely volatile and sensitive to external shocks (related to fluctuations in revenues, security threats, or the emergence of new rival destinations), while those infrastructures are not necessarily used in other activities, in case of decline in tourism demand.

When a destination reaches the physical limit of the possible number of visitors, the *consolidation* phase is reached. In this case, the management of the destination tends to shift from the objective of attracting more visitors to the efforts to diversify the portfolio of services, in order to enlarge the value chain of the tourism sector, to reinforce the connections with other economic sectors, or to reduce the impacts of seasonability. The growth rates of tourism demand tend to decline, until the stabilization of the number of tourists, which corresponds to the phase of *stagnation*.

Several options are possible for the evolution of a tourism destination after a period of *stagnation*, according to the TALC model. If there is a significant degradation of territorial resources due to overuse, this can imply an irreversible *decline*, with important negative consequences related to the subsequent sub-utilization of built facilities and infrastructures. Nevertheless, if the resources are still attractive but the region has lost its competitive position due to the emergence of rival destinations, new marketing strategies, focused on different markets or development of innovative products, can lead to a process of *rejuvenation*, as observed, among others, by Kozak and Martin (2012).

Despite its important limitations in order to offer an exact identification of each stage in the evolution of a destination or its limited predictive possibilities, the TALC model appears as a useful tool to understand the evolving character of tourism areas, as stressed by Haywood (1986) – who offers an early attempt to integrate some flexibility within this deterministic approach. As also observed by different authors (Wall 1982, Haywood 2006, and even Butler 2009), the model can integrate different additional aspects, such as those related to demand fluctuations (Nejad and Tularam 2010), entrepreneurship dynamics (Russel 2006), residents' perceptions (Diedrich and García-Buades 2008), and also new methodologies related to complex models to process information (McKercher 1999; Cole 2009).

In particular, the importance given in tourism studies to the aspects related to the sustainable use of resources also contributed to the popularization of the TALC model, by integrating concepts like *intensity* or *regulation* within the analysis of tourism dynamics and planning process (Weaver, 2010). Other relevant applications related to the concept of sustainability were proposed by Coccossis (2002), identifying different dimensions (environmental, social, and economic) for the definition of the carrying capacity of a destination, or by Avdimiotis (2009), proposing a model to anticipate possible problems and opportunities related to tourism dynamics in order to support planning processes for investments, promotional strategies, accessibilities, or limits to the utilization of sensitive resources. In a similar sense, the European Commission (2002) defined an "Early Warning System" to prevent the decline of destination by spreading the best practices to maintain the socio-economic contributions of tourism.

With different perspectives, the TALC model can offer useful insights to analyze the cycles and processes of economic growth in areas where tourism plays a relevant socio-economic role, as observed in Case Study 1.3. In fact, the empirical applications of the TALC model cover a wide range of subjects and different types of tourism areas. These studies include mass tourism destinations (Rodriguez, Parra-Lopez and Yanez-Estevez 2008) but also particular tourism attractions like natural parks (Zhong, Deng and Xiang 2008) or cultural resources (like urban heritage where excessive tourism flows can deteriorate local material cultural resources, as noted by Malcolm-Davies 2006), focusing on the identification of limits to their utilization. The analysis proposed by Russo (2001) for the city of Venice emphasized how the life cycle of tourism development of the city imposed different types of new cycles on the surrounding areas.

2.4 Tourism and Regional Growth

More broadly, the relation between tourism dynamics and economic growth has been analyzed in a large number of studies, in different parts of the world and focusing on different territorial levels. Although the local level (closer to the concept of destination) is often difficult to analyze (due to the lack of relevant statistical information), these relations between the evolution of the tourism sector and the processes of economic growth in the territory have been the object of attention of numerous researchers, with focus on the regional, national, or international levels. Examples of very early efforts to analyze these questions were offered by Carlson (1938) or Ullman (1954), as observed in the detailed systematization of the historical evolution of tourism research proposed by Butler (2015).

Until recently, it was possible to observe a general consensus in the literature around the concept of *tourism-led growth*, a hypothesis tested and confirmed in a large number of studies, as pointed out by Brida, Cortes-Jimenez, and Pulina (2016), who offer a systematic compilation of these studies. Concluding that tourism dynamics effectively contributes for territorial economic growth, at different levels, these studies were generally based on methodologies relying on time series or cross-sectional data (like panel data methods), in order to analyze the evolution of a destination along time.

At the international level, Chen and Chiou-Wei (2009) focused on Taiwan and Korea, Cortes-Jimenez and Pulina (2010) analyzed the cases of Spain and Italy, while Dritsakis (2004) compared the performance of seven Mediterranean countries. At the national level, several studies were focused on Taiwan (Kim, Chen and Jang 2006), Greece (Dritsakis 2004; Eeckels, Filis and Leon 2012), or Spain (Balaguer and Cantavella-Jordá 2002). At the regional level, Risso, Barquet, and Brida (2010) analyzed the case of Trentino, in Italy. Following different methodologies, all these works (focusing on territories where tourism is an important economic activity) confirmed the tourism-led growth hypothesis, claiming that tourism growth exerts positive impacts on the economies concerned.

Nevertheless, more recent studies, using larger datasets and analyzing longer periods, revealed different results for the relation between tourism and economic growth, suggesting that these impacts tend to vary as the tourism area evolves along its life cycle. One example is offered by Capó, Font, and Nadal (2007a) when analyzing this relation with a long-term perspective at the Canary Islands (a major tourism destination in Spain). The authors observed important transformations within the regional economic structure, as tourism mobilizes local resources and achieves higher importance, replacing other economic sectors. At the international level, a study conducted by Adamou and Clerides (2009), involving a large number of countries (162) observed during a relatively long period (1980–2005), pointed out that the positive impacts of tourism on economic growth tend to disappear in the long run, as a result of the structural economic transformations occurring within the national economies. Like in the previous case, the results suggest that the positive impacts of tourism depend on the evolutionary life cycle of tourism destinations.

The transformations that can occur within the economic structure of a tourism destination during the development stage of its life cycle are related to the high attractiveness of the tourism sector for investments, with expected high returns in the short run, due to the high levels of growth of tourism demand. This concentration of resources into tourism activities can imply a reduction of investment (and production) in other existing sectors, like the primary sector (in certain areas, shifting from agricultural production to golf courses or rural tourism) or the manufacturing sector (normally requiring higher levels of investment in technology and more skilled labor while offering lower expectations for high profits in the short run).

This type of analysis of the transformations within regional economic structures as a result of an intensive growth of tourism is rooted in the concept of *Dutch disease*, as proposed by Corden (1984) to describe how the overexploitation of natural resources (in this case, the extraction of natural gas in a region of the Netherlands) had contributed to a loss of importance of the regional manufacturing activities, while boosting the provision of non-tradable products and services. The author concluded that these structural transformations contributed to a long-term loss of welfare in the long region.

Similarly, the tourism sector can be seen as depending on the "extraction" of territorial resources (climate, beach, natural parks, cultural heritage, etc.), also creating the expectation for high returns of investment in very short time, while potentially contributing to reinforce the importance of the non-tradable sector (Copeland 1991; Chao et al. 2006). Some recent studies have addressed this question, taking advantage of the existence of long temporal datasets and aiming at identifying how these resources could possibly contribute to promote a long-term transformation in the regional economic structures, by reducing the importance of the tradable sectors (agriculture and manufacturing), while boosting non-tradable activities (construction and services).

A study developed by Capó, Font, and Nadal (2007b), focused on two of the most important tourism regions in Spain (the Balearic and the Canary islands) and assuming tourism-related natural resources (the beaches and the climate) as comparable to the natural gas (in the origin of the concept of *Dutch disease*), concluded that the regional economies of both islands suffered important structural transformations, with a clear decay of manufacturing activities and progressively lower impacts of tourism on regional growth.

Nevertheless, other recent studies have shown contradictory (or ambiguous) results. In fact, the possible implications of tourism dynamics as a cause of the decline of agriculture or industrial activities is far from being consensually supported by the existing literature. Holzner (2011) tested the possible existence of a *beach disease* process related to tourism development by analyzing 134 countries between 1970 and 2007, concluding that no process of deindustrialization could be causally linked to the dynamics of the tourism sector. Also focusing on a large set of countries and a long series of data, Lee and Chang (2008) concluded that the causalities were different in different countries, not being possible to define a common tendency, while Du et al. (2016) found that the contribution of the tourism sector for a long-term process of economic growth depends on its integration into the broader economic dynamics. With a different perspective, when performing a regional analysis in the United States, Tang and Jang (2009) did not find any significant relation between tourism dynamics and regional economic growth.

Nevertheless, it should be observed that these studies consider a period of stable growth of economic development and tourism dynamics, without relevant external shocks influencing the socio-economic performances or the evolution of the tourism sector. After the international crisis starting in 2007, this situation would change and several studies analyzed its impacts on tourism. Important declines in tourism activities were observed in Europe (Smeral 2009) and in Asia (Song and Lin 2010), while Caletrío (2012) observed that visits abroad (which were continuously growing for 25 years) reduced significantly in the United Kingdom in 2008. In fact, the external shock resulting from the international crisis clearly revealed how strong the fluctuations (elasticity) of tourism demand can be when in face of a sudden decrease in income.

Case Study 2.2 (Romão, Guerreiro, and Rodrigues 2016), focusing in a tourism-dependent region in the South of Portugal and considering a relatively long period (1995–2012), takes into account the possible transformations of the economic structure of the region along a process of intense development of tourism and also takes into account the impacts of the international crisis. For this case, it is possible to observe that the region suffered a process of deindustrialization (similar to the concept of *Dutch disease*), with a clear gain of importance of the construction activities and the non-tradable sector, stimulated by tourism dynamics. The emergence of the crisis – with a very short-term negative impact on tourism, with quick recovery – had a strong and more permanent impact on construction, leading to an important increase in the regional unemployment.

The different results obtained in different places and different moments suggest that the relation between tourism development and economic growth is far from being deterministic and fully predictable, depending on the specific conditions and structures of the regional economies. In that sense, the availability of longer series of data can contribute for a more detailed analysis and clarification of these questions.

2.5 Evolutionary Economic Geography: History and Place in Tourism Development

It is clear that territorial characteristics related to climate, nature, landscapes, culture, or heritage determine to a very large extent the type of tourism attractions, products, and services existing in a destination. In that sense, tourism is a place-dependent activity, in which the uniqueness of each destination relies on the singularity of its territorial resources. In this context, it is not surprising that many studies on tourism come from the field of geography, even when focused on the socio-economic impacts of tourism development.

Moreover, as observed in the previous sections, the evolution of a tourism destination along time has deep implications on the impacts of tourism on local communities, in a varied set of aspects: socio-economic benefits and costs, pressure on sensitive environmental resources, and interference on daily life of residents or shared use of public spaces and facilities. In that sense, history also matters when analyzing a tourism destination, and this historical evolution is a crucial dimension that must be taken into account in the planning processes of tourism development or, more broadly, when defining territorial development strategies.

As it was also previously observed, the negative impacts on tourism dynamics and economic growth arising from the international economic crisis that started in 2007 revealed different types of reactions in different tourism-dependent regions, depending on the specific characteristics of their economic structures. In fact, despite the quick recovery observed in tourism demand, in a large number of regions where tourism plays a prominent role (e.g., the Southern European area), problems related to high levels of unemployment or low economic growth persisted for a much longer period.

This context – in which an external shock (the international financial crisis) caused important disturbances in regional economic systems – was favorable for the emergence and wide utilization of the concept of *resilience* within economic analysis. Defining resilience in the sense proposed by Modica and Reggiani (2015) – the ability of a system to recover to a stable evolution path after a negative external shock – the concept is particularly relevant for tourism studies, mostly when tourism is seen as a crucial sector within strategies of regional development.

An important example of this importance is the analysis conducted by Milio (2014), pointing out that, in the European context, the less resilient regions were those with higher levels of specialization in tourism and construction (which confirms the conclusions presented in Case Study 1.2). Moreover, it was also observed in the work presented in Case Study 2.3 (Romão and Nijkamp, forthcoming) that, at the European level and considering the period between 2004 and 2011 (including the international crisis started in 2007 and the subsequent relative recovery), Southern European regions are generally those where tourism demand is higher and also those where GDP per habitant tends to be lower, both in terms of its absolute value and also when observing its growth rate, suggesting that high tourism dynamics is not necessarily related to high levels of economic growth and also revealing the relatively low socio-economic resilience of these regions.

The different mechanisms and adaptation processes undertaken in different regions in face of a similar external shock also contributed to reinforce the importance of the approaches linked to the *evolutionary economic geography* (EEG) theoretical framework, which emphasizes the importance of place (geography) and time (history) – with their implications on the characteristics of different economic systems – for the analysis of regional processes of development (Boschma and Martin 2010 offer an overall and systematic presentation of this conceptualization).

Considering tourism as a place-dependent activity, where the evolutionary process of the life cycle of tourism destinations plays a decisive role, the EEG approach has also been recently seen as a useful tool for the analysis of tourism dynamics, in particular when the concept of resilience becomes a central aspect for tourism-dependent regions. In particular, Ma and Hassink (2013) or Sanz-Ibáñez and Clavé (2014) established a clear connection between EEG and the analysis proposed by Butler (1980) for the life cycle of tourism areas, while Cárdenas-García and Sánchez-Rivero (2015) confirmed the importance of the local territorial characteristics of each economic system when analyzing the relation between tourism and economic growth. In more general terms, Brouder and Eriksson (2013) compiled in a systematic way the main contributions that EEG can offer to the field of tourism.

As a consequence of the central importance of history and geography within the EEG framework, the concept of *path dependence* (Boschma and Martin, 2010) stresses how strategic choices implemented in the past and historical processes of evolution influence and constrain the possible decisions and choices for the future. In that sense, this approach can help to identify and to analyze the unequal spatial distribution of economic activities and the different results and performances obtained in different regions, even when subject to similar external shocks or disposing of similar resources.

These processes of path dependence have different causes, as summarized by Martin (2014). Focusing on their importance for the tourism sector, path dependence can be the result of:

– Available natural resources (regions where tourism attractiveness mostly depends on natural assets – ecotourism, sun and sea, or winter sports – are clearly dependent on those resources to define their portfolio of tourism products and services)
– Sunk costs of local productive, physical, and infrastructural assets (large-scale investments, like those related to ports, airports, or theme parks, can be useful in order to prompt tourism activities but can also have very low utilization in case tourism activities drop)
– Agglomeration economies, local external economies of specialization, or localized spin-off firm birth (high specialization in tourism, mostly when the region is in the development stage, with high growth rates of tourism demand, influences the creation of new businesses around the same sector)
– Interregional linkages and dependencies (tourism often implies cooperation between regions, as tourists visit more than one place, not necessarily within the same administrative territorial unit or even in the same country; this process can reinforce interregional economic dependencies in the long term)
– Local technological lock-in (concentration of knowledge production and innovation capabilities in a prominent sector can reduce innovation dynamics in the long term, mostly if the sector is not connected with other economic activities)

Combining these aspects with the formulation proposed by Butler (1980) for the life cycles of tourism destinations, we can observe that the initial stages of evolution of a destination are normally linked to the first aspect (existence of natural – or cultural – resources), whose importance is emphasized if the region achieves the stage of development, with large investments in infrastructures (potential sunk costs), creation of agglomeration economies (increasing the specialization in tourism), reinforcement of interregional linkages based on tourism activities, and lack of technological development and innovative capabilities, once tourism tends to be a sector with relatively low incorporation of knowledge and technology, despite the high potential that will be discussed in detail in Chap. 4.

In this context, when the process of tourism development tends to reach a limit, tourism demand stabilizes, the economic dynamics tends to decline, and the difficulties for the region to find other development paths, based on different patterns of production and specialization, tend to increase. In fact, as observed by Essletzbichler and Rigby (2005), the EEG conceptualization sees the evolution of an economic system as a process of mutation, in which interaction between agents and the resulting knowledge spillovers determine the possibility for the emergence of new (different) types of business. In that sense, an overspecialization in tourism can imply a lack of economic alternatives in the long run.

These aspects can also be observed when looking at the results obtained in Case Study 2.3. The spatial correlation between the endowment in natural resources and tourism dynamics appears, in fact, as a relevant source of path dependency lock-in. On the other hand, the high levels of specialization in tourism observed in these regions (both in terms of the share of this sector in the regional employment and gross value added) suggest high sunk costs related to facilities and infrastructures, which are not necessarily useful for other sectors.

Moreover, the persistence of high levels of investment in the tourism sector shows a different lock-in process, as a result of the existing conditions of specialization and agglomeration spillovers existing in these regions. In this context, a structural transformation of these regional economies aiming at higher levels of efficiency in the utilization of their resources appears as highly constrained by the prevailing specialization in tourism products and services with relatively low value added. Finally, the spatial effects identified suggest that close regions with similar characteristics tend to show similar patterns of evolution, revealing the importance of interregional linkages as another source of path dependence lock-in. In that sense, promoting structural changes in the regional economies seems to require supra-regional forms of collaboration and strategic approaches.

It is also important that tourism is a place-based activity, with some specific characteristics that differentiate it from other economic activities, like *co-terminality* (direct interaction between producer and consumer), *spatiality*, and *temporality* (consumption and production of tourism services occur in the same place at the same time). As it will be seen in more detail in Chap. 4, these characteristics imply a permanent interaction and exchange of information, a process prompted by the development of information and communication technologies (ICT) and their wide application in tourism services.

Thus, and also taking into account that tourism destinations comprise a wide range of products and services to satisfy the needs and expectation of different types of visitors, the tourism sector has a high potential to mobilize resources, products, and services from other sectors (apart from ICT, obvious examples are agriculture, food industries, transports, energy, or creative activities, in broad sense). Once this integration of different products and services is made with permanent interaction, at the local level, with the users, there is a high potential for the development of practice- and place-based innovative services, integrating knowledge and technology, while adapting the existing services and resources to the requirements of demand.

In this sense, the concepts of *relatedness*, *variety*, and *regional branching*, also proposed by the EEG framework (Boschma et al. 2016), provide useful tools to explore the potential of tourism activities to engage in systematic processes of interconnection with other (related) sectors, which is only possible if the region disposes a variety of economic activities that can comprise an interrelated innovative network. In that sense, as it will be discussed with more detail in Chap. 4, tourism and its potential broad scope of activities can prompt the development of new regional branches and to contribute for a diversification of the regional economies, with higher incorporation of knowledge and technology and generating higher value added.

2.6   Concluding Remarks

This chapter was focused on the importance of tourism in contemporary economies, a critical overview of the techniques to assess and to measure this importance, the implications of the evolving character of tourism destinations, the relations between tourism dynamics and economic growth, and the potential contributions of the conceptual framework proposed by the evolutionary economy geography in this context.

In particular, this chapter focused on:

– General identification of a path of sustained growth at the international level for the tourism sector, with important socio-economic impacts all over the world
– Possible methods and limitations to estimate these impacts within the overall economy (*tourism satellite accounts*, input-output tables, or CGE and SAM models)
– Different techniques to assess the economic value of nonmarketable tourism-related assets, like nature or cultural heritage (hedonic prices or contingent valuation), or immaterial aspects like the loyalty of visitors
– Discussion of the communal character of many tourism resources, with the consequent appropriation and provision problems characterizing the common pool resources
– Analysis of the historical dimension of tourism development, through the evolutionary aspects of the life cycle of tourism destinations and their implications on socio-economic impacts and planning processes
– Analysis of the contribution of tourism for economic growth (tourism-led growth) and its limitations in the long run
– Discussion on the negative long-term consequences of specialization in tourism
– Exploration of the potential contributions of the evolutionary economic geography for tourism studies, considering tourism as a place-based activity and destinations as evolutionary systems
– Discussion of the role of tourism within the context of a regional economy and its relations with other sectors, activities, and innovation dynamics

Case Study 2.1: Market Segmentation and Tourism Economic Impacts

Neuts B, Romão J, Nijkamp P, Shikida A (2016) Market segmentation and their economic impacts in an ecotourism destination: An applied modelling study on Hokkaido, Japan. Tourism Economics 22(4):793–808

This article develops a market segmentation approach for the UNESCO World Natural Heritage Site of Shiretoko Peninsula (in the northeast part of Hokkaido, Japan), a unique place due to its unique geological and biological characteristics (volcanic origin and biodiversity, including threatened species). Bear watching and whale and dolphin spotting are particularly relevant to attract tourists. It is an important ecotourism destination, attracting more than 1.8 million tourists per year, whose activities include sea cruises, kayak trips, mountain hiking, hot springs, landscape observation, and a rich gastronomy. Shiretoko attracts a diverse range of tourist groups, and this work is based on a survey made for the users of boat tours: large-scale boats, smaller boats, and sea kayaking. All these segments have their specific advantages and disadvantages.

Segmentation is a valuable marketing tool to focus attention on the most advantageous clusters of visitors. In an ecotourism destination, the attractiveness of tourists may be defined by their ecological awareness but also their (potential) economic impact, since there is a need to balance ecological sustainability and economic viability. This article proposes a model-based latent class analysis of visitors' preferences and choices in order to identify different demand clusters, which can be used to make informed decisions about management strategies on tourist heterogeneity in order to maximize benefits for the local economy. The model identifies four different clusters of tourist activities, differing in their motivations, information search patterns, preferred boat routes, and secondary activities.

From this, it was possible to identify that certain clusters, in this case the bear watchers and active explorers, are much more active throughout the region than others. On the other hand, tourists participating on a tour limit their visit to a boat ride, which suggests the possibility to extend their visits. For another cluster (non-organized tourists), there is also a potential to extend their visit by motivating them to visit more secondary sites. Since these people are mainly self-informed through Internet and guidebooks, additional research might benefit from identifying the most important digital and printed information sources in order to ensure incorporation of additional visitor information.

While large-scale tours offer large number of tourists that are required by larger tourist organizations, their spending throughout the region is limited and their activities are focused on a few suppliers. On the other hand, younger tourists, perhaps less affluent and more individualistic, seem to spread their expenditure over a larger area, while using more services. In the same way, family trips and smaller group trips in small boats can benefit regional development, if coupled with non-boating activities. It is therefore important to treat these diverse segments differently and independently, since both types of expenditure pattern are needed for a healthy tourist industry.

Although the organized market is very important (with around 30% of the total sample visiting as part of a group), their importance is limited to a specific area (Utoro town), not offering financial benefits to other parts of the peninsula. Getting tour organizers to enlarge their routes can extend potential economic income in the region, although the lack of sizeable accommodation to host a large number of visitors is a weakness. Therefore, primary attention should be put on enlarging local involvement in the value chain, by incorporating local products and services such as local fisheries. This would not only limit leakages and increase regional wellness and employment creation but could also add to the authenticity of the tourist experience.

While the users of sea kayaks are the smallest of the four segments, they offer economic benefits to the wider region. However, from an environmental management perspective, it would be unwise to focus on attracting a higher number of visitors in this category, since a large number would have a negative impact on the wilderness experience they depend on by potentially exceeding the social carrying capacity.

An important management concern is directed to the bear watchers and organized tour groups, with respect to their visitor motivations. Although they reveal a strong primary motivation for bear watching, a large number of them choose a boat route (to Cape Shiretoko) with low chances of spotting bears. More importantly, tour groups taking larger boats are too far off the coast to see the bear population. Therefore, these visitors might come to Shiretoko Peninsula and entering a cruise with wrong expectations. It is a concern that tour operators should provide the right information, which is useful to choose a suitable tour, based on primary visitor motivations. On the other hand, tourists primarily motivated by the landscape features are also likely to be interested in wilderness settings. Thus, boat operators can inform these tourists about other wilderness activities such as sea kayaking as well as land-based tours. This will serve to further raise the economic value of these tourists for the area while also possibly improving the visitor experience. These aspects related to information will be discussed with more detail in Chap. 4, while aspects related to the management of natural sites will be discussed in Chap. 3.

Case Study 2.2: Tourism and Regional Resilience

Romão J, Guerreiro J, Rodrigues P (2016) Tourism Growth and Regional Resilience: the "Beach Disease" and the Consequences of the Global Crisis of 2007. Tourism Economics 22(4):699–714

As a consequence of the international financial crisis in 2007, the region of Algarve (South of Portugal), where tourism plays an important economic and social role, suffered a decrease in tourism demand, while unemployment increased sharply. Although tourism activities registered a quick recovery, unemployment levels continued to grow. This work analyses thes central role of tourism within the regional economy of Algarve and identifies its major sectorial impacts, discussing the possible implications on regional resilience and unemployment.

Tourism in Algarve is concentrated in the summer period (75% of the overnights in 2012 were registered between April and September) and depending on a few large issuing markets (the United Kingdom, Germany, the Netherlands, and Portugal were responsible for 75.5% of the overnights in regional hotels and similar establishments). After the international financial crisis in 2007, regional tourism demand decreased between 2007 and 2009, while a substitution of foreign tourists by national visitors was observed between 2007 and 2010. This had important consequences on the regional unemployment levels: from 15.7 thousand persons in 2008, this number increased to 32.7 thousand in 2011, with a reduction of the overall number of employed persons after 2008 and a relevant decline in the construction sector, suggesting a lack of resilience of the regional economy.

This analysis focuses on the period between 1995 and 2012, considering four main economic sectors: most of the tradable products, including agriculture, fisheries, extractive industries, and manufacturing (A); construction (B); most of activities related to tourism and leisure, including accommodation, restaurants, transports, and retail (C); and other non-tradable services, including real estate, information and communication technologies, design, education, arts, culture, and public management (D). Sectors C (tourism) and D (non-tradable services) were predominant within the regional gross value added in 1995, and their importance increased until 2012, corresponding to a significant decrease of the importance of tradable goods. Nevertheless, this sector (A) did not suffer a negative impact from the international crisis. The GVA for all other sectors decreased in 2008, but, although sectors C and D started to recover in 2009, that did not occur with B (construction), which continued to decrease, becoming the smallest sector under analysis. In terms of employment, sectors C and D are also clearly dominant, and their importance remains stable during the period under analysis. Apparently, only the construction (sector B) absorbed the workers from the tradable sector (A) between 1995 and 2012. Nevertheless, it is observed that, with the exception of the non-tradable services (D), employment has decreased in all sectors as a consequence of the crisis. This affected tourism and related activities (C) and, to a larger extent, construction (B).

In order to understand how the evolution in each sector impacted the other sectors of the regional economy, two Bayesian vector autoregressive models were estimated based on the previous data: the first includes the sectorial regional employment and the second the sectorial regional gross value added, leading to very similar conclusions: these results reveal the existence of self-reinforcing mechanisms among three sectors (construction, tourism, and non-tradable services), justifying the importance they have gained over the last 20 years, both in terms of regional employment and the regional gross value added, along with the growth of tourism activities. It is also visible that the tradable sector (A) is completely excluded from this process, not receiving any positive impact from the development of the other sectors of the regional economy, leading to a decay of employment in agriculture, fisheries, and manufacture over this period.

With the introduction of a dummy variable in the models, the impacts of the international crisis of 2007 on the different sectors could be captured. The results clearly show negative impacts on employment in the tradable sector (A), tourism (C), and, to a much larger extent, the construction sector (B). These negative impacts are clearly not compensated by the positive impact on the non-tradable products and services (D). Regarding the gross value added, only on the construction sector, a relevant (and negative) impact was observed. As a result, construction assumed a growing importance in the regional employment structure during these two decades, even if its contribution for the regional value added did not increase in a similar proportion. When this sector declined sharply after 2008, its employment was not absorbed by the other sectors, leading to a dramatic increase in the regional unemployment rate, revealing the lack of regional resilience against a negative external shock.

The concentration of the positive effects of tourism on the employment and gross value added of the non-tradable services and construction activities is linked to a dynamic process of evolution of the regional economy where these three sectors have been "feeding" each other over the last 20 years. The tradable sector did not benefit from this dynamics, leading to a significant decrease of its importance over the last two decades. Thus, a process similar to the *beach disease* conceptualization can be identified in the region during this period.

Case Study 2.3: Tourism and Regional Growth

Romão J, Nijkamp P (forthcoming) Spatial Impacts Assessment of Tourism and Territorial Capital: A Modelling Study on Regional Development in Europe

This study focuses on the relation between tourism dynamics and regional economic growth across Europe. Despite the large number of papers focusing on similar issues, the results are often contradictory or, at least, ambiguous. Moreover, most of the studies have analyzed periods of relatively stable growth, both in terms of the economic and tourism performance of the regions. In this case, the period under analysis (2004 and 2011) includes a first stage of growth, the impacts of the international economic crisis started in 2007 and a stage of recovery after that. The study includes of a large number of regions (237), with very diverse characteristics, both from the point of view of the importance of tourism and also from the perspective of economic development. All the NUTS 2 regions (following the classification defined by Eurostat) from Austria, Belgium, Bulgaria, Czech Republic, Denmark, Estonia, Finland, France, Germany, Greece, Hungary, Italy, Latvia, Lithuania, Luxemburg, the Netherlands, Poland, Portugal, Romania, Slovakia, Slovenia, Spain, and the United Kingdom were included. The relevance of this territorial level (larger than the scale of the destination) relates to the existence of regional governance institutions, both at the tourism and economic policy levels, which enables to address relevant implications for development strategies.

The relation between tourism demand (number of nights spent in accommodation establishments) and economic growth (GDP per capita) is contextualized through the introduction of other explanatory variables describing the territorial capital of each region. This includes material features (natural resources, measured according to the share of the territory classified as an ecological area within the European network *Natura 2000*; and cultural assets, the number of World Heritage Sites classified by UNESCO), patterns of tourism specialization (gross fixed capital formation in tourism and share of tourism services within the regional workforce and gross value added), and immaterial endowments (qualifications of the workforce, measured by the share of the workforce with tertiary education, and innovation capabilities, measured by the regional investment in R&D activities).

The study includes an exploratory spatial analysis based on local indicators of spatial autocorrelation. A bivariate analysis is performed, identifying spatial correlation effects between the regional GDP growth (non-lagged variable) and the scores observed (for other variables) in the neighborhood (spatially lagged). This analysis shows that only in part of France and the North of Italy high tourism demand (and also specialization) is correlated with high economic growth, while low specialization in tourism and high economic growth is observed in a large group of regions (in Germany and other Northern areas). Moreover, the opposite situation (high levels of tourism specialization spatially correlated with low economic growth) is observed in most of the Southern European area. Cumulatively, high levels of investment in tourism are also observed in these regions, despite the relatively low economic impacts, within the European context.

Regarding the immaterial aspects of the territorial capital, the analysis shows that there is almost no region where high levels of GDP per habitant coexist with low investments in R&D. On the other hand, most of the Southern European regions exhibit abundance of natural and cultural resources, generally correlated with low economic growth. As it was also seen that these regions also have high tourism demand, these results suggest that natural and cultural resources tend to be integrated into massive forms of tourism supply, with low socio-economic benefits and potential high negative environmental impacts.

This exploratory analysis is complemented with an explanatory spatial econometric model, where GDP per habitant is the dependent variable and all the others are explanatory variables. Confirming the results observed at the local level, the general tendency identified shows that specialization in tourism and regional endowment in natural resources are negatively correlated with regional economic growth. Additionally, the model identifies positive spatial *spillovers*, suggesting that the dynamics observed in one region tends to be influenced by the performance of its neighbors, which shows the importance of interregional coordination policies, an aspect that is generally not taken into consideration.

In conclusion, the analysis shows a process of divergence between Northern and Southern regions, in which the second group tends to reveal higher levels of specialization and lower achievements in terms of economic growth. Although this tourism dynamics can be rooted in the natural endowments of the territories, it is reinforced by high levels of investment, leading to (and being reinforced by) high levels of specialization in tourism, which constrains the possibilities for diversification of the regional economic structures. In fact, most of the sources of *path dependence* lock-in can be observed in this case.

References

Adamou A, Clerides S (2009) Prospects and limits of tourism-led growth: the international evidence. The Rimini Centre for Economic Analysis – Working Paper 41-09

Agarwal S (1997) The resort cycle and seaside tourism: an assessment of its applicability and validity. Tour Manag 18(2):65–73

Andersson T, Armbrecht J, Lundberg E (2012) Estimating use and non-use values of a music festival. Scand J Hosp Tour 12(3):215–231

Avdimiotis S (2009) From development to decline. Tracing the life circle notifications of a destination. J Environ Prot Ecol 10(4):1205–1217

Balaguer J, Cantavella-Jordá M (2002) Tourism as a long-run economic growth factor: the Spanish case. Appl Econ 34(7):877–884

Boschma R, Martin R (2010) The aims and scope of evolutionary economic geography. In: Boschma R, Martin R (eds) The handbook of evolutionary economic geography. Edward Elgar, Cheltenham, pp 3–39

Boschma R, Coenen L, Frenken K, Truffer B (2016) Towards a theory of regional diversification. Pap Evol Econ Geogr 16:17

Briassoulis H (2002) Sustainable tourism and the question of commons. Ann Tour Res 29(4):1065–1085

Brida JG, Cortes-Jimenez I, Pulina M (2016) Has the tourism-led growth hypothesis been validated? A literature review. Curr Issue Tour 19(5):394–430

Brouder P, Eriksson R (2013) Tourism evolution: on the synergies of tourism studies and evolutionary economic geography. Ann Tour Res 43:370–389

Brown G, Mendelsohn R (1984) The hedonic travel cost method. Rev Econ Stat 66(3):427–433

Butler R (1980) The concept of a tourism area life cycle of evolution: implications for management of resources. Can Geogr 24(1):5–12

Butler R (2009) Tourism in the future: cycles, waves or wheels? Futures 41:346–352

Butler R (2015) The evolution of tourism and tourism research. Tour Recreat Res 40(1):16–27

Caletrío J (2012) Simple living and tourism in times of 'austerity'. Curr Issue Tour 15(3):275–279

Capó J, Font A, Nadal J (2007a) Tourism and long-term growth: a Spanish perspective. Ann Tour Res 34(3):709–726

Capó J, Font A, Nadal J (2007b) Dutch disease in tourism economies: evidence from the Balearics and the Canary Islands. J Sustain Tour 15(6):615–627

Cárdenas-García P, Sánchez-Rivero M (2015) Tourism and economic development: analysis of geographic features and infrastructure provision. Curr Issue Tour 18(7):609–632

Carlson AS (1938) Recreation industry of New Hampshire. Econ Geogr 14:255–270

Chao C, Hazari B, Laffargue J, Sgro M, Yu E (2006) Tourism, Dutch disease and welfare in a open dynamic economy. Jpn Econ Rev 57(4):501–515

Chen C, Chiou-Wei S (2009) Tourism expansion, tourism uncertainty and economic growth: new evidence from Taiwan and Korea. Tour Manag 30(6):812–818

Choi Y, Lee W, Lee C, Dattilo J (2015) Valuation of mudflats in nature-based tourism: inclusion of perceived value of festival experience. Tour Econ 21(4):833–851

Coccossis H (2002) Tourism development and carrying capacity. In: Apostoulos G, Gayle D (eds) Island tourism and sustainable development. Praeger, Westport, pp 131–144

Cohen E (1972) Towards a sociology of international tourism. Soc Res 39:164–182

Cole S (2009) A logistic tourism model: resort cycles, globalization, and Chaos. Ann Tour Res 36(4):689–714

Copeland B (1991) Tourism, welfare and de-industrialization in a small open economy. Economica 58(232):515–529

Corden W (1984) Booming sector and Dutch disease economics: survey and consolidation. Oxf Econ Pap 36:359–380

Cortes-Jimenez I, Pulina M (2010) Inbound tourism and long-run economic growth. Curr Issue Tour 13(1):61–74

Crompton JL, Jeong JY, Dudensing RM (2016) Sources of variation in economic impact multipliers. J Travel Res 55(8):1051–1064

Diedrich A, García-Buades E (2008) Local perceptions of tourism as indicators of destination decline. Tour Manag 30:512–521

Dritsakis N (2004) Tourism as a long-run economic growth factor: an empirical investigation for Greece using causality analysis. Tour Econ 10(3):305–316

Du D, Lew AL, Ng PT (2016) Tourism and economic growth. J Travel Res 55(4):454–464

Dwyer L, Forsyth P, Spurr R (2004) Evaluating tourism's economic effects: new and old approaches. Tour Manag 25:307–317

Eeckels B, Filis G, Leon C (2012) Tourism income and economic growth in Greece: empirical evidence from their cyclical components. Tour Econ 18(4):817–834

Essletzbichler J, Rigby D (2005) Competition, variety and the geography of technology evolution. Tijdschr Econ Soc Geogr 96(1):48–62

European Commission (2002) Early warning system for identifying declining tourist destinations. European Commission, Luxembourg

Haywood K (1986) Can the tourist-area life cycle be made operational? Tour Manag 7:154–167

Haywood K (2006) Legitimizing the TALC as a theory of development and change. In: Butler R (ed) The tourism area life cycle, vol 2.: Conceptual and theoretical issues. Channel View Publications, Clevedon, pp 29–44

Holzner M (2011) Tourism and economic development: the beach disease? Tour Manag 32(4):922–933

Kim H, Chen M, Jang S (2006) Tourism expansion and economic development: the case of Taiwan. Tour Manag 27(5):925–933

Kozak M, Martin D (2012) Tourism life cycle and sustainability analysis: profit-focused strategies for mature destinations. Tour Manag 33:188–194

Lagiewsky R (2006) The application of the TALC model: a literature survey. In: Butler R (ed) The tourism area life cycle, , vol 1: applications and modifications. Channel View Publications, Clevedon, pp 27–50

Lee C, Chang C (2008) Tourism development and economic growth: a closer look at panels. Tour Manag 29(1):180–192

Lee C, Han S (2002) Estimating the use and preservation values of national parks' tourism resources using a contingent valuation method. Tour Manag 23:531–540

Liu J, Nijkamp P, Lin D (2017) Urban-rural imbalance and tourism-led growth in China. Ann Tour Res 64:24–36

Loomis JB (2014) Economic valuation: concepts and empirical methods. In: Fischer M, Nijkamp P (eds) Handbook of regional science. Springer, Berlin, pp 973–992

Ma M, Hassink R (2013) An evolutionary perspective on tourism area development. Ann Tour Res 41:89–109

Malcolm-Davies J (2006) The TALC and heritage sites. In: Butler R (ed) The tourism area life cycle, vol. 1: Applications and modifications. Channel View Publications, Clevedon, pp 162–180

Martin R (2014) Path dependence and the spatial economy. In: Fischer M, Nijkamp P (eds) Handbook of regional sciences. Springer, New York, pp 609–629

McKercher B (1999) A chaos approach to tourism. Tour Manag 20:425–434

Milio S (2014) Impact of the economic crisis on social, economic and territorial cohesion of the European Union, , vol. 1. Directorate-general for internal policies. Policy Department B: Structural and Cohesion Policies, Luxembourg

Modica M, Reggiani A (2015) Spatial economic resilience: overview and perspectives. Netw Spatial Econ 15(2):211–233

Nejad S, Tularam G (2010) Modeling tourist arrivals in destination countries: an application to Australian tourism. J Math Stat 6(4):431–441

Neuts B, Romão J, Nijkamp P, Shikida A (2016) Market segmentation and their potential economic impacts in an ecotourism destination: an applied modelling study on Hokkaido, Japan. Tour Econ 22(4):793–808

Ostrom E (2010) The challenge of common-pool resources. Environment 50(4):8–20

Plog S (1972) Why destination areas rise and fall in popularity. Hotel Restaur Admin Q 14:55–58

Polo C, Valle E (2012) Input-output and SAM models. In: Dwyer L, Gill A, Seetaram N (eds) Handbook of research methods in tourism: quantitative and qualitative approaches. Edward Elgar Publishing, Cheltenham, pp 227–260

Risso W, Barquet A, Brida J (2010) Causality between economic growth and tourism expansion: empirical evidence from Trentino-Alto Adige. TOURISMOS Int Multidisciplinary J Tour 5(2):87–98

Rodriguez J, Parra-Lopez E, Yanez-Estevez V (2008) The sustainability of island destinations: tourism area life cycle and teleological perspectives. The case of Tenerife. Tour Manag 29:53–65

Romão J, Nijkamp P (Forthcoming) Spatial impacts assessment of tourism and territorial capital: a modelling study on regional development in Europe

Romão J, Guerreiro J, Rodrigues PMM (2016) Tourism growth and regional resilience: the "beach disease" and the consequences of the global crisis of 2007. Tour Econ 22(4):699–714

Russel R (2006) The contribution of Entrepreneurship theory to the TALC model. In: Butler R (ed) The tourism area life cycle, vol. 2: Conceptual and theoretical issues. Channel View Publications, Clevedon, pp 105–123

Russo A (2001) The "vicious circle" of tourism development in heritage cities. Erasmus University, Rotterdam

Saayman M, Saayman A (2014) Who is willing to pay to see the big 7? Tour Econ 20(6):1181–1198

Sanz-Ibáñez C, Clavé S (2014) The evolution of destinations: towards an evolutionary and relational economic geography approach. Tour Geogr 16(4):563–579

Smeral E (2009) The impact of the financial and economic crisis on European tourism. J Travel Res 48(1):3–13

Song H, Lin S (2010) Impacts of the financial and economic crisis on tourism in Asia. J Travel Res 49(1):16–30

Tang C, Jang S (2009) The tourism-economy causality in the United States: a sub-industry level examination. Tour Manag 30(4):553–558

Ullman EL (1954) Amenities as a factor in regional growth. Geogr Rev 44:119–132

UNWTO (2018) Tourism highlights. UNWTO, Madrid

Wall G (1982) Cycles and capacity: incipient theory or conceptual contradiction? Tour Manag 3:188–192

Weaver D (2006) The "plantation" variant of the TALC in the small-island Caribbean. In: Butler R (ed) The tourism area life cycle, vol. 1: Applications and modifications. Channel View Publications, Clevedon, pp 185–197

Weaver D (2010) Indigenous tourism stages and their implications for sustainability. J Sustain Tour 18(1):43–60

Weaver D, Lawton LJ (2007) Twenty years on: the state of contemporary ecotourism research. Tour Manag 28:1168–1179

Wright WCC, Eppink FV (2016) Drivers of heritage value: a meta-analysis of monetary valuation studies of cultural heritage. Ecol Econ 130:277–284

Zhong L, Deng J, Xiang B (2008) Tourism development and the tourism area life-cycle model: a case study of Zhangjiajie National Forest Park, China. Tour Manag 29:841–856

Chapter 3
Tourism, a Place-Based Activity

Contents

Abstract The uniqueness of natural and cultural features constitutes a central aspect for a strategy of destination differentiation in contemporary tourism, requiring particular care, planning, and monitoring processes when integrated into products and services. This chapter analyzes the potential contribution of these sensitive resources for local sustainable development processes, along with a discussion on the potential negative impacts exerted by tourism activities. This can be observed for the possible degradation or destruction of natural resources and ecosystems and also when looking at questions related to the uniqueness, authenticity, and evolving character of local cultural heritage, taking into account the different perceptions,

---

Case study 3.1: Nature, Culture, and Tourism Demand
Romão J (2015) Culture or Nature: a space-time analysis on the determinants of tourism demand in European regions. Discussion Papers Spatial and Organizational Dynamics 14
Case study 3.2: Nature, Culture, and Value Added by Tourism
Romão J, Guerreiro J, Rodrigues PMM (2017) Territory and sustainable tourism development: a space-time analysis on European regions. Region 4(3):1–17
Case study 3.3: Motivations, Segmentation, Loyalty, and Urban Cultural Heritage
Romão J, Neuts B, Nijkamp P, Shikida A (2014) Determinants of trip choice, satisfaction and loyalty in an eco-tourism destination: A modeling study on the Shiretoko Peninsula, Japan. Ecological Economics 107:195–205
Case study 3.4: Motivations and Segmentation in Ecotourism
Romão J, Neuts B, Nijkamp P, Leeuwen ES van (2015) Culture, product differentiation and market segmentation: a structural analysis of the motivation and satisfaction of tourists in Amsterdam. Tourism Economics 21(3):455–474

© Springer Nature Singapore Pte Ltd. 2018   37
J. Romão, *Tourism, Territory and Sustainable Development*, New Frontiers
in Regional Science: Asian Perspectives 28,
https://doi.org/10.1007/978-981-13-0426-2_3

backgrounds, and motivations of each individual (resident or tourist), which implies a permanent process of negotiation between different perspectives and eventually conflictual values. In the context of tourism, the importance of interpretation is emphasized, as a tool to ensure the *(co-)creation* of different types of significant experiences for different types of tourists, stressing the importance of market segmentation processes as a complement to the strategies of territorial differentiation based on local uniqueness. The sensitiveness of these resources and their importance as structural aspects of the daily life of residents and local identities reinforce the importance of community involvement and participatory decision-making mechanisms for the management of natural and cultural resources in tourism activities.

Keywords Natural resources · Sustainable tourism · Heritage tourism · Significance · Differentiation · Segmentation

3.1   Introduction

Travelling is an ancient activity, as it is the study of temporary human flows for recreational or cultural reasons, the choice of destinations, or the motivations underlying it. This is witnessed in different types of analysis, including literary texts or contributions from different scientific disciplines, like geography, sociology, anthropology, environmental studies, economics, marketing, or management. This long history of travelling and studying travel behaviors offers a wide and varied source of information about the contemporary tourism industry and the relations between the characteristics of places and the motivations of travellers. In fact, tourism is clearly a place-dependent activity: contrary to most of the other economic activities, tourism services are produced and consumed in the same location, while the provision of these services is highly dependent on the specific resources existing in each destination.

In particular, the natural characteristics of the places have always been – and still are – major determinants for the attraction of visitors. With different impacts depending on the evolution of each destination, the utilization of natural resources for tourism purposes raises important questions in terms of their preservation and the contribution for the well-being of the populations of the destinations where they are located. Depending on resources that must be preserved, tourism based on natural assets requires an adequate management, including the definition of limits according to the carrying capacity of each site. In this context, nature has a potential high contribution for the differentiation of a destination (once natural conditions are not possible to replicate in other places) and requires a precise strategy of segmentation of demand (once there are limits to the utilization of resources, it is important to attract the tourists who are aware of their characteristics and the need to preserve them).

Although the importance of the preservation of sensitive natural resources (along with some critical views on their destruction and degradation due to overuse related to leisure activities) was acknowledged within tourism studies much before, these aspects gained renewed interest after the publication of *Our Common Future* (World Commission on Environment and Development 1987) and the generalization of the concept of sustainable development. Along with the concern with the protection of resources, the importance of the contribution of tourism for the improvement of the socio-economic conditions of the host communities was also emphasized. Consequently, the idea of competitiveness of destinations, when faced in a long-term perspective, also included concerns related to the sustainability of tourism, both in terms of the preservation of resources and also in terms of its impact on the living conditions of host communities.

In a similar way, the cultural characteristics and heritage existing in a destination contribute to shape its uniqueness, also providing a solid basis for a strategy of destination differentiation. Like it happens for the natural environment, cultural heritage is unique in each place and impossible to replicate elsewhere. Cultural aspects reinforce the character of tourism as a place-based activity, justifying the adoption of international guidelines by different institutions (in particular, ICOMOS, UNESCO, and the World Tourism Organization), in order to define an adequate conceptual framework and appropriate management tools for its integration into the processes of tourism development. This also includes immaterial aspects, linked to local knowledge, traditions, and lifestyles, which assume raising importance within post-Fordist societies, where cultural values tend to be closely linked to economic products and services and the focus on the role of personal experiences tends to replace the focus on resources and material products.

It is also noteworthy that natural and cultural resources are object of a process of *commodification* when used for tourism purposes: in fact, these aspects only become available to tourists when transformed (or integrated) into products and services. This commercial exploitation can lead to overuse and degradation, when not supported by adequate planning processes, which should involve the local communities, as expressed by most of the international institutions (although, in fact, not effectively implemented in most of the tourism destinations). For the particular case of cultural heritage, it should be noted that questions like *identity* or *authenticity* – which are crucial for the marketing strategies of differentiation of a destination – are not static or objective elements. Instead, they are the result of dynamic processes, involving conflictual views among members of the local communities, while being used by visitors according to their own characteristics, motivations, and perceptions.

As the specific characteristics of the places – both regarding their natural and cultural aspects – constitute core elements for tourism attractiveness, they are usually considered the *pull factors* motivating the choice of a destination. In this sense, nature and culture are at the core of the processes of differentiation that make a destination unique. The integration of this unique supply into global processes of monopolistic competition requires, on the other hand, the ability to attract the specific market segments which are interested in these features and motivated for the

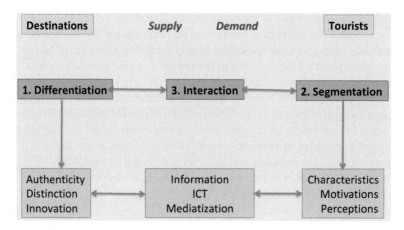

Fig. 3.1 Differentiation, segmentation, and information in tourism

visit. Thus, place-based differentiation must be linked to a strategy of market segmentation, so as to guarantee a satisfactory provision of adequate services to the right type of consumers, with different characteristics, motivations, and perceptions regarding the ecological or cultural values of each site.

This chapter is organized as follows. Section 3.2 discusses the relation between natural resources and tourism development, the importance of their preservation, and their role for the sustainable development of the host communities. Section 3.3 focuses on the integration of culture and cultural heritage into tourism dynamics, taking into consideration the importance of the immaterial aspects and the role of the *experience* in the contemporary processes of consumption. Starting from a discussion of the concept of *authenticity*, Sect. 3.4 emphasizes the importance of interpretation of the local values (both natural and cultural) taking into account different types of perceptions and motivations from different visitors. Finally, Sect. 3.5 establishes a link between the differentiation of destinations and the strategies of market segmentation. Four Case Studies are presented, with empirical illustrations of some of the conceptualizations discussed along the chapter. Figure 3.1 represents this double process of destination differentiation and market segmentation, mediated by the role of information, to be discussed in detail in Chap. 4.

3.2 Nature and the Sustainable Use of Resources

The enjoyment of nature and natural landscapes is an ancient motive for travelling and a core element of the tourism experience, as it is widely analyzed in the literature. Thermal waters attracted visitors in many parts of Europe after the seventeenth century, leading to the creation of holiday resorts in different countries, including notorious destinations in Germany (like Baden-Baden), the United Kingdom (Bath), or France (Vichy). These are just some examples of places where the socio-economic elites found conditions for their leisure activities, combining a health-oriented approach based on the properties of the water with the enjoyment of natural landscapes and entertainment, often including facilities like casinos (Patmore 1968, Walton 2013). In countries like Japan, short travels from urban centers to rural areas to enjoy the *onsen* (traditional Japanese bath) experience constitute an ancient tradition, at the least in the last 3,000 years (Graburn 1995). Also for the population of the Roman Empire, the utilization of thermal waters was part of the daily life, and it was common for the Roman social elites to move toward mountain areas during summer, as observed by Butler (2015) in his systematization of historical touristic movements around the world. These aspects will be discussed with more detail in Chap. 5.

With the development of rail transportation networks along the nineteenth century and the increasing utilization of automobiles during the twentieth century, a shift in the tourism fluxes toward the coastal areas has been observed in many countries (including Southern Europe), starting a process of development of the *sun and sea* destinations. The yearly movements of the Russian tsar and his court to the South of France during the final part of the nineteenth century are often seen as the birth of modern tourism. Later on, with the development of the welfare state over the twentieth century (in different moments and grades in different parts of the world), the assumption of the workers' right to paid holidays, the reduction in working time, or the increasing discretionary income contributed to the massification of tourism, with *sun and sea* destinations becoming extremely popular in places where the weather conditions are more suitable for summer holidays. This also has raised the interest for scientific research in tourism, as confirmed by early studies proposed by Gilbert (1939) or Stansfield (1972).

Clearly representing a wide process of democratization of leisure and tourism, this massive tourism development in coastal areas also implied a process of degradation of sensitive ecological areas, excessive construction of accommodation facilities and other tourism-oriented infrastructures, or different types of relevant impacts on the lifestyle and living conditions of the local populations. As it has been observed in Sect. 2.3 (when discussing the life cycle of tourism destinations), such a process of tourism development normally starts with positive socio-economic impacts on the local economies, but negative impacts may emerge during the stages of development of a destination, mostly when tourism growth is not adequately supported by economic and territorial planning. This lack of planning was, in fact, observed in many coastal areas with strong tourism development during the later decades of the twentieth century.

On the other hand, the reinforcement of a local or regional specialization pattern based on the tourism sector can lead to a process of lock-in path (as discussed in Sect. 2.4), related to the regional economic dependence on the overexploitation of sensitive natural resources. As it was observed in Case Study 2.2 (Romão et al. 2017), this type of development can lead, in the long run, to a transformation of the regional economic structures, with tourism and the production of non-tradable products and services replacing other activities, like those related to agriculture, fisheries, or manufacture.

Moreover, as it is presented in Case Studies 2.1 (Romão 2015) and 2.2 (Romão et al. 2017) – which offer a comprehensive analysis, at the European level, of the contemporary relations between the regional endowment on natural resources and tourism dynamics in Europe – Southern European regions generally show a very high level of tourism demand with relatively low value added by tourism activities. This suggests that these regions – with a very rich biodiversity within the European context and a tourism demand very dependent on the *sun and sea* travel motivation – have generally implemented massive forms of tourism development, with relatively low socio-economic benefits for the local communities and potential high environmental impacts on the territories.

The negative impacts of mass tourism development, mostly those observed in coastal areas after the 1960s, in different parts of the world, have led to the emergence of different types of critical approaches, both in terms of the social conflicts emerging between residents and visitors of mass tourism destinations and also within the academic literature. In fact, the *host-guest* conflict as a scientific research topic has a relatively long history. Already during the 1970s, Doxey (1975) proposed the *Irridex* – an *index of irritation* measuring the negative reaction of local residents regarding tourism development – as an early effort to address this problem. Even before the conceptualization of the evolutionary approach to a tourism destination proposed by the *Tourism Area Life Cycle* conceptualization (Butler 1980), Doxey took into consideration the evolving impacts of tourism on the daily life of the residents, describing a path "from euphoria to antagonism" in the relation between local residents and tourists. Thirty years later on, Wall and Mathieson (2006) would describe it as a process from "euphoria to xenophobia." With the massification of urban tourism observed in the last years, this tension has also spread to the city context, as observed, among others, by Bimonte and Punzo (2016).

With the emergence and global acceptance of the idea of sustainability, after the publication of the document "Our Common Future" (World Commission on Environment and Development, 1987), this concept was also applied in tourism studies, emphasizing the importance of the preservation of territorial resources when used for tourism purposes. Sharpley (2009) summarized the early efforts to integrate this idea into the field of tourism studies, by mentioning the examples of the "Strategy for Sustainable Tourism Development" (a report published after a tourism Conference in Vancouver in 1990), the "Sustainable Tourism Development Conference" (the first conference oriented to this specific topic, in Edinburgh in 1990), the publication by the English Tourist Board (1991) of *The Green Light: A Guide to Sustainable Tourism*, the creation of the *Journal of Sustainable Tourism* in 1992, or the publication of *Sustainable Tourism Development: Guide for Local Planners* by the World Tourism Organization (1993).

In an initial stage, the concept of sustainability applied to tourism activities was clearly linked to the promotion of *niche* forms of tourism: small-scale tourism segments, oriented to the concept of differentiation, one of the generic strategic formulations proposed by Porter (1985) for achieving a competitive position. This was suggested, among others, by authors like Poon (1994), opposing this strategic option to an alternative based on cost leadership, related to mass tourism, with low prices, low value added for the regional economies and high negative externalities.

Nevertheless, Butler (1999) would later on claim that sustainability and the principles of sustainable development should be applied to all types of tourism development and planning, including mass tourism, observing that the excessive use of sensitive territorial resources can also occur in small-scale forms of tourism activities. This author would also point out the important distinction between the sustainable utilization of territorial resources for tourism activities (which is the focus of this chapter) and the impacts of tourism on sustainable development, which includes the achievement of socio-economic benefits for the local populations living in tourism destinations (as it will be discussed with more detail in Chap. 5).

Despite the existence of (much) earlier attempts to address these questions (Meinecke 1929, ORRRC 1962, Wagar 1964), the research on these topics increased significantly at the global level during the subsequent years. Different authors analyzed the relations between competitive strategies for differentiation in tourism and the importance of unique territorial resources (often linked to the ecologic characteristics of the destinations), along with the importance of the preservation of these sensitive assets. This type of analysis had important implications in terms of the definition of limits for the utilization of these resources, taking into consideration the carrying capacity of each site. Buhalis (1999), Hassan (2000), or Page and Dowling (2002) offered relevant examples of this type of approach, while Miller and Twining-Ward (2005) or Weaver (2006) offered exhaustive analysis of these problems, also proposing indicators for their measure.

Later on, Williams and Ponsford (2009) would define as the *environmental paradox* this double process of exploitation and protection of resources: the supply of tourism products depends on the exploitation of resources that must be preserved. Moreover, with the recent global awareness regarding climate change and its high potential impacts on coastal areas, the study of the environmental aspects of tourism dynamics gained a renewed interest, as observed by authors like Weaver (2011). In a more critical perspective, Douglas (2014) would point out that the integration of environmental or cultural territorial features into tourism products implies their commercialization, with the subsequent potential problems related to their excessive use, degradation, or even destruction, as it will be discussed with more detail later on. Jovicic (2014) offers a systematic overview of these contributions. It is also noteworthy that the definition of tourism competitiveness proposed by Ritchie and Crouch (2003) – and generally accepted in the subsequent literature – aims at integrating the concept of sustainability (both in terms of the sustainable use of tourism resources and the impacts of tourism on sustainable development) into the competitive strategies, by assuming a long-term perspective (as it will be discussed in Chaps. 4 and 5).

Despite the diversification of recreational, leisure, and tourism activities observed in the last decades, natural resources still constitute a major asset for tourism in contemporary societies. Along with the persistence of *sun and sea* tourism or sports tourism related to activities in the sea (sail, kayak, surf, diving, etc.) or in the mountains (sky and other winter sports), other types of nature-based tourism have gained importance recently, including ecotourism (in different types of natural parks) and active and adventure tourism (hiking, biking, *radical* activities, etc.), along with the redevelopment of thermal resources oriented to new wellness practices and health-oriented activities (as it will be analyzed with more detail in Chap. 5). The dependence of all these activities on the integrity of the natural resources constituting the core of the destination attractiveness calls for a careful planning for their utilization.

3.3   Culture and Tourism in the *Experience Economy*

As it was discussed for the natural characteristics and resources of destinations, cultural features also contribute decisively for tourism attractiveness based on the uniqueness of each place. In this sense, these assets also have a high potential contribution for the achievement of a differentiated position within tourism markets, once the specific cultural characteristics prevailing in each territory are normally impossible to replicate in different places. In fact, cultural motives are also documented as ancient reasons for travelling, for example, when related to religious aspects, as observed by Butler (2015).

The tendency for the incorporation of cultural, affective, and symbolic values into products and services (or, in broader terms, into the contemporary production and consumption systems) constitutes an important characteristic of *post-Fordist* societies, as witnessed by a large number of authors (Scott 2007). Consequently, the relation between local or regional development and the cultural dynamics or artistic production gained renewed attention over the past years, as Fusco-Girard and Nijkamp (2009) observed. In the particular field of tourism – normally including a varied set of creative activities, eventually requiring qualified or specialized human resources – this tendency has been clearly revealed through the increasing importance of the concept of *experience* (Tussyadiah 2014), replacing the importance of the availability of specific resources as core determinants of destination attractiveness. Consequently, the focus of tourism management and policies has gradually shifted from resource and facility management to questions related to livability or cultural interaction, with implications on territorial and destination design. These questions will be discussed with more detail in Chap. 4.

Culture is a broad concept, comprising a wide range of elements, both material and immaterial, often used with different meanings in tourism studies. For the purposes of this discussion, culture is considered as the "set of distinctive spiritual, material, intellectual and emotional features of society or a social group, that encompasses, not only art and literature, but lifestyles, ways of living together, value systems, traditions and beliefs," as defined by UNESCO (2001). Assuming this definition, two broad cultural domains can be identified: the economic (comprising the production of cultural goods and services) and the social (comprising the participation in cultural activities), which are both relevant in the context of tourism activities. These domains are interrelated within a *cultural cycle*, a set of practices, activities, and resources required to transform ideas into cultural goods and services for consumers, participants, or users, involving different stages: creation (ideas and concepts), production (realization and reproduction), dissemination (to exhibitors, users, or consumers), transmission (related to places for transmission of knowledge and skills), and consumption (activities of audiences and participants). The integration of cultural aspects into tourism dynamics has implications on all these stages of the cycle.

With particular importance for the context of tourism, the related concept of cultural heritage has evolved significantly over the last decades. When the Venice Charter (ICOMOS 1965) updated the Athens Charter (approved in 1931), this UNESCO-related organization enlarged the concept of historic monument in order to "embrace not only the single architectural work but also the urban or rural setting in which is found the evidence of a particular civilization, a significant development or a historic event. This applies not only to great works of art but also to more modest works of the past which have acquired cultural significance with the passing of time."

Acknowledging the importance of cultural heritage for tourism activities, the International Cultural Tourism Charter (ICOMOS 1999) defined its scope, its role for the differentiation of tourism destinations in a context of globalization, and its relation with the ecological features of the places, by pointing out that "heritage is a broad concept and includes the natural as well as the cultural environment. It encompasses landscapes, historic places, sites and built environments, as well as bio-diversity, collections, past and continuing cultural practices, knowledge and living experiences. It records and expresses the long processes of historic development, forming the essence of diverse national, regional, indigenous and local identities and is an integral part of modern life."

Stressing the importance of an adequate management in order to preserve the integrity of the sites, this document also suggests that heritage constitutes a "dynamic reference point and positive instrument for growth and change. The particular heritage and collective memory of each locality or community is irreplaceable and an important foundation for development, both now and into the future." In this sense, heritage-based tourism should offer relevant socio-economic benefits for the local communities while requiring their active participation in the management of heritage resources and tourism dynamics at the local level, in collaboration with public authorities, private companies, and technical experts.

In fact, this document constitutes a major reference for the management of cultural heritage in tourism destinations, defining six major principles: encouraging public awareness of heritage (as a way to promote intercultural exchanges between hosts and guests), managing a dynamic relationship between heritage places and tourism (which involves conflicting values), ensuring a worthwhile visitor experience (satisfying the needs and motivations of tourists), involving host and indigenous communities (in planning processes for heritage conservation and tourism), providing benefits for the local community (through job creation and valorization of local products), and defining responsible promotion programs (protecting and natural and cultural heritage). Although these principles were defined almost 20 years ago, they still offer a useful framework for the integration of local heritage into contemporary tourism dynamics. It also possible to observe that the principles of community involvement and participation into the management of heritage and tourism dynamics at the local are, in general, far from satisfactory.

In a similar way, also international tourism related institutions implemented recommendations for the utilization of cultural resources and heritage into tourism dynamics (OECD 2009, 2014). In particular, the Global Code of Ethics for Tourism (UNWTO 2001) emphasizes the role of tourism as a "vehicle for individual and collective fulfillment" and its contribution to "mutual understanding and respect between peoples and societies," by using the cultural heritage while contributing to its enhancement. In this context, the document stresses the right to travel of any person, along with the responsibilities and obligations of all the stakeholders involved in the tourism sector, as a precondition for the achievement of benefits for the local communities and the contribution for a process of sustainable development. Thus, cultural heritage is seen both as a tourism resource requiring adequate management and also as an outcome of tourism activity, as a result of its utilization and valorization, with potential positive impacts on sustainable development.

The immaterial aspects of cultural heritage that were implicit in previous documents would be more explicitly addressed by UNESCO (2003), when defining *intangible cultural heritage* as "practices, representations, expressions, knowledge, skills – as well as the instruments, objects, artifacts and cultural spaces associated therewith – that communities, groups and, in some cases, individuals recognize as part of their cultural heritage." This document also defines the scope of activities comprised within immaterial heritage, by mentioning oral traditions and expressions, performing arts, social practices, rituals or festive events, knowledge or practices concerning nature and the universe, or traditional craftsmanship.

This definition of immaterial cultural heritage would be integrated into institutional guidelines for tourism activities by UNWTO (2003), emphasizing the potential role of tourism for its preservation and economic valuation, while reinforcing the sense of pride and belonging of local communities. In this context, the document points out some major challenges for heritage tourism, implying a long-term strategy: understanding the links between these two concepts; defining tourism products based on heritage; identifying stakeholders, creating partnerships, and establishing participation mechanisms; maintaining authenticity and setting limits of acceptable change; balancing education and entertainment; ensuring cultural dynamism; and implementing research and monitoring systems.

The utilization and preservation of cultural resources is also a matter of major concern when looking at major internationally recognized sites, as it is the case of those classified as World Heritage. As observed by Bandarin (2005), although the applications for this status are normally based on the definition of conservation strategies, this classification tends to increase the attractiveness of the place and the number of visitors, increasing the risks of damage – *a double-edged sword*, as the author points out. Thus, despite the existence of relevant potential benefits for the local economies, the management of this type of site also presents important challenges related to the limits of their utilization, according to their carrying capacity, in a similar way as it was observed before for natural resources.

3.4   Authenticity, Interpretation, and Perceptions

Along with these evolving definitions of culture and cultural heritage, also their analysis within tourism studies evolved along the last decades. In particular, it was observed that the visit to a particular heritage site does not imply that this is the main motivation for the trip: in fact, a tourist can be primarily motivated by other aspects of the destination (e.g., the beach, a natural park, sports facilities, nightlife, business, etc.) but still take the opportunity to visit a museum or a monument. Based on this idea, Poria et al. (2001) shifted the focus of the definition of heritage tourism from the resources of the destination to the motivations of the travellers, assuming it as a form of tourism which is more related to the motivations and perceptions of the visitor than to the attributes of the site. In this sense, they define heritage tourism as "a subgroup of tourism, in which the main motivation for visiting a site is based on the place's heritage characteristics according to the tourists' perception of their own heritage."

The definition proposed by these authors emphasizes the importance of the personal cultural background of each tourist, as a major factor determining the motivations and perceptions about the attributes of the site. These aspects would be analyzed in a subsequent work (Poria et al. 2003), identifying different types of behavior of tourists (before, during, and after the visit to a heritage site), depending on the attributes of the site, along with personal characteristics or awareness and perceptions regarding the heritage elements concerned. In particular, the authors observed that tourists perceiving a heritage site as part of their own heritage tend to reveal significantly different types of behavior when compared with tourists who do not perceive the same way. This aspect stresses the importance of the emotional elements of the experience of visiting a heritage site, as long as it reveals the importance of taking into consideration different motivations, expectations, and perceptions of tourists for the management and tourism marketing strategies of heritage sites.

In a broader context, the perception of the importance of the spatial settings where heritage sites are located – and contributing to understand their meaning and their relation with local communities – has been also reinforced as a crucial element for their preservation and interpretation (ICOMOS 2005), enlarging the scope of heritage from a specific individual site to a broader geographical area, eventually including several heritage sites. This document – updating the Venice Charter (ICOMOS 1965) – reinforces the importance of interpretation for a full understanding and appreciation of the characteristics of historical heritage, while defining planning tools and practices for the management of heritage settings, rather than individual sites.

This dynamic character of cultural heritage, along with the different interpretations and utilizations potentially made by different persons regarding the same cultural asset or setting, has particular importance in the case of tourism, once it implies different processes of communication according to the different perceptions and motivations of different tourists. Moreover, the integration of cultural elements into the touristic dynamics of each place requires a process of commodification – through the transformation or integration of cultural assets and values into tourism products and services – which potentially implies a process of transformation along time, thus reinforcing the dynamic character of cultural heritage.

As observed by Wait (2000), when used in the context of tourism, heritage assets and locations also offer the setting for other travel motivations. Thus, the commoditized version of cultural heritage offered to tourists tends to be adapted to this type of motivation, raising the question of the *authenticity* of the heritage tourism experience, once every representation of cultural heritage is necessarily partial, selective, and depending on subjective factors, not only related to the recipient of information (the traveller) but also to the managers and marketers of heritage sites. In this context, commoditization can be seen as a "process by which things (and activities) come to be evaluated primarily in terms of their exchange value, in a context of trade, thereby becoming goods (and services)," as defined by Cohen (1988).

In a similar perspective, Harrison (2005) points out that the meanings associated with cultural heritage are continuously redefined within a complex process of social interaction and negotiation, as the integration of history within an experience (touristic or not) is necessarily subjective, reflecting dominant perspectives (related to social class, power relations, or local and nationalistic feelings) existing in each society at each moment. This author compares the processes of *commodification* of cultural heritage inherent to their integration into tourism products to the exhibition of artistic or cultural objects in museums and art galleries, once these objects were also subject to processes of trade aiming at performing specific functions for an audience. Nevertheless, although tourism tends to exacerbate such a process of commodification in a similar way, it must be noted that the impacts of large-scale forms of tourism can be significantly higher than those related to the impacts of exhibitions in museums and art galleries. It must be also noted that in both cases, the performative utilization of such artistic or cultural objects may contribute for the preservation of skills and traditions that could have disappeared in their absence.

In the context of this double process of permanent rediscussion and renegotiation about cultural heritage – both within local communities (where individuals or groups with different and often conflicting values and preferences dispute their hegemony) and in the relation between local communities and visitors (also an heterogeneous group, with different preferences and motivations, as will be discussed later on), neither the interpretation nor the right to access to monuments or other cultural sites can be seen as permanent or universal, as observed and discussed by Evans (2005). Thus, an effective community involvement appears as a crucial element for the management of cultural heritage, both in terms of the potentially conflictual views existing within local communities and also in terms of the preservation of local characteristics in face of the commodification processes related to its integration into tourism products. In fact, this utilization of heritage by the tourism industry tends to be promoted by a limited number of stakeholders, with their specific motivations and values, normally related to commercial interests (in the case of private companies) or preservation of political power (in the case of public institutions).

Although this reinforcement of the power and control of local communities over cultural heritage is also claimed by most of the international institutions with relevant work on this field, community involvement is still far from being a generalized practice in heritage management for tourism. As a consequence, as Wait (2000) observes, when contributing to create a stage for the broad set of activities performed by tourists, heritage settings tend to be used for tourism marketing purposes as a unified set, corresponding to a specific view of the historical aspects or cultural values, so that it can easily be placed in the market and perceived by consumers. Thus, conflictual views of local history or culture tend to be avoided, in order to generate a unique – and manipulated – vision, corresponding to the prevailing commercial or political interests involved and presented as *authentic* within touristic markets.

Aspects related to the *authenticity* of cultural tourism experiences have been analyzed – at least – since the sociological studies of tourist motivations and experiences proposed by MacCannell (1973), who discussed the contradiction between the desire of the tourists for authentic cultural experiences and the fact that all the setting of a tourism destination is prepared in advance to host the tourists, thus implying the impossibility of an *authentic* experience. This discussion has been developed by Cohen (1988), by observing that the transformation of cultural experiences into tourism products, a process of commodification, as observed before, implies that *authentic* cultural experiences, in the context of tourism, are represented, in fact, by a process of *staged authenticity* – a representation of the local culture oriented to the motivations of the travellers, implying a selection of specific cultural manifestations and, eventually, a transformation of the cultural meanings and values involved.

While observing that this process can occur in areas where tourism is in the earlier stages of its development (with native population performing specific parts of their culture) and also in mass tourism destinations (where all the setting is prepared to accommodate tourists), this author also claims that *authenticity* is not an objective fact – both for the tourists and also for the local residents. In fact, cultural heritage is subjective to multiple contradictions within any community: history and memory are always matters of social and political dispute, and even if some aspects can be commonly shared among their members, other aspects can have different meanings, interpretations, and importance. Thus, *authenticity* is perceived by local residents as a subjective and dynamic aspect, normally with relevant transformations over time and significant differences between social groups.

Paradoxically, in the context of tourism development, *staged authenticity* – oriented to commoditized consumption by tourists – can emerge as a unifying element of local culture, within the dynamic process of historical evolution of a tourism destination. The case of Disneyland or other similar built facilities for tourism attraction are examples of this process: starting as a process of *staged authenticity*, performed for visitors and without strong roots within the local communities, these places may become – as times passes – important symbols of the local culture, being recognized as such by local residents. This process, defined by Cohen (1988) as *emergent authenticity*, can be seen as an *invention of tradition*. In this context, authenticity is a socially constructed concept, implying a permanent negotiation and transformation, both when considering the local communities and also their interaction with tourists.

3.5   Destination Differentiation and Market Segmentation

Natural and cultural characteristics of each place contribute for its uniqueness. The impossibility to replicate these aspects opens the possibility for a monopolistic process of competition between destinations, each of them offering singular attractions to potential visitors. Nevertheless, a tourism destination comprises a much wider set of services and facilities, which can be linked to these unique territorial aspects. In that sense, a tourism destination can be seen as a multi-service complex oriented to multiple segments of the tourism market, exploring its uniqueness with the adequate type of services for each type of tourists. Defining a mix of products and services for the needs and motivations of specific segments of the tourism market is crucial for contemporary tourism marketing and destination management, in a global and highly competitive environment (Matias et al., 2007).

It is also noteworthy that tourists tend to develop an overall perception of their satisfaction with a destination, despite the fragmentation of their experiences, using different services provided by diverse companies or enjoying public and common places, spaces, infrastructures, and facilities (Buhalis 2000). From this perspective, a solid and coherent coordination between the local unique resources and the multiple services offered in a destination is a crucial aspect for the achievement of a differentiated position within the international tourism markets. Moreover, the adaptation of these services to the specific needs and motivations of different groups (business or leisure visitors; solo travellers, groups or families; young and older tourists; etc.) is also a decisive aspect to take into account in the tourism destination marketing strategies (Kozak and Rimmington 2000; Castro et al. 2007). In fact, each tourist creates a personal perception (image) about different places which will determine the decision to travel, the choice of a destination, or the specific aspects, products, and services to explore and to consume during the trip (Chen and Tsai 2007).

Travelling – considered as a search for a personal enrichment, which contributes for the realization of the individual's potential – can be included within the *self-actualization* level of needs, on the top of the Maslow's hierarchy (Maslow, 1943). The motivations for travelling have been extensively analyzed and systematized within the tourism literature over the past decades. Among the most popular conceptualizations is the distinction between *pull* and *push* factors proposed by Crompton (1979), defining that *push* factors (Iso-Ahola 1989) are those influencing the decision to travel (related to personal preferences and intrinsic motivations of tourists, like relaxation, entertainment, escape from routine, adventure, sports, etc.), while *pull* factors determine the choice of a specific destination. According to this conceptualization, *pull* factors are those related to the specific characteristics of each place, including its cultural assets, natural resources, climate, landscape, or facilities. This type of formulation has been used in a large number of studies in very different destinations, once the identification of the *pull* factors appears as a crucial element to identify what kind of travellers (market segments) can be attracted by the specific characteristics and services of a specific destination (differentiation) or to decide about the services and facilities required to attract them (Dann 1981, Bansal and Eiselt 2004, Yoon and Uysal 2005).

On the other hand, Martin Armario (2008) considers this interactive selection process between the motivations of the tourist and characteristics of the places as the first phase of the travel, while the second phase consists in the experience at the destination. As it will be discussed in Chap. 4, a third phase can also be taken into account, referring to the feedbacks of the traveller after the tourism experience, which tend to assume higher importance within contemporary tourism with the generalization and massive utilization of information and communication technologies (in particular, the so-called social networks).

It should be also noted that the pull factors defining a place clearly indicate the expectations of the tourists about the destination. Therefore, an adequate process of positioning and branding the destination and its features within the global tourism market appears as a precondition to guarantee the satisfaction of the visitors. In fact, satisfaction with the tourism experience can only be achieved if the resources, services, and facilities available at a destination can meet the expectations and perceived images of the visitors before the travel. As observed by Chi and Qu (2008) or Lee (2009), the analysis of the relation between the pull factors of the destination and the satisfaction levels of tourists achieved with each of them is a crucial aspect for the strategies of market segmentation.

Satisfaction with the destination – seen as the overall result of the satisfaction achieved with the multiple aspects and services experienced during a travel – offers a decisive contribution for the loyalty of tourists, as observed by Castro et al. (2007) or Lee (2009). Defined as the intention to revisit the place or to recommend it to friends and families (Oppermann 2000, Yoon and Uysal 2005; Chen and Tsai 2007), achieving high levels of loyalty is normally one of the major aims of marketing strategies, as this type of tourist offers very reliable promotion of the destination without any cost (which is an increasingly important aspect, with the development of ICT) and also because their increased knowledge about the place, when revisiting, normally allows them to achieve a better enjoyment of the local services and amenities.

The segmentation of tourism markets assumes special importance for ecotourism destinations, as it is discussed in Case Study 3.3 (Romão et al. 2015). The tourism supply in these destinations is highly dependent on sensitive resources, requiring careful utilization by their users. Thus, marketing strategies must be precisely oriented to the specific groups of tourists who are aware of the characteristics of the sites and motivated for activities that do not affect their value and integrity. Moreover, the carrying capacity of these places is normally limited, implying restrictions to the number of visitors. In this context, this type of tourists should be also willing to contribute for the preservation and maintenance costs of these sensitive assets. As it will be discussed in Chap. 4 (Case Study 4.1), information can play a crucial role for this match between the characteristics of these places and type of tourists attracted for visiting them. Additionally, information is also crucial for the understanding and full enjoyment of the ecological aspects of the places.

This matching process between the features of the sites and the characteristics and motivations of tourists is even more important in the context of travels where culture and cultural heritage play an important role as motives of the visit. This aspect is discussed in Case Study 3.4 (Romão et al. 2014), clearly revealing how different characteristics of travellers (and their motivations about cultural heritage) in a specific destination influence the perception of the visitors, their satisfaction with the cultural experiences, and their loyalty to the destination. In particular, this case study reveals that – even when the experiences with the material and immaterial aspects of the travel are both highly satisfactory – immaterial cultural heritage can exert higher impacts on the decision to revisit or to recommend the destination. Thus, tourism marketing and management of destinations where cultural heritage plays an important role must pay careful attention, not only to the built environment (museums, art galleries, monuments, etc.) but also to the immaterial aspects of culture (local knowledge and traditions, lifestyles, etc.).

The importance of questions related to the interpretation of the meaning of culture and cultural heritage discussed before also has implications for the differentiation of the destination (in order to guarantee a unique supply which cannot be replicated in a different place) and the segmentation of tourists (in order to attract the specific groups of visitors who are interested in a specific cultural aspect while offering them the information and the tools to understand and to interpret the features of the place).

In this context, some previously mentioned documents published by ICOMOS define relevant guidelines for the implementation of adequate means of interpretation of heritage sites, both in terms of their educational purposes and also in terms of their utilization for tourism activities, taking into consideration the different types of users, with their specific characteristics, motivations, cultural background, or personal involvement with the heritage concerned. In particular, ICOMOS (2008a) focuses on the access and understanding of heritage sites, the provision of relevant information sources, the contextualization of the site within a spatial setting, the preservation of authenticity, or the planning processes for a sustainable use. On the other hand, ICOMOS (2008b) is oriented for the creation of cultural routes integrating different heritage sites and providing guidelines for the definition of their contents within a specific territorial, cultural, and historical context, the importance of their significance, and interpretation for visitors with different cultural backgrounds and motivations or their dynamic and evolving character.

Different types of definitions have been used within tourism studies in order to define the relation between tourists and cultural heritage. Pearce (1996) distinguished between intrinsic (related to the individual) and extrinsic (related to the sites) motivations, while Apostolakis (2003) described this relation as *experientially based* (focusing on the individual characteristics of the experience at a site) or *descriptive* (when focused on the heritage sites displayed). Taking these conceptualizations into account, Timothy and Boyd (2003) distinguish an analysis centered on the characteristics of supply (the heritage assets) from an analysis centered on demand (the motivations of travellers). This focus on demand and the intrinsic motivations of tourism for an experiential contact with cultural heritage is in accordance with the definition of heritage tourism proposed by Poria et al. (2001) previously discussed, clearly being the most relevant in terms of the processes of market segmentation for tourism destination management.

An early study by Cohen (1979) proposes a categorization of the travel motivations with particular relevance for the case of heritage tourism. This author distinguishes the *recreational mode* (related to trips faced as entertainment, without meaningful cultural purposes), the *diversionary mode* (related to trips aiming at escaping from daily life routines, also without meaningful cultural intentions), the *experiential mode* (related to trips aiming at a search for a lost sense of authenticity which is pursued by witnessing the authenticity of others), the *experimental mode* (search for authenticity through the tourist's own experiences in a different cultural context), and the *existential mode* (aiming at a full immersion in a different culture). These different types of motivations clearly influence the way tourists observe and enjoy local cultures and heritage, along with their concerns regarding the authenticity of the cultural encounters.

Nevertheless, in a later work, Cohen (1988) observes that – in a context of commodification of cultural experiences and performative approaches to heritage oriented to their enjoyment by tourists – travellers revealing higher concerns with cultural heritage (experiential, experimental, and existential) are often not prepared to make informed judgments about the authenticity of their cultural experiences, as they do not have the adequate tools and methods of analysis to do it. In this sense, these travellers can embrace experiences of *staged authenticity* without a critical look, while the other types of tourists (recreational or diversionary) do not have this type of concern. Thus, marketing strategies for destinations where cultural heritage plays an important role must take into account these different motivations and perceptions, so as to provide satisfactory experiences for different types of travellers.

Other types of studies focus on another important aspect of marketing segmentation in heritage tourism: the personal relation of the visitors with the cultural values concerned. Poria et al. (2003) distinguish four different possibilities to define this relation between tourists and heritage assets: visitors who are not aware of the heritage attributes of the site, visitors who are aware of the heritage attributes of the site but are motivated by other attributes, visitors who are motivated by the heritage attributes of the site but do not perceive them as part of their own heritage, and visitors who are motivated by the heritage attributes of the site and perceive them as part of their own heritage. The authors empirically observe different types of behavior on site according to these characteristics, requiring different types of information, interpretation, and services. Moreover, the authors also concluded that higher levels of satisfaction and loyalty are obtained by the travellers who aware of the characteristics of the site and perceive it as part of their personal heritage, which clearly reinforces the importance of effective marketing strategies oriented to specific groups who can be more closely related (and interested) in the characteristics of a specific site. In a different study based on a similar conceptualization, Poria et al. (2006) also observe that the motivation to visit a site increases when it is perceived as part of personal heritage of the visitor.

Taking into consideration the different motivations of heritage travellers and their diverse relations with the sites concerned, Poria et al. (2009) analyzed the role and importance of interpretation in the context of heritage tourism. The authors observed that some visitors (mostly those without personal relation with the heritage under analysis) look for objective information to contextualize the site (acquiring knowledge), while others (mostly those with personal relation with the place) look for an emotional experience, requiring a different type of information (interpretation as a mediator for emotions). Thus, the authors recommend a strategy of customization of the information provided at the sites, requiring innovative approaches to ensure the satisfaction of different visitors. In this sense – and following the previous definition of cultural heritage centered on the demand side (the characteristics and motivations of tourists) – the authors define interpretation as "the process of the transmission of knowledge, its diffusion, and its reception and perception by the individual," clearly emphasizing the central role of the tourists as "active receptors," demanding different types of information according to their needs and motivations.

Inspired by the classification of different levels of authenticity proposed by Wang (1999), Laing et al. (2013) analyze the specific context of wellness tourism, distinguishing *intrinsic authenticity* (a single determination of genuineness), *existential authenticity* (focused on the perception of the tourists, who look for an opportunity to find authentic selves, apart from them daily routines); and *corporeal authenticity* (focused on the physical senses). Wellness services can be rooted in different cultural traditions (the Arabic or Turkish *hammam*, the Finish *sauna*, or the Japanese *onsen* are some examples) and – like in the case of cultural heritage – tourists can have different interests and motivations regarding them. In this case, travellers can look for local knowledge about wellness practices (intrinsic), perceive their own behavior in a non-familiar environment (existential), or enjoy the physical feelings related to the wellness practices (corporeal).

This variety of perceptions, behaviors, and relations established between tourist and heritage sites (and generally occurring, in similar ways, in other type of destinations, once knowledge and cultural values are generally embedded in any kind of tourism experience) also have implications on the analysis of authenticity, its dynamic role, and its different perception, understanding, and meaning for different types of (groups of) tourists. In this sense, Chambers (2009) proposes to shift the focus from the concept of authenticity to the concept of *significance*. This shift allows to consider the multiple and eventually contradictory views about authenticity (even within the local communities, as it was discussed before), along with the diverse motivations, perceptions, needs, and behaviors of tourists. In this context, cultural heritage is appropriated in different ways by different travellers, according to their specific interests, implying the existence of multiple processes of interpretation and utilization of cultural heritage. Thus, providing adequate information and tools for different uses of local heritage implies special care with the preservation of the inherent values of the site. As it will be discussed in Chap. 4, information plays a decisive role in this context.

3.6   Concluding Remarks

This chapter was focused on the importance of natural and cultural assets for contemporary tourism, taking into account the sensitiveness of these resources, mostly when they are transformed into commercial products and services for tourism purposes. As these resources constitute basic elements for a strategy of destination differentiation, a unique and simplified version of their authenticity and contribution for the local identity tends to be adopted for marketing purposes. Assuming heritage as a negotiation process involving conflictual views (even within the local population) and providing tools for an appropriate interpretation of heritage and its contradictions and conflicts, along with the understanding of the different motivations of different segments of the tourism global market and the effective involvement of local population, appear as crucial elements for the preservation of the integrity of these resources.

In particular, this chapter focused on:

– The role of nature as a core element for destination differentiation
– The importance of preserving natural resources when commodified for utilization in tourism processes of development
– The possible negative impacts of tourism on natural resources, along with their potential contribution for local sustainable development
– The importance of combining the concepts of sustainability and competitiveness in a strategy of tourism development
– The role of cultural identity and heritage shaping the uniqueness of a place and supporting a strategy of destination differentiation
– The conflictual views and dynamic negotiation processes within the local communities regarding cultural identity and authenticity
– The role of the characteristics, motivations, and perceptions of tourists when using commodified cultural resources within tourism activities
– The importance of interpretation for multiple perceptions about identity, authenticity, and the different types of tourists visiting heritage sites or using heritage settings for recreational activities
– The need for market segmentation as a complement of the strategies of territorial differentiation based on local uniqueness
– The importance of community involvement for the management of natural and cultural resources in tourism activities

Case Study 3.1: Nature, Culture, and Tourism Demand

Romão J (2015) Culture or Nature: a space-time analysis on the determinants of tourism demand in European regions. Discussion Papers Spatial and Organizational Dynamics 14

Taking advantage of the existence of geo-referenced data at the European level, the development of adequate estimation methods, and the corresponding software tools, this work offers a global overview, at the European level, of the relations between tourism demand and the regional endowment in natural and cultural resources. By using spatial econometric techniques (a panel data model combining spatial and temporal information), the analysis leads to the identification of spatial clusters of regions with similar characteristics, along with relevant processes of spatial heterogeneity among European regions. Spillover effects between regions are also clearly identified by using this type of methodology.

The study includes 237 NUTS 2 regions, according to the Eurostat classification, corresponding to the level at which regional authorities define strategic development policies. All NUTS 2 regions from Austria, Belgium, Bulgaria, Cyprus, Czech Republic, Denmark, Estonia, Finland, France, Germany, Greece, Hungary, Italy, Latvia, Lithuania, Luxemburg, Malta, the Netherlands, Poland, Portugal, Romania, Slovakia, Slovenia, Spain, and the United Kingdom have been analyzed, with the exception of islands (as the distance or absence of contiguity imposes severe problems of estimation within spatial analysis).

The endowment in natural resources was measured according to the percentage of the regional territory of each region classified within the Natura 2000 network (European protected areas, due to their ecological characteristics). Although these are not necessarily tourism products or attractions, they offer a good proxy for the environmental characteristics of the places and the richness of their biodiversity. Moreover, due to the protective regulations applying to these regions, tourism activities are often highly conditioned.

On the other hand, cultural resources were measured according to another international standard classification: the number of World Heritage Sites classified by UNESCO within each region. Also, this indicator has some limitations, as there are other types of material (museums or monuments) and immaterial (traditions, local knowledge, events, etc.) cultural resources that may have a relevant role on tourism dynamics, not being considered in this analysis (due to the limitations related to available data for international comparisons). Nevertheless, the number of classified World Heritage Sites offers a reasonable proxy for the richness of cultural heritage in each region.

The first results of this work relate to the identification of spatial clusters, based on local indicators of spatial association (which compare the score for one region with the score obtained by its neighbors). Reflecting the importance of tourism demand, high shares of the territory within the Natura 2000 network and high number of heritage sites (within the European context) of Southern European regions, this exploratory spatial univariate analysis (considering only one variable) has shown that most of the spatial clusters related to these aspects are located in this area. Moreover, when performing a bivariate analysis (comparing the score of one region for one variable with the score of the neighbors for a different variable), the results have been similar, with Western regions of South Europe showing a clear link between tourism demand and the endowment on natural and cultural resources in the neighborhood. Nevertheless, many *outliers* (regions with very diverse patters of spatial association) have been identified for the relation between natural resources and tourism demand.

Finally, by using a spatial panel model, the correlation between tourism demand and natural and cultural resources, along with other variables, like the abundance of accommodation establishments, has been estimated. As a result of the diversity (outliers) of spatial patterns related to natural assets, the positive impact identified for this parameter was not statistically relevant. Nevertheless, all the other variables had significant statistical impacts, as expected.

Additionally, positive spatial *spillovers* were also identified, suggesting that the interaction between neighbor regions tends to generate more positive impacts than the potential negative impacts related to competitive processes. This has important implications in terms of interregional cooperation, stressing the importance of coordination of policies for resource and infrastructure management or for promotion and marketing policies. In fact, tourists tend to travel through different destinations during one trip, not being necessarily confined by the administrative boundaries of one region.

Case Study 3.2: Nature, Culture, and Value Added by Tourism

Romão J, Guerreiro J, Rodrigues PMM (2017) Territory and Sustainable Tourism Development: a Space-Time Analysis on European Regions. Region 4(3):1–17

This study focuses on the same wide set of European regions and uses the same spatial econometric methods as the work presented in Case Study 2.1. Also, natural resources (measured as the share of the regional territory classified under Natura 2000) and cultural assets (measured according the number of classified World Heritage Sites in each region) follow the same approach, while the contextual variables considered (number of beds available in accommodation establishments and gross fixed capital formation in the tourism sector) are also the same.

The difference here is that, instead of analyzing the impact of natural and cultural resources on tourism demand, the attention goes now to their economic impacts on regional gross value added. This focus on the economic impacts is closer to the idea of tourism competitiveness, as the gross value added is a better indicator to analyze the economic benefits arising from tourism activities in a destination or region. Thus, this analysis aims at identifying the impact of natural and cultural resources on regional tourism competitiveness at the European level.

In fact, tourism demand (as analyzed in Case Study 3.1) can be high because the prices are very low, which suggests a weak competitive position, while normally implying high environmental costs on sensitive natural or cultural resources. As it will be discussed in Chap. 5, the preservation of a competitive position in the long run also depends on the preservation of the core resources contributing for the attractiveness of a tourism destination.

Like in Case Study 3.1, an exploratory spatial analysis based on local indicators of spatial association has been conducted. Among the main results, it was observed that high values for the gross value added in tourism and high tourism demand tended to cluster in Southern regions of Europe, while low values for both variables were observed in Eastern Europe. Moreover, low value added in tourism spatially associated with high tourism demand was also found in clusters of regions in the South, suggesting the existence of large-scale tourism flows with low economic benefits and potential high negative environmental impacts.

In similar sense, spatial clusters of regions where high investment in tourism sector coexists with low value added by this sector tend also to occur in the Southern part of Europe, suggesting that tourism is seen as an economic priority, despite the low economic achievements. This aspect clearly shows the evolutionary path-dependence process discussed in Chap. 2, with the specialization in tourism imposing its own reinforcement.

Other path dependence aspects can also be seen when looking at the relations between gross value added in tourism and the endowment in natural and resources, as South Europe is again the place where abundance of these resources is often associated with a low gross value added by tourism activities. As these are also regions where tourism demand and investments are high, these results reveal an unsustainable process of tourism development – based on low-cost mass tourism with negative impacts on sensitive ecological and cultural resources – and still a tendency to reinforce the role of this sector within the regional economies (as it was also seen in Case Study 2.3, in Chap. 2).

This work also offers an explanatory regression model based on spatial econometric techniques, revealing (at the general European level) that tourism demand and investment tend to exert a positive impact on the gross value added generated by tourism in each region. Nevertheless – and combining this result with the exploratory spatial analysis – it is clear that different dynamics and spatial patterns are observed within European regions.

Moreover, the model reveals a negative correlation between the endowment in natural resources and the gross value added by the tourism sector, confirming the observations made for Southern European regions and revealing relevant problems, both in terms of the sustainable use of resources and the competitive position (apparently more dependent on the low cost than on the quality of services and sophistication of tourism supply).

Case Study 3.3: Motivations, Segmentation, Loyalty, and Urban Cultural Heritage

Romão J, Neuts B, Nijkamp P, Leeuwen ES van (2015) Culture, product differentiation and market segmentation: a structural analysis of the motivation and satisfaction of tourists in Amsterdam. Tourism Economics 21(3):455–474

This work offers a conceptual model to analyze the relation between the characteristics, motivations, satisfaction, and loyalty of tourists (demand side) with the characteristics of an urban destination (supply side). With a particular focus on the role of cultural heritage, the analysis distinguishes between the immaterial (local knowledge, lifestyle, or events) and material (museums, monuments, or architecture) cultural aspects of the city of Amsterdam, with relevant implications on the results obtained. By using a structural equation model (SEM), the analysis includes a segmentation of the tourism demand, taking into account the characteristics of tourists, their motivations, the satisfaction achieved with each aspect of the city, and the implications on loyalty to the destination.

The characteristics of tourists taken into account were related to their age; sex; income; level of education; nationality (from the Netherlands or abroad), being a member of a heritage society; and also the purpose of the visit (business or leisure). Based on an exploratory factor analysis, the motivations were grouped into three types: culture (including archeology, museums, landscape, and urban atmosphere), entertainment (comprising shopping and nightlife), and business. Moreover, following a similar methodology, the levels of satisfaction were classified into two broad groups related to cultural heritage: material assets (archeology, monuments, museums, and landscape) and immaterial factors (traditions and local customs and knowledge).

Among the main results, important differences were observed between Dutch and foreign visitors, as the cultural motivation was not very relevant for tourists from the Netherlands, although they revealed clear intentions to revisit the city. This can be related with the business motives but also with personal connections motivating the visit to friends or relatives. On the other hand, young and low-income visitors revealed high levels of satisfaction and loyalty, revealing the attractiveness of the city for young travellers. Although their income is low and the economic impact tends to be limited, they will probably revisit the destination in the future.

The study also observed that tourists visiting Amsterdam for business have this activity as a primary motive, while revealing higher income levels and higher satisfaction with the intangible cultural aspects of the city. On the other hand, although visitors on holiday have culture and entertainment as the primary motives, they also achieve higher levels of satisfaction with the immaterial aspects of cultural heritage, even if their motivation relies both on the material and immaterial aspects. Nevertheless, as they show good satisfactory levels with these two aspects, it is possible to conclude that Amsterdam clearly fulfills the expectations of cultural tourists. The contrary was observed for the tourists with shopping and nightlife as their primary motivations, who do not seem satisfied with the material aspects of cultural heritage.

A very important conclusion arising from this analysis relates to the implications on loyalty arising with the satisfaction achieved with the different aspects of cultural heritage. Although the levels of satisfaction were generally very high both regarding the material and immaterial aspects of the cultural heritage of the city, visitors satisfied with the immaterial aspects appear to be more loyal to the destination (by expressing their intention to revisit and/or to recommend the visit to family and friends) than those who were more satisfied with the material aspects. In a similar vein, it was also observed that members of heritage societies tend to be less loyal to the city as a tourism destination, as their motivations were mostly focused on the material aspects of cultural heritage.

This result can be related with the fact that visiting and experiencing material aspects (monuments or museums) do not justify another visit, while the enjoyment of immaterial aspects (lifestyle, local traditions) motivates the intention to revisit. This conclusion has important implications in terms of tourism planning for urban destinations: despite the importance of the built environment and quality of cultural facilities to be visited, an enjoyable urban tourism destination also depends – even to a larger extent – on the immaterial aspects comprising daily live in the city.

Case Study 3.4: Motivations and Segmentation in Ecotourism

Romão J, Neuts B, Nijkamp P, Shikida A (2014) Determinants of trip choice, satisfaction and loyalty in an eco-tourism destination: A modeling study on the Shiretoko Peninsula, Japan. Ecological Economics 107:195–205

Ecotourism has experienced a sustainable growth in the last decades, with the ecological characteristics of non-urban areas attracting travellers interested in the natural features of the territories. Also, natural heritage has been recently seen as an important asset to be preserved, with the creation of a list of sites classified by UNESCO as World Heritage. Nevertheless, if the presence of a site in this list ensures that more resources and specific measures are oriented to its protection, it also reinforces the attractiveness of the place, potentially contributing to increase the number of visitors and the pressure on sensitive resources.

In this context, the tourism attractiveness and competitiveness of an ecological site requires its promotion as a valuable natural resource but also the definition of limits to its utilization, according to its carrying capacity. As the number of visitors is necessarily limited, it is crucial for an eco-tourism destination to identify the most suitable segments of the tourism market, taking into account their awareness of the ecological relevance of the concerned resources, the importance of their preservation, and also the economic impacts that can make economically viable the construction and maintenance of the infrastructures and services required for the visit. In this sense, also loyal visitors are of extreme importance, as they tend to know better the characteristics of each site, using it in an adequate way and promoting the place in accordance with its sensitive characteristics.

The work focuses on the development of specific tourism services (different types of boat trips) to visit the World Heritage Site of Shiretoko Peninsula, in Hokkaido (North of Japan). The study takes into account the characteristics and motivations of visitors, their satisfaction with the trip, and the implications of their option for a specific kind of boat trip for their loyalty toward the destination, assuming that these marketing tools are essential elements for the management of a sensitive site like this one. The analysis is divided into two stages, starting with the analysis of the relation between the characteristics of the visitors (motivations, source of information used, eventual previous experiences, or season) and the boat trip selected (type of boat and route). In a second stage, the authors analyze the implications of this trip choice on the satisfaction with different aspects of the visit and also on the loyalty to the destination (the intention to repeat the visit or to recommend it).

It was observed that 84.4% of the visitors came from other areas of Japan than the Hokkaido Prefecture, mostly travelling with family (61.2%) or groups (29.5%) and generally (79,4%) staying at least one night in the area. Almost two thirds (61.2%) were visiting Shiretoko for the first time and almost half of them (47%) collected the information on the Internet or guidebooks, while one third (33,2%) was informed through the acquisition of tour package to Hokkaido.

Regarding the type of boat, large vessels were chosen by a majority of visitors (49,4%), while one third opted for a small boat (32,3%) and the remaining used a sea kayak (18,3%). In terms of routes, Cape Shiretoko was the most popular (61.8%), while Kamuiwakka Fall (26.8%) and Rusha Bay (10.9%) also had relevant scores (the other three routes were almost not mentioned). It was also observed that 77,6% of the tourists visited the paths near the lakes (revealing the importance of water-related resources for the attractiveness of the site).

By using an exploratory factor analysis, three main motivations for the visit were identified: the landscape (87.9%), wildlife (65.5%), and the boat experience itself (20%). It is noteworthy that only 39.3% of the visitors expressed their satisfaction with the observation of wildlife, which suggests the existence of unrealistic expectations regarding the effective experience to be undertaken. In fact, a major element of dissatisfaction was not seeing the things that were expected, pointed out by 23% of the visitors. Nevertheless, 95% of the visitors still revealed the intention to revisit and to recommend the visit, showing that there was a very high satisfaction with the visit as a whole.

It was also observed that large groups tend to prefer large boats to Cape Shiretoko (66.9%) or to Kamuiwakka Fall (30.7%), which is related to the option for a fixed tour program. On the other hand, solo travellers seem to prefer a sea kayak (40.3%), which is a tendency also observed for the young visitors or by persons primarily motivated by the boating experience in itself. Tourists essentially motivated by wildlife tend to prefer tours on small boats (mostly to Rusha Bay and Cape Shiretoko), so that they travel more close to the shoreline and it can be possible to observe the bears. For the marine animals, observing whales and dolphins is mostly related to the option for a large boat (travelling more far from the coastline).

The lack of satisfaction with wildlife encounters is one of the few problems identified in this study. As this is an aspect that cannot be controlled by the managers of the site, it is important to provide adequate information about the expectation related to each type of boat and route, so that the visitors can chose in accordance with their specific motivations. The role of information within this context of matching the needs of particular groups of tourists with the resources, products, and services available in each destination will be discussed with more detail in Chap. 4.

References

Apostolakis A (2003) The convergence process in heritage tourism. Ann Tour Res 30(4):795–812

Armario ME (2008) Tourist satisfaction: an analysis of its antecedents. Asociación Española de Dirección y Economía de la Empresa 17:367–382

Bandarin F (2005) Foreword. In: Harrison D, Hitchcock M (eds) The politics of world heritage: negotiating tourism and conservation. Channel View Publications, Clevelon, pp 5–6

Bansal HS, Eiselt H (2004) Exploratory research of tourist motivations and planning. Tour Manag 25:387–396

Bimonte S, Punzo L (2016) Tourist development and host-guest interaction: an economic exchange theory. Ann Tour Res 58:128–139

Buhalis D (1999) Limits of tourism development in peripheral destinations: problems and challenges. Tour Manag 20:183–185

Buhalis D (2000) Marketing the competitive destination of the future. Tour Manag 21:97–116

Butler R (1980) The concept of a tourism area life cycle of evolution: implications for management of resources. Can Geogr 24(1):5–12

Butler R (1999) Sustainable tourism: a state-of-the-art review. Tour Geogr 1(1):7–25

Butler R (2015) The evolution of tourism and tourism research. Tour Recreat Res 40(1):16–27

Castro C, Armario E, Ruiz D (2007) The influence of market heterogeneity on the relationship between a destination's image and tourists' future behavior. Tour Manag 28:175–187

Chambers E (2009) From authenticity to significance: tourism on the frontier of culture and place. Futures 41:353–359

Chen C, Tsai D (2007) How destination image and evaluative factors affect behavioral intentions? Tour Manag 28:1115–1122

Chi C, Qu H (2008) Examining the structural relationships of destination image, tourist satisfaction and destination loyalty: an integrated approach. Tour Manag 29:624–636

Cohen E (1979) A phenomenology of tourist experiences. Sociology 13:179–201

Cohen E (1988) Authenticity and commoditization in tourism. Ann Tour Res 15:371–386

Crompton J. (1979) Motivations for pleasure vacations. Annals of Tourism Research VI(4):408–424

Dann G (1981) Tourist motivation: an appraisal. Annals of Tourism Research VIII(2):187–219

Douglas JA (2014) What's political ecology got to do with tourism? Tour Geogr 16(1):8–13

Doxey G (1975) A causation theory of visitor-resident irritants: methodology and research inferences. Proceedings of the 6th annual conference of the travel and tourism research association. In: San Diego. Travel and Tourism Research Association, Whitehall

Evans G (2005) Mundo Maya: from Cancún to City of culture. World heritage in post-colonial Mesoamerica. In: Harrison D, Hitchcock M (eds) The politics of world heritage: negotiating tourism and conservation. Channel View Publications, Clevelon, pp 35–49

Fusco-Girard L, Nijkamp P (2009) Cultural tourism and sustainable local development. Ashgate, Aldershot

Gilbert EW (1939) The growth of inland and seaside resorts health resorts in England. Scott Geogr Mag 55:16–35

Graburn N (1995) The past in the present in Japan: nostalgia and neo-traditionalism in contemporary Japanese domestic tourism. In: Butler R, Pearce D (eds) Change in tourism people, places processes. Routledge, London, pp 47–70

Harrison D (2005) Contested narratives in the domain of world heritage. In: Harrison D, Hitchcock M (eds) The politics of world heritage: negotiating tourism and conservation. Channel View Publications, Clevelon, pp 1–10

Hassan S (2000) Determinants of market competitiveness in an environmentally sustainable tourism industry. J Travel Res 38(3):239–245

ICOMOS (1965) International charter for the conservation and restoration of monuments and sites (The Venice Charter). Adopted in the 2nd International Congress of Architects and Technicians of Historic Monuments, Venice

ICOMOS (1999) International cultural tourism charter: managing tourism at places of heritage significance. Adopted at the 12th General Assembly of ICOMOS, Mexico City

ICOMOS (2005) Xi'An declaration on the conservation of the settings of heritage structures. Adopted by the 15th General Assembly of ICOMOS, Xi'an

ICOMOS (2008a) The ICOMOS charter for the interpretation and presentation of cultural heritage sites. Ratified by the 16th General Assembly of ICOMOS, Québec

ICOMOS (2008b) The ICOMOS charter on cultural routes. Ratified by the 16th General Assembly of ICOMOS, Québec

Iso-Ahola S (1989) Motivation for leisure. In: Jackson EL, Burton TL (eds) Mapping the past, charting the future. Venture Press, Pennsylvania, pp 247–279

Jovicic DZ (2014) Key issues in the implementation of sustainable tourism. Curr Issue Tour 17(4):297–302

Kozak M, Rimmington M (2000) Tourist satisfaction with Mallorca, Spain, as an off-season holiday destination. J Travel Res 38:260–269

Laing J, Voigt C, Frost W (2013) Fantasy, authenticity and the spa tourism experience. In: Voigt C, Pforr C (eds) Wellness tourism. Routledge, London, pp 220–234

Lee T (2009) A structural model to examine how destination image, attitude, and motivation affect the future behavior of tourists. Leis Sci 31:215–236

MacCannell D (1973) Staged authenticity: arrangements of social space in tourist settings. Am J Sociol 79(3):589–603

Maslow AH (1943) A theory of human motivation. Psychol Rev 50(4):370–396

Matias A, Nijkamp P, Neto P (2007) Advances in modern tourism research. Springer, New York

Meinecke EP (1929) The effect of excessive tourist travel on California redwood parks. California State Printing Office, Sacramento

Miller G, Twining-Ward L (2005) Monitoring for a sustainable tourism transition: the challenge of developing and using indicators. CABI Publishing, Oxfordshire

OECD (2009) The impact of culture on tourism. OECD, Paris

OECD (2014) Tourism and the creative economy. OECD, Paris

Oppermann M (2000) Tourism destination loyalty. J Travel Res 39:78–84

Outdoor Recreation Resources Review Commission (ORRRC) (1962) Report of the ORRRC vols 1–27. Outdoor Recreation Resources Review Commission, Washington DC

Page SJ, Dowling RK (2002) Ecotourism. Prentice Hall, Harlow

Patmore J (1968) The Spa towns of England and Wales. In: Beckinsale G (ed) Problems of urbanisation. Methuen, London, pp 168–194

Pearce PL (1996) Recent research in tourists' behaviour. Asia Pacific J Tour Res 1(1):7–17

Poon A (1994) The 'new tourism' revolution. Tour Manag 15(2):91–92
Poria Y, Butler R, Airey D (2001) Clarifying heritage tourism. Ann Tour Res 28(4):1047–1049
Poria Y, Butler R, Airey D (2003) The core of heritage tourism. Ann Tour Res 30(1):238–254
Poria Y, Reichel A, Biran A (2006) Heritage site perceptions and motivations to visit. J Travel Res
   44:318–326
Poria Y, Biran A, Reichel A (2009) Visitors' preferences for interpretation at heritage sites. J Travel
   Res 48(1):92–105
Porter M (1985) Competitive advantage – creating and sustaining superior performance. The Free
   Press, New York
Ritchie J, Crouch G (2003) The competitive destination: a sustainable tourism perspective. CABI
   International, Oxfordshire
Romão J (2015) Culture or Nature: a space-time analysis on the determinants of tourism demand
   in European regions. Discussion Papers Spatial and Organizational Dynamics 14
Romão J, Neuts B, Nijkamp P, Shikida A (2014) Determinants of trip choice, satisfaction and loy-
   alty in an eco-tourism destination: a modeling study on the Shiretoko Peninsula, Japan. Ecol
   Econ 107:195–205
Romão J, Neuts B, Nijkamp P, van LES (2015) Culture, product differentiation and market seg-
   mentation: a structural analysis of the motivation and satisfaction of tourists in Amsterdam.
   Tour Econ 21(3):455–474
Romão J, Guerreiro J, Rodrigues PMM (2017) Territory and sustainable tourism development: a
   space-time analysis on European regions. Region 4(3):1–17
Scott AJ (2007) Capitalism and urbanization in a new key? The cognitive-cultural dimension.
   Social Forces 85(4):1465–1482
Sharpley R (2009) Tourism development and the environment: beyond sustainability? Earthscan,
   London
Stansfield CA (1972) The development of modern seaside resorts. Park Recreat 5(10):14–46
Timothy DJ, Boyd SW (2003) Heritage tourism. Prentice Hall, Harlow
Tussyadiah IP (2014) Toward a theoretical foundation for experience design in tourism. J Travel
   Res 53(5):543–564
UNESCO (2001) Universal declaration on cultural diversity. UNESCO, Paris
UNESCO (2003) Convention for the safeguarding of the intangible cultural heritage. UNESCO,
   Paris
UNWTO (2001) Global code of ethics for tourism. UNWTO, Madrid
UNWTO (2003) Study on tourism and intangible cultural heritage. UNWTO, Madrid
Wagar J (1964) The carrying capacity of wildlands for recreation forest science, Monograph No.
   7. Society of American Foresters, Washington, DC
Wait G (2000) Consuming heritage – perceived historical authenticity. Ann Tour Res 27(4):835–862
Wall G, Mathieson A (2006) Tourism: change, impacts and opportunities. Pearson, Essex
Walton JK (2013) Health, sociability, politics and culture – spas in history, spas and history: an
   overview. In: Walton JK (ed) Mineral springs resorts in global perspective. Routledge, London,
   pp 1–14
Wang N (1999) Rethinking authenticity in tourism experience. Ann Tour Res 26(2):349–370
Weaver D (2006) Sustainable tourism: theory and practice. Elsevier, Oxford
Weaver D (2011) Can sustainable tourism survive climate change? J Sustain Tour 19(1):5–15
Williams P, Ponsford I (2009) Confronting tourism's environmental paradox: transitioning for sus-
   tainable tourism. Futures 41:396–404
World Commission on Environment and Development (1987) Our common future. Oxford
   University Press, Oxford
Yoon Y, Uysal M (2005) An examination of the effects of motivation and satisfaction on destina-
   tion loyalty: a structural model. Tour Manag 26:45–56

Chapter 4
Tourism: A Knowledge-Based Activity

Contents

Abstract Contemporary production and consumption systems increasingly integrate immaterial aspects related to knowledge or cultural values and symbols into products and services, often through processes of *co-creation*, leading to a personalization and adaptation of supply to the needs and motivations of consumers. Tourism plays a prominent role within this emergent *creative economy*, and the focus on the immaterial aspects of the experience tends to prevail over the material aspects of the destinations, while information and communication technologies appear as crucial tools for the match between differentiation of destinations and

---

Case Study 4.1: Information and Satisfaction in an Ecotourism Destination
Neuts B, Romão J, Nijkamp P, Shikida A (2014) A quality assessment of tourist information: the case of nautical tourism at Shiretoko Peninsula. Almatourism 9:24–34
Case Study 4.2: E-Services in Urban Tourism
Romão J, Neuts B, Nijkamp P, Leeuwen ES van (2015) Tourist Loyalty and e-Services: A Comparison of Behavioral Impacts in Leipzig and Amsterdam. Journal of Urban Technology 22(2):85–101
Case Study 4.3: Tourism, Innovation, and Regional Specialization
Romão J, Nijkamp P (2017) A spatial econometric analysis of impacts of innovation, productivity and agglomeration on tourism competitiveness. Current Issues in Tourism. DOI: 10.1080/13683500.2017.1366434
Case Study 4.4: Urban Attractiveness for Tourists and Residents
Romão J, Kourtit K, Neuts B, Nijkamp P (2017) The Smart City as a Common Place for Tourists and Residents: a Structural Analysis on the Determinants of Urban Attractiveness. Cities. DOI: 10.1016/j.cities.2017.11.007

© Springer Nature Singapore Pte Ltd. 2018
J. Romão, *Tourism, Territory and Sustainable Development*, New Frontiers
in Regional Science: Asian Perspectives 28,
https://doi.org/10.1007/978-981-13-0426-2_4

market segmentation. The intense development observed in these technologies during the last few decades contributes for the enhancement of *co-created* tourism
experiences while opening new opportunities for the reinforcement of linkages
between tourism and other creative activities, along with the potential reinforcement of regional innovation networks, potentially involving a large number of small
and decentralized tourism providers. On the other hand, agglomeration effects
related to recent urban development contribute for the concentration of creative
activities in cities, along with the emergence of a varied supply of flexible and creative tourism products and services. This fast growth of tourism in contemporary
cities also raises new challenges for urban planning, not only related to the shared
use of spaces, facilities, and infrastructures but also regarding the impacts of tourism on local markets and especially on the housing markets in large-scale urban
tourism destinations.

Keywords Information · Smart tourism · Co-creation · Smart specialization ·
Creative economies · Urban tourism

4.1 Introduction

Although tourism services are provided at the local level by a large variety of different and independent companies comprising a decentralized value chain, destinations normally follow a differentiation strategy by exploring the uniqueness of their
territorial assets, both material and immaterial. On the other hand, tourists constitute a multifaceted market, with different characteristics, perceptions, motivations,
and needs. In this context of differentiation of destinations and market segmentation, information plays a determinant role in order to ensure an adequate match
between tourism demand and supply. This importance is enhanced by the potential
interaction between suppliers and consumers, which has increased with the recent
developments in information and communication technologies (ICT), promoting
new forms of *co-creation* of tourism services, experiences, and destinations.

These interactive processes may emerge in different stages of the travel: before
travelling, during the visit, and after the travel, different types of digital tools and
e-services can contribute to personalize and share tourism experiences, making
tourism markets more flexible, adjustable, and transparent. At the same time, the
destination becomes a "repository" of decentralized information about the preferences, behaviors, and satisfaction of tourists, which may be used for innovative
practices and the consolidation of innovation networks. Thus, the concept of *coopetition* – a process of cooperation between rival companies – emerges as especially
important in the context of the small companies operating in tourism destinations:
normally with small-scale and unstructured forms of integration of knowledge into
their production systems, cooperation between them may contribute to accumulate

information and to reinforce the overall attractiveness of the place, through the creation of learning networks.

Tourism services also have high potential to establish connections with other economic activities. Apart from digital technologies, the emergent creative sectors oriented to the integration of knowledge and cultural values intro tradable goods and services also have clear impacts on the enrichment of the tourism experiences. Transport and mobility services, energy-saving equipment, water management, food production, ecological services, sports, or other types of recreational and educational activities can also benefit from the tourism market while contributing to improve the diversity and quality of the services available in each destination. In this sense, tourism can achieve a prominent role within smart specialization strategies, by using unique territorial knowledge and resources in order to reinforce the linkages with related economic activities, while contributing for the development and consolidation of regional systems of innovation. Nevertheless, these results do not seem to be achieved (at least in accordance to their full potential) in the contemporary forms of tourism, as it will be discussed.

Following the emergence and development of this *creative economy*, the economic role of cities has clearly gained importance in the last few decades. Due to agglomeration effects and location externalities, urban areas tend to concentrate the production of these creative sectors while attracting skilled and qualified labor. Thus, contemporary cities are also the setting where creative oriented infrastructures and environments can be found, along with a large market of local residents, whose increasing discretionary incomes allow the consumption of products and services related to these creative sectors, which tend to embed knowledge and cultural values and symbols into the production systems. Thus, cities can provide a varied set of creative services, amenities, and infrastructures, reinforcing their tourism attractiveness by offering different consumption opportunities for diverse market segments. However, it must be noted that the integration of cultural values into production and consumption systems implies a process of commodification, transforming local culture and heritage into products and services, which (as discussed in Chap. 3) is a major question in the context of massified forms of tourism.

Other cultural and socio-economic problems related to the fast development of tourism in contemporary cities are currently observed. Along with the questions related to the shared used of public spaces, services, and infrastructures, tourism tends to be concentrated in specific parts of the urban areas (normally including the most unique historical districts), which, apart from the issues related to uniqueness, identity, and authenticity discussed before, also creates inflationary effects, potentially contributing for the emergence of places with high concentration of tourists and low presence of local residents, who prefer other (more quiet and affordable) locations.

In fact, tourism tends to reinforce the processes of spatial reorganization observed in the central areas of many cities, where former industrial buildings are renovated to accommodate creative activities, while the former residents tend to be replaced by new creative professionals. This process of *gentrification* in contemporary cities can be reinforced by the dynamics of tourism, both through the construction of

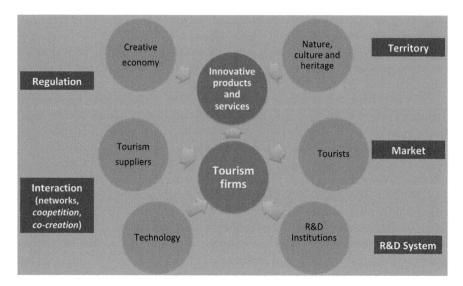

Fig. 4.1 Innovation in tourism

hotels and also through the expansion of the so-called *shared economy*. Enhanced by diverse online platforms, this type of housing became an important solution for tourism accommodation, offering the opportunity for small-scale entrepreneurial initiatives and higher interaction between hosts and guests but also implying inflationary processes in the housing markets and lack of houses for the local population. In this case, participatory processes of tourism and city planning may contribute to reduce or to eliminate potential conflicts between tourists and the local communities.

This chapter is organized as follows. Section 4.2 discusses the role of information and communication technologies (ICT) promoting the match between differentiation of destinations and tourism market segmentation while creating the conditions for the emergence of co-created tourism services and experiences. Section 4.3 contextualizes tourism within contemporary creative economies, stressing its potential role to establish linkages with related sectors within smart specialization strategies aiming at reinforcing regional innovation systems. Section 4.4 analyzes how the dynamics of contemporary cities are especially important for the emergence and development of creative economies, including new tourism activities and experiences based on local cultural heritage and knowledge, physically anchored in specific locations with unique characteristics. As this dynamics is not exempt of potential negative consequences, Sect. 4.5 problematizes different aspects related to the fast and intense growth recently observed in urban tourism. Empirical applications of some of these conceptual analyses are presented in four case studies. A diagram representing the major elements constituting a regional innovation system in tourism is depicted in Fig. 4.1.

4.2   ICT, Smart Tourism, and Co-creation of Images, Experiences, and Destinations

Tourism services have two important and distinctive characteristics – spatiality and temporality – implying that the production and consumption of tourism products occur in the same place, at the same time (as it was discussed in the previous chapter). The implications of a third distinct characteristic of tourism are now discussed: co-terminality, implying the existence of a direct interaction between producers and consumers. Related to this permanent process of interaction, there is a flux of information with a high potential to contribute for the adaptation of tourism services to the specific needs of each consumer. The fast development of ICT opened new opportunities for the intensification of this interaction between multiple types of tourists visiting a destination and diverse service providers, not only during the consumption process but also before and after the travel.

The strategic importance of differentiation of a destination, related to the supply of products and services based on the uniqueness of its territorial resources, along with the market segmentation processes related to the identification of the adequate consumers, attracted and motivated by those specific features, was also discussed in the previous chapter. As it will be analyzed now, information plays a decisive role within this double process of differentiation and segmentation, as it is the vehicle to generate an adequate match between the specific features of each destination and the heterogeneous characteristics, motivations, and needs of different market segments (Kozak and Rimmington 2000; Castro et al. 2007), as it is exemplified in Case Studies 4.1 (Neuts et al. 2014, focusing on an ecotourism destination) and 4.2 (Romão et al. 2015a, analyzing two urban destinations). Thus, the permanent interaction between producers and consumers within the tourism experience – enhanced by the role of ICT – can be an extremely useful tool for this matching and for the planning processes within the tourism sector, both at the company and at the destination level. In fact, this flow of information potentially constitutes a new source of competitive advantage, as the destination tends to become a decentralized repository of information about the motivations, preferences, needs, behavior, and satisfaction of the visitors. The emergence of the concept of *big data* – related to the accumulation of large quantities of information regarding individual behaviors – is particularly relevant in the case of tourism, with some companies taking advantage of the opportunities opened by online platforms to accumulate user-generated data about travel behaviors, motivations, and preferences, which allows them to offer personalized services adjusted to the perceived needs of each consumer.

The fast, intense, and diversified development of ICT in the last decades has exerted a profound impact on tourism activities, as analyzed by a large number of authors (Lin and Huang 2006; Buhalis and Law 2008; Hall and Williams 2008; Aldebert et al. 2011; Lo et al. 2011). The development of multiple tools based on geographical information systems, the *global distribution systems* and *computer reservation systems* applied to transportation, accommodation, or other services; the massification of the Internet; the increased interactivity resulting from the tools related to the *Web 2.0* (social media); the generalization of its mobile utilization in portable devices (*Web 3.0*); the development of easy-to-use tools for multimedia production and communication; the increasing speed, reliability, and amount of information transmitted; and the generalization of online payment systems have created new opportunities for marketing and distribution strategies, also generating new sources of competitive advantage in tourism activities.

These new processes of interaction between tourism companies and travellers contribute to a better knowledge about the needs and motivations of tourists, helping the companies to reach specific market targets with personalized information about adequate services (Sabiote-Ortiz et al. 2016). On the other hand, these new forms of interaction also impact the demand side of the tourism markets, by increasing the autonomy and bargaining power of the consumers, contributing for a more diversified, flexible, and transparent process of adjustment between supply and demand of tourism services (Tussyadiah and Fesenmaier 2009; Neuts et al. 2013; Wang et al. 2016a). The implications of the development of ICT on tourism can be identified before, during, and after the trips.

Before the trip, (potential) tourists look for different sources of information related to possible destinations that fill their *push* motivations (corresponding to their inner reasons to travel, like adventure, relaxation, learning, romantic experiences, physical activities, etc., as described in Chap. 3). After this first selection, also the *pull* motivations (related to the specific characteristics and services existing in each destination) are taken into account, considering different aspects involved in the travel plan (solo traveller, group, family, couple, with or without children, age, gender, cultural background, income level, etc.). Thus, from the point of view of the service providers in each destination, it is important to provide accurate information regarding the characteristics of the service and how they are framed into the specific and unique features of the destination. For the traveller, there are normally abundant tools allowing for an independent selection and acquisition of a varied set of services, including transportation, accommodation, tickets for events, or access to diverse amenities and facilities.

At this stage, it is crucial that the image of the destination and the expectations about the services created by the tourist closely correspond to the real experience they will enjoy, so that they can achieve high levels of satisfaction. In this context, the possibilities for interaction between suppliers and consumers have a high potential for the creation of a flexible and personalized supply of services, adapted to the specific characteristics, motivations, needs, and requests of individual travellers. This can be seen as a process of *co-creation* of tourism experiences (Binkhorst and Dekker 2009), as the final services to be provided can correspond to an interactive process leading to personalized solutions, which integrate consumer's preferences into the pre-existing available services. Different types of websites and applications, booking and payment tools, maps and geo-visualization tools, or multimedia presentation are useful elements in this stage of the (pre)visit.

During the trip, the applications and tools oriented to mobile utilization gain higher importance, as the tourist is normally moving in the destination, as observed by Wang et al. (2016b). Offering easy and cost-effective solutions for Internet access in mobile devices is now crucial to ensure that visitors have easy access to information about the opportunities at the destination. This includes aspects related to mobility and transportation, location of facilities and amenities, events, monuments, and other aspects of cultural heritage or features related to nature and landscape. In this context, access to geo-referenced information and *augmented reality* tools (providing contextual information about elements of the destination visited by tourists) in mobile devices appear as crucial elements to increase the satisfaction of the visitor with the experience at the destination. As observed by Chen and Tsai (2007), different types of e-services can contribute to enhance the satisfaction of visitors with their tourism experiences.

Finally, it is also possible to observe that the processes of interaction through ICT still can continue after the visit. From the point of view of suppliers, it is possible to implement processes of customer relation management (CRM), by providing information about special offers and promotional campaigns or new products and services adjusted to the perceived needs and motivations of each visitor. On the other hand, tourists can provide feedbacks about their experiences, both through direct interaction with suppliers and mostly through the publication of their experiences, both in specialized travel websites and blogs (by reviewing and rating services, facilities, or locations), or by sharing their experiences using their personal webpages in social networks (Kim and Fesenmaier 2017). With very easy-to-use tools for multimedia production and distribution, this process of convergence between different media and platforms (Jenkins 2006) and *mediatization* of the tourism experiences (Mansson 2011) clearly enhances the role and importance of travellers shaping the image of a destination, as their perceptions tend to be very reliable within their circles of friends and acquaintances. In fact, sharing tourism experiences in social networks or travel blogs is very common nowadays.

In this context of generalized utilization of ICT before, during, and after the travels, new entrepreneurial practices oriented toward personalized experiences – the *co-creation* of destinations and experiences – potentially contribute for the development and implementation of innovative practices and services (as observed regarding the *big data* approach), along with new forms of tourism governance mobilizing the different stakeholders involved (Sigala 2012; Sigala and Marinidis 2012). Contemporary tourists have abundant opportunities to choose between different types of service providers and to request adaptations in order to fit their requirements, while they can also contribute for the (positive or negative) promotion of destinations. Thus, *co-creation* can be seen as a process to increase the flexibility and transparency of tourism markets while also having important implications on the commodification (and authenticity) of the experiences discussed in the previous chapter. Very recent developments in tourism research enlarge the scope of *co-creation* processes, by taking into account the interactions between different customers as a source of product and service development – *the customer-to-customer co-creation* (Rihova et al. 2018).

Taking into account that each tourism destination comprises a network of small and large companies (and eventually public institutions) providing different services, Sigala (2009) defines the interactive tools related to *Web 2.0 (social networks)* as "tools of mass collaboration," as they enhance the opportunities for large-scale processes of interaction between suppliers and consumers and also for the coordination between service providers and regulatory institutions operating in a destination. This process of collaboration of rival companies within a tourism destination is refereed in the literature as *coopetition*, implying cooperation between companies, which are, at the same time, competing. *Coopetition* appears as a crucial aspect of contemporary tourism dynamics, as local companies must cooperate in order to promote the destination and to ensure the overall satisfaction of visitors while competing between them for their preference.

These concepts of interaction between a network of different local stakeholders involved in processes of *coopetition* and the tourists visiting a destination, the adaptation and co-creation of tourism services and experiences for highly informed and independent visitors, or the convergence of media and communication tools allowing tourists to shape the image of a destination are taken into account by Boes et al. (2016) to define the concept of *smart tourism destinations*, seen as "ecosystems for tourism destination competitiveness." While emphasizing the enabling role of ICT, these authors consider these elements as the basis for the implementation of place- and knowledge-based innovation strategies, relying on the specific resources, knowledge, and information available in each region. In this sense, a *smart destination* can be defined at three levels: ICT, leadership, and participatory governance; fluid interactions between economic, social, and technological actors; and different dimensions of innovation based on territorial resources. As it was discussed in the previous chapter, these elements are crucial for the supply of significant tourism experiences based on local unique resources requiring careful management by local communities.

4.3   Tourism, Creativity, and Regional Innovation Systems

As it was seen, although tourism destinations are presented under the same brand and tend to create a unified image, each of them integrates a large variety of products and services, produced by independent suppliers (Daskalopoulou and Petrou 2009). In this sense, a destination generates multi-products, oriented to diverse market segments (Romão et al. 2015a, 2015b). Despite this fragmented supply of tourism products and services, tourists normally perceive the destination as a whole, even if their overall satisfaction results from the cumulative impacts of each of the services experienced during the travel (Buhalis 2000).

It is also noteworthy that the interaction between suppliers and consumers involves a large quantity of informal information, which needs to be codified in order to be useful for the management of those services or to the implementation of innovative practices. Nevertheless, most of the tourism services are provided by small and medium companies (SME), whose formal learning processes are often not structured. Thus, this type of company finds particular obstacles for the development of innovation processes, as observed by Tödtling and Kaufmann (2001). In this context, the development of regional innovation networks (as proposed by Hjalager 2010) is a major challenge for the competitiveness of tourism destinations, by using the interaction between small firms to accumulate large quantities of decentralized information, in order to overcome the low scale and lack of formal learning structures of individual SME.

Taking these aspects into consideration, the European Commission (2006) proposed the concept of "Tourism Learning Area," offering guidelines for the coordination between agents and reinforcement of local networks for innovation in tourism, assuming this dynamics as a process of collective learning at the local level. It is assumed that innovative processes within the tourism sector are the result of systematic interactions between companies with different dimensions and purposes, between firms and their clients and also from the development of different technologies, both arising from cooperative actions undertaken with research and development (R&D) institutions or from outside the tourism sector, including the developments in ICT. In this sense, tourism supply and demand tend to integrate higher amounts and complexity of information, by using sophisticated means of communication and interaction, implying that tourism is increasingly becoming a knowledge-based activity, as exemplified by different companies operating in the business sector with an intensive utilization of *big data* based on user-generated contents.

Although tourism is an economic activity globally distributed and innovations within this sector can easily have a global diffusion (Millar and Choi 2011), local networks are still crucial elements for innovation. The general approach to regional innovation systems proposed by different authors (Cooke 2001; Asheim and Coenen 2006; Asheim et al. 2011) – clusters of organizations (firms, public institutions, or research centers) aiming at producing and diffusing new knowledge, skills, and best practices – can also be applied to the tourism sector. As stressed by Wiliams and Shaw (2011), the importance of these local networks in tourism is related to the specificity of the interactive process developed among tourism service providers and consumers at the destination and the opportunities arising from this accumulation of information. Moreover, the tacit knowledge accumulated by small and medium companies (SME) is the most difficult to incorporate in an organization, but it is also the most difficult to imitate in different contexts.

Considering the fragmentation of the supply of tourism services and the importance of SME, policy efforts for the creation and coordination of these networks assume special importance, as discussed by Hall and Williams (2008). The consolidation of these kinds of network is expected to contribute to develop innovative practices, to create new business, and to raise the productivity levels at the destination, by creating new added value within the value chain of the local tourism supply. On the other hand, as Liu et al. (2017) observe, the attraction of tourists to a destination may contribute for the creation of agglomeration economies, potentially opening the possibility for the emergence and development of new markets for innovative products and services, not necessarily confined to the tourism sector. In this context, different activities with a broader scope can benefit from the increasing dimension of local markets arising from the presence of tourists, in particular in rural areas with low population density. The creative sector is clearly one of most likeable to benefit from these externalities, along with different applications of ICT or services for common use by tourists and local residents (transportation and mobility, water management, or energy production and consumption).

Despite the difficulties in measuring the different aspects defining the regional innovation systems and their relation with the tourism sector (Rodríguez et al. 2014), different studies critically analyze this dynamics (Medina-Muñoz et al. 2013), including the effects of cross-border regional innovation systems, related to the exploitation of common opportunities between neighbor regions with similar characteristics (Weidenfeld 2013). Innovation processes normally imply the integration of novelty into existing elements and factors (continuity), in order to generate new combinations (Lundvall 2002). In this sense, innovation can be seen as an evolutionary and path-dependent process, in which the involved institutions are, themselves, subject to evolution (Malakauskaite and Navickas 2010). The specific characteristics of the territorial capital available in each region – generally defined by Capello et al. (2011) as the ability to transform local resources into competitive products and services – clearly determine the potential of each region to undertake successful innovative practices and strategies.

In this sense, the analysis performed in the Case Study 4.3 (Romão and Nijkamp 2017, focusing on a large number of European regions) reveals a relatively weak innovative performance of the regions where tourism plays a more prominent role, once they are normally related with low levels of technological development and qualification of the labor force. In fact, Hansen and Winther (2011) observe that the most research-intensive European economic sectors (which do not include the activities more directly related to tourism) tend to be spatially concentrated, contributing to increase regional inequalities while revealing the dependence of each region on its geographical and historical characteristics influencing development trajectories (Martin 2014). With similar implications, Milio (2014) observed that regions with high levels of specialization in tourism and construction revealed more difficulties to recover their levels of production and employment after the international crisis started in 2007.

On the other hand, questions related to the qualifications of workers also received recent attention within tourism studies, in a context where labor relations tend to be much more flexible and informal than in other economic sectors, due to the effects of volatility or seasonality of demand or the requirements to perform multiple and flexible tasks in small organizations. By analyzing the relation between the characteristics of the work force and the performance of high-ranked hotels, Yang and Cai (2015) identified very high positive impacts of qualifications and specialization of the workers on the results of this particular type of hospitality service. In a different context, Úbeda-García et al. (2014) identified those positive impacts of qualified human resources only for the hotels following a clear strategy of differentiation. These results suggest that qualified human resources positively impact the performance of tourism organization when they are oriented toward high-quality services or they follow a strategy of service differentiation.

Questions related to the mobilization of local knowledge, innovation capabilities, and qualified human resources are at the core of the strategies of *smart specialization* recently adopted by the European Commission (Foray et al. 2012) and currently undertaken by the regions of the European Union. Boschma (2016) synthetizes this concept accurately, by pointing out that such strategies aim at a process of niche specialization in a limited number of sectors, supported by research and development activities based on endogenous resources (both material and immaterial and including human resources), potentially generating inter-sectorial spillovers. While stressing that the application of ICT for the modernization of the tourism industry can be a relevant example of smart specialization, Piirainen et al. (2017) suggest that such processes can follow different paths even within the same sectors, depending on the conditions and characteristics of each region.

As it was discussed in Chap. 2, regional development is an evolutionary process, with different processes of path dependence related to their particular historical and geographical conditions (Martin 2014). In the case of tourism, these processes can be caused by the available natural resources; sunk costs of local productive, physical, and infrastructural assets; agglomeration economies, local external economies of specialization, or localized spin-off firm birth; interregional linkages and dependencies; and local technological lock in. Strategically, the *smart specialization* approach proposes to reinforce the connections between closely related sectors of economic activity (*related variety*, as defined by Neffke et al. 2009) in order to explore the synergies between them to generate a path of economic growth. In the case of tourism, apart from the accommodation, transportation, and food sectors, also the ICT and multimedia production can be considered related activities, along with other cultural and creative activities (discussed with more detail in Sect. 3.3), ecological services, energy production and consumption technologies, or water-saving equipment, which can contribute to develop the regional technological capabilities while contributing to the reinforcement of the image of sustainability of the destinations, which is a raising concern of contemporary travellers.

It should be also noted that, although tourism activities can have multiple related sectors, many of them requiring the incorporation of advanced technologies and knowledge, along with qualified labor, this is not often achieved in the most consolidated destination, as it was observed in Case Study 3.3 (Romão et al. 2015b). In fact, even in Europe – one of most developed continents of the world – specialization in tourism seems to be related with low technological development, lack of qualified human resources, and low value added by the regional economies. In this context, the concluding chapter of this book will discuss some challenges for the future of tourism development. Moreover, it is also observed by Neffke et al. (2009) that the potential synergies associated with related variety can also have a negative effect on regional resilience, as defined by Modica and Reggiani (2015) and discussed in Chap. 2: if a negative external shock affects the demand of one of the sectors, this can easily spread to the related sectors. In this context, the authors point out that a balanced regional economic structure, involving several unrelated clusters of related activities, seems to offer better perspectives for regional sustainable development.

4.4   Creative Tourism and the Smart City

Contemporary economies are characterized by a strong convergence between the cultural and the economic domains, through increasing integration of information, knowledge, and symbolic values into tradable goods and services, as observed, among others by Scott (2007). In this context, cultural production is increasingly *commodified* and oriented to markets, while the production of commodities (both goods and services) tends to integrate more aesthetic and semiotic meanings, beyond the traditional utilitarian aspects. This double process of commodification of culture is linked to significant transformations on the demand side, related to the increase in discretionary income for large parts of the population and transformations in life-styles, with higher importance given by consumers to aspects related to entertainment, cultural interaction, education, self-esteem, wellness, or personal valorization. OECD (2014b) refers to this type of dynamics as the emergence of a *knowledge economy* or *creative economy*, linked to a strong development of creative industries, whose growth has been continuously higher than the global economy during the last years, as expressed by the evolution observed for the trade in creative goods and services, with an average growth of 8.8% per year between 2002 and 2011 (UNCTAD 2013).

According to OECD (2014b), *creative industries* comprise "knowledge-based creative activities that link producers, consumers and places by utilizing technology, talent or skill to generate meaningful intangible cultural products, creative content and experiences." While requiring the integration of knowledge, technology, and highly qualified workers related to specialized skills, these activities normally engage in systematic innovation processes in different sectors of activity. Although the scope of *creative activities* is often difficult to define (in fact, the levels of creativity, integration of knowledge, technological development, and innovation can vary within the same sector), normally creative products and services are identified with the outputs of multimedia production and distribution, ICT (hardware and software), architecture and design, communication and advertising, and fine and performing arts or cultural production and distribution, along with some leisure activities, like interactive games, gastronomy, or tourism. In a similar sense, for UNESCO (2009), *creative activities* are "those in which the product or service contains a substantial element of artistic or creative endeavour" while emphasizing that the consumption of these products and services is often linked to interactive processes with suppliers, often leading to processes of *co-creation* and personalized products adjusted to the needs and motivations of consumers. Similar approaches are adopted by other institutions, like the British Council (2010) or the European Commission (2011).

These global societal and economic transformations also had deep implications on the tourism sector. The raising discretionary income and the increasing leisure time contributed to a significant growth in the number of travels and the revenues generated by the tourism industry, as discussed in Chap. 2. On the other hand, a shift from the focus of tourism from the supply of territorial resources to the demand for experiences has also been observed (Tussyadiah 2014), as mentioned in Chap. 3, raising the importance of the immaterial aspects of the visit (UNWTO 2003; UNESCO 2003), including cultural interaction with local knowledge and traditions, aspects related to *livability*, concerns with local communities, or the significance of contacts with different cultural contexts, depending on the characteristics, background, and motivations of each tourist. In this context, tourism has a high potential to generate linkages with other creative activities, including communication and advertising, multimedia production, software development and its mobile applications, new modes of transportation, architecture and landscape design, or, in a broad sense, cultural and environmental services. Thus, tourism development can also promote the linkage between the creative products and services (often with easy access to mechanisms of global distribution) and the places where they are produced, contributing to reinforce local networks, knowledge externalities, and the consolidation of local clusters (Richards 2013).

Considering these societal transformations observed in contemporary societies related to production systems and consumption patterns, the emergence of the concept of *creative tourism* is not surprising. As suggested by OECD (2014b), creative tourism enlarges the scope of cultural heritage, by linking the physical aspects of each place to the intangible aspects of local cultures, knowledge, and lifestyles, in order to generate a tourism experience deeply rooted on the uniqueness of the destinations. Such a process implies innovative approaches in order to integrate (and to anchor) these immaterial aspects within the physical aspects of the tourism supply, including branding and promotional strategies. Taking advantage of the interaction opportunities offered by ICT, processes of co-creation must also be enabled, allowing the visitors to develop their own creative processes while experiencing the different aspects of the destinations. Thus, cities – with their networks of connected creative agents and a varied set of cultural and creative amenities and infrastructures – offer the ideal setting for these new forms of personalized and creative forms of tourism experiences.

Along with the emergence of this new economic dynamics related to knowledge and creativity, cities and metropolitan areas become more important in a global context, with more than 50% of the world population living today in urban settlements, a figure that can reach 70% by the mid of this century. The concentration of creative activities (as defined before) in urban areas tends to attract qualified (and also nonqualified, as it will be discussed later on) human resources, reinforcing those creative spatial clusters through agglomeration effects related to the externalities and efficiency benefits arising from proximity and co-location. In his detailed analysis of the evolution of cities, Scott (2017) defines this stage as the "third wave" within the evolution of urban settlements. In this sense, contemporary cities (and especially large metropolitan areas) are reinforcing their central role within the global economy, taking advantage of both scale (related to dimension) and variety (related to convergence of a wide scope of creative activities). On the other hand, the context of global competition for the attraction of qualified human resources and investment flows also reinforces the importance of public policies for urban promotion, branding, and attractiveness.

In this context, cities are not only the place where cultural industries tend to concentrate, but they are also the place where higher quantities of infrastructures for cultural consumption (museums, art galleries, theatres, concert halls, and also other type of creative environments, like locations oriented to accommodate start-up companies or historical neighborhoods) can be found. Along with these infrastructures, the concentration of population, with higher discretionary income, opens the opportunities for the development of markets related to these creative products and services, in accordance with the new urban lifestyles, as observed by Currid-Halkett and Scott (2013). Finally, contemporary concerns with environmental questions, mobility and transports, green spaces, or, in broad terms, *livability* – defined as a measure of quality of live, comprising social aspects and the urban environment, as proposed by Kashef (2016) – tend to reinforce the attractiveness of cities and to justify important public investments.

The importance of creative economies and digital technologies in urban areas also contributed to emergence of the concept of *smart city*, used in the literature with different meanings, often related to the utilization of ICT for city management and planning. Nevertheless, this concept can be used with a broader perspective, as proposed by Caragliu et al. 2011 when stating that a city is smart "when investments in human and social capital and traditional (transport) and modern (ICT) communication infrastructure fuel sustainable economic growth and a high quality of life, with a wise management of natural resources, through participatory governance." This multidimensional approach considers economic, social, environmental, and technological issues, generally including the ideas of livability (as defined before) and sustainability (both in terms of the preservation of sensitive resources and the contribution for socio-economic development). With similar purposes, Case Study 4.4 (Romão et al. 2017) adopts the concept of *sustainable smart city* (proposed by Ahvenniemi et al. 2017), emphasizing the role of livability, social conditions, or natural and cultural assets (framed within the concept of sustainable city), along with the aspects related to the creative economies and digital technologies (framed within the concept of smart city). Balsas (2004) or OECD (2014a) propose similar approaches while suggesting principles and indicators to measure the performance of contemporary cities.

The spatial clustering of creative activities, infrastructures, labor, and markets in contemporary cities eventually leads to processes of economic specialization, through the co-location of related activities in specific cities (or neighborhoods). Currid-Halkett and Scott (2013) offer some examples of such *place-in-product* promotional processes, in which the characteristics or images of places are linked to products or services (Paris fashion, Hollywood or Bollywood movies, etc.) in order to generate value through the creation of a distinctive brand. In this sense, this double relation between culture and creativity and city branding (the city benefits and promotes itself through the uniqueness of certain creative products and also the products benefit from the fascination arising from their location in some specific cities) implies that the perceived quality of a product or service depends not only on the performance of individual firms but also on the dynamics of a local cluster of creative economic activities. These aspects of city branding, in a context of globalized competition for the attraction of financial resources, high-tech companies, or skilled and creative labor, are often linked to significant investments in public infrastructures and amenities (transports, green areas, cultural facilities, etc.) and also to the construction of "iconic buildings" designed by internationally recognized architects (*starchitecture*), as discussed in detail by Scott (2017).

While reinforcing the fascination and uniqueness of the cities in order to increase the cultural environment and urban livability, these regeneration processes also contribute to reinforce the attractiveness of the cities from the perspective of tourism. As it was discussed in Chap. 3, branding places according to their unique and specific characteristics contributes to the creation of a differentiated tourism destination, which competes with other urban centers within a monopolistic (or *Chamberlinian*) process, once each of them includes features that are not possible to imitate or to replicate elsewhere. In this sense, clusters of creative activities reinforce the uniqueness of the tourism experience in urban destinations. On the other hand, the concentration of diverse cultural amenities and recreational or educational activities, along with highly developed infrastructures and raising importance of green areas and livability, clearly contributes for the quick development of urban tourism in contemporary societies. As observed by UNWTO (2012), by reducing the transaction costs due to agglomeration effects, cities offer a varied supply of tourism services for diverse segments of tourism demand, as discussed by Mazanek (2010) and exemplified in the Case Studies 4.2 (Romão et al. 2015a) and 3.4, in Chap. 3 (Romão et al. 2015b).

In this context, the role of cultural heritage is becoming increasingly important for urban tourism, as witnessed in different studies. Some examples are offered by Zhang et al. (2011), when analyzing the importance of classified heritage (and, in particular, the impacts of integrating the World Heritage list) for tourism in cities or, by Al Haija (2011), when discussing the role of *historical towns* for urban tourism attractiveness. Domicelj (1992) offered an early analysis of the importance of cultural activities for the emergent *experiential tourism* within travels to urban destinations, with implications for planning processes. With a broader perspective, Fusco-Girard and Nijkamp (2009) or Riganti (2009) analyzed the contribution cultural heritage for local economic development, including aspects related to tourism. Moreover, in a recent work, UNESCO (2016) addressed questions related to the *historic urban landscape* (HUL) in the context of the digital transformations and the emergent trends on urban creativity in contemporary societies, by enlarging the scope of heritage in order to include aspects like the engagement with local communities, the creative reutilization of heritage buildings, and the reinforcement of local identities linked to immaterial cultural aspects or specific economic dynamics, along with the overall urban structure, including open spaces, gardens, infrastructures, or other elements defining urban livability.

4.5   Tourism and Contemporary Urban Social and Spatial Inequalities

The rising importance of knowledge and creativity in the production and consumption systems – through the incorporation of symbolic and cultural values into products and services and the intensification of the utilization of intellectual and creative work – is part of a wider transformation observed in the contemporary (*Post-Fordist*) economic systems, as analyzed by Scott (2007). This author proposes the concept of "cognitive capitalism" to define the current stage of development of global production systems, identifying other structural aspects underlying these transformations, like their leading sectors (related to cultural products and technology-intensive manufacturing and services), or the technological foundations (digital technologies). Small and decentralized production units tend to prevail, while production tends to be customized and oriented to personal needs, within processes of monopolistic competition between producers exploring specific unique assets and characteristics. As it was discussed, the recent high growth levels observed in the tourism sector are also related to these transformations.

As a result of the agglomeration effects and creative externalities generated in urban contexts, contemporary cities attract large quantities of people, including less qualified workers, without creative skills, lacking opportunities in other places, often coming from different (and less developed) countries and without the social capital normally required for an adequate integration into labor markets. At the same time, labor markets also have changed, becoming less stable, with more flexible, deregulated, and precarious work relations. The transformation in the production systems and the technological developments related to ICT or artificial intelligence implied a significant loss of intermediate positions in the labor markets (job polarization), with a concentration of jobs on the top level (highly qualified and specialized) and the low level (nonqualified), with the consequent inequalities in wages and revenues. These inequalities have direct impacts on the propensity to travel, with the increasing discretionary income of high-waged workers contributing significantly for contemporary tourism growth, while low-waged workers have limited options to travel.

In this context of high concentration of economic activities in urban areas, linked to significant inequalities among the population, cities become a place where the contradictions of contemporary societies are more clearly exposed, as observed by Sassen (2010). In fact, although most of the processes described before (transformations in production processes, deregulation of labor markets or job polarization, and wage inequalities) are not specifically urban (as they affect the society as a whole), the fact that firms and population increasingly converge to urban settings makes cities a particular focal point for the analysis of contemporary social problems and conflicts, as they are the location where the major societal trends assume their material expression – in terms of the economic, technological, cultural, social, or political terms. Paradoxically, the author observes the process of globalization contributed to a certain loss of influence of the nation-state as a policy actor while enhancing the role of cities and metropolitan areas. On the other hand, as pointed out by Meijer and Thaens (2018), creative processes of innovation in contemporary smart cities cannot be analyzed with an exclusive focus on the technological dimension, requiring an integrated approach that takes into consideration the interrelations between social and technological aspects, in order to develop collaborative processes.

One important impact of these economic and societal transformations on the urban structures of contemporary cities relates to the processes of *gentrification* – functional changes and reoccupation by different populations – as discussed in detail by Scott (2017). With the loss of importance of obsolete industrial units, empty buildings tend to be reused in accordance with the needs of creative activities (hosting firms related to these new emergent sectors or cultural facilities), also involving public investments for urban renovation (infrastructures, green areas, accessibility and mobility, etc.). The creative externalities created in these new areas (sometimes reinforced by large-scale buildings designed by famous architects, as mentioned before), along with their renovated status, tend to generate an increase in housing prices, implying the displacement of the former industrial workers to peripheral urban areas, while the (renewed) residences are occupied by new professionals from the creative sectors. On the other hand, the attraction exerted by cities on low-skilled and less qualified workers contributes for the concentration of large parts of the population in peripheral areas of the city. These processes tend to increase spatial inequalities in contemporary cities, with high quality (and occasionally closed to public access) in residential areas of the center, coexisting with low-quality and poorly infrastructured areas in the periphery. In less developed economies, such a process can lead to the development of large suburban areas with very low quality of life, including informal construction and lack of the basic infrastructures, as pointed out by Davis (2006), when discussing the intense growth of *slums* in large metropolitan areas of the Global South.

An example of such a process of *creative gentrification* is described in detail by Avdikos (2015), when observing the renovation of a former industrial area in the center of Athens, informally occupied by creative independent professionals. Their activities contributed to create a new reputation for that zone, leading to an agglomeration of creative activities and stimulating public interventions on transport networks and public spaces, reinforcing its livability. In a context of deep economic crisis, real estate prices in that area increased significantly above the rest of city, and those creative activities were gradually replaced by high-quality (and highly priced) residential buildings, along with spaces occupied by other companies, in different types of services related to the creative economy, including hotels. Thus, the creative externalities generated by the first creative agents moving to the area lead to the emergence of "monopoly rents" related to the new reputation of the area, which were, in fact, appropriated by landowners. The study shows that the *creative newcomers* who started the process of renovation of the area could not – after a relatively short time – afford to live or to work in that place. An implicit question underlying this dynamics – the private appropriation of benefits resulting from collective action – will be discussed in Chap. 5, in the context of the *common pool resources* approach to tourism.

The role of tourism within these processes of gentrification is not only related to the appearance of hotels inside these renovated creative areas of cities. Also the *sharing economy*, reinforced by the development of global online platforms in the last years, has strong implications, related to the utilization of residential units for tourism purposes. As observed by OECD (2014b), these platforms contributed to develop different forms of tourism experiences (*live like a local*, through the opportunity of sharing a house with a local family in a residential area), along with new opportunities for small-scale entrepreneurial initiatives at the local level, contributing for higher benefits of the host communities in tourism destinations. Nevertheless, different negative consequences also have been observed as this type of tourism tends to increase: a lack of sense of community within local neighborhoods (as part of the new neighbors are temporary residents, staying for very short periods), lack of care with public spaces and facilities, or noise and other forms of disturbance in residential units. While stressing that house sharing constitutes a relevant economic opportunity, a more sustainable form of consumption and a possible path to a more decentralized, equitable, and sustainable economy, Martin (2016) also points out different problems, like the creation of unregulated marketplaces or the creation of an unstructured field for innovation.

In fact, as noted in different cities like Venice, Lisbon, Barcelona, Amsterdam, or Berlin, this type of accommodation has gradually shifted from the share of a part of a house to the rental of full apartments, with important implications on the housing markets, as the revenues obtained are significantly larger than those arising from regular long-term rental contracts. In this sense, this new form of tourism clearly contributed for inflationary process in the housing markets, accelerating the displacement of local populations from central areas of the cities and creating new problems for local residents to find affordable housing solutions. Thus, these processes may generate an objective loss of welfare for the residents who do not get direct economic benefits from tourism services. On the other hand, the replacement of permanent local residents by temporary visitors contradicts the concept of *live like a local* underlying this type of tourism experience. In this context, it is not surprising that many cities are currently implementing new regulation in order to control and to limit this kind of tourism accommodation. Examples from different European cities where tourism plays an important role are presented and discussed by Dredge et al. (2016).

Thus, although urban tourism has a high potential to generate new economic and entrepreneurial dynamics related to the creative sectors, its growth also implies the emergence of new problems in contemporary cities. These problems also relate to the cumulative use of public spaces, facilities, services, and infrastructures by the local population and the visitors, often with significant problems of congestion and lack of mobility in the most attractive urban areas. In this context, different types of protests have emerged in different cities, sometimes including actions of civil disobedience aiming at the boycott of tourism development or, at least, at creating the acknowledgment, among tourists, of the negative impacts of their presence (Colomb and Navy 2017). These emerging conflicts have also led some cities to implement participatory processes of tourism planning, aiming at reaching a balance between tourism dynamics and the preservation of urban livability for local communities, as it is the case of the plans developed by the Barcelona City Council (2017). It is also relevant that recent studies apply the concept of *carrying capacity* (normally used in the context of sensitive ecological sites with tourism utilization) to the urban context, as proposed by Wei et al. (2015). Case Study 4.4 (Romão et al. 2017) analyzes the impact of different factors related to livability (environment, accessibility, and living conditions) and the creative economy (cultural interaction, innovation, and economic dynamics) on the urban attractiveness (for residents and international tourists).

The potential of tourism for urban development is also analyzed by UNWTO (2012), stressing that cities can offer diverse and flexible tourism products and services, while tourism can promote urban vitality and dynamism, contribute for a renewed urban landscape, enhance personal relations, create jobs (also in related sectors, like those linked to the creative economy), generate income, and contribute for the maintenance of urban infrastructures and public services. Nevertheless, the problems of urban tourism discussed before are also addressed, leading to the identification of several major challenges for tourism development in contemporary cities: adequate management of the increasing number of tourists, ensuring quality of life and socio-economic benefits for the local population, control of the environmental impacts through appropriate development plans, and implementation of participatory decision-making processes, mobilizing the local populations. In fact, several cities start to implement planning processes to address these problems, including the regulation of shared houses originally aiming at residential purposes.

The impacts of the recently observed high growth of city tourism on the urban cultural heritage are also object of particular attention, once the uniqueness of historical and cultural assets is often an important motive attracting visitors, implying a process of commodification that can change their meaning and authenticity, as discussed in Chap. 3. In this sense, ICOMOS (2016) recently addressed these questions, from the point of view of the contribution of the *historic urban landscape* for the sustainable development of cities, also stressing the importance of the immaterial aspects of cultural heritage. According to this organization, the contemporary processes of intense urbanization and globalization, along with the strong development of tourism, potentially contribute for a loss of authenticity at the local level, implying planning processes oriented to preservation of ecological characteristics of urban settings and the respect for the local community rights regarding heritage, its utilization for economic purposes, and the benefits resulting from its exploitation. These concerns are clearly in accordance with the problematic of urban tourism discussed in this chapter, while their implications for sustainable development processes will be discussed with more detail in Chap. 5.

4.6   Concluding Remarks

This chapter was focused on the role of tourism within the context of the contemporary creative economies and the related transformations observed both in the production and the consumption systems, with increasing importance of immaterial aspects related to knowledge or cultural values and symbols, along with personalized experiences oriented to specific needs and motivations of travellers. In this context, the recent and continuous developments in ICT clearly contribute for the enhancement of co-created tourism experiences while opening stronger opportunities for the reinforcement of linkages between the tourism sector and other creative activities, along with the potential reinforcement of regional innovation networks. In particular, the agglomeration effects related to urban development contribute for the emergence of a varied supply of flexible and creative tourism products and services, contributing for the strong growth recently observed in city tourism. Nevertheless, these large influxes of visitors into contemporary cities also raise new problems and challenges for urban planning, not only related to the shared use of spaces, facilities, and infrastructures but also regarding the impacts on local markets and particularly on the housing market in large-scale urban tourism destinations. This conceptual analysis is complemented by four case studies with empirical applications.

In particular, this chapter focused on:

- The importance of information for the match between differentiation of destinations and market segmentation
- The role of ICT promoting interaction between producers and consumers for the *co-creation* of tourism experiences
- The opportunities for the creation and consolidation of local networks of tourism-related innovative activities, by integrating and sharing information about the behaviors and preferences of tourists
- The fragmented, diversified, and decentralized character of the value chain of tourism services in each destination, with potential connections to other sectors, including the dynamic contemporary creative activities
- The potential central role of tourism within smart specialization strategies for the development of regional innovation processes in connection with related sectors
- The raising importance of knowledge and culture in the contemporary economy and in the specific case of tourism
- The importance of urban agglomerations for the emergence and development of the knowledge economy, creative activities, and new tendencies in the tourism sector, based on the uniqueness of each place and in the context of a global competition
- The importance of cultural heritage (including its immaterial aspects) for the creative economy and urban tourism development
- Different problems of tourism in cities related to shared use of public spaces and infrastructures, commodification of cultural values, degradation of community

values, inflationary processes, acceleration of gentrification processes, or shortage of housing for the local population
- New challenges for urban tourism planning, in face of the economic opportunities and also the problems related to the massification of tourism in cities
- Specific challenges for cultural heritage management in urban context, requiring active participation of the local population in tourism and urban planning processes

Case Study 4.1: Information and Satisfaction in an Ecotourism Destination

Neuts B, Romão J, Nijkamp P, Shikida A (2014) A quality assessment of tourist information: the case of nautical tourism at Shiretoko Peninsula. Almatourism 9:24–34

As a consequence of the rising importance of interactive ICT tools in tourism, communication between service providers and tourists has gained renewed attention within tourism studies and entrepreneurial practices. By using a structural equations model, this work analyzes the impacts of using different information sources when booking a cruise tour in an ecotourism destination (the natural World Heritage Site of Shiretoko, in Hokkaido, Japan). Information appears as a crucial element in this type of destination, as the activities largely depend on a set of factors not controllable by tourism companies (like climate conditions influencing the visibility of natural assets, or the behavior of animals expected to observed).

Shiretoko Peninsula was classified by UNESCO as a World Heritage Site in 2005, constituting a complex ecosystem due to its biodiversity (a large variety of wildlife can be seen, including whales, dolphins, sea lions, bears, eagles, owls, and a varied set of birds), along with particular geological characteristics. Different types of boat trips (large boats, small boats, and kayaks, with options for different routes) are among the attractions offered to visitors, and the information used for this study (1170 questionnaires) was collected during 2 consecutive years among the users of these cruises, including information about the different phases of the experience (before, during, and after the trip).

It was observed that the Internet and guidebooks were the main sources of information (47.0%); recommendations from friends or family (11.1%) or local sources like hotels and tourist information centers or shops (13.4%) were much less representative. Almost one third of the visitors (33.2%) did not choose a specific cruise plan, once it was already included in the travel package acquired for the trip. A large boat (travelling relatively far from the coastline) was used by 49.4% of the visitors, while small boats (32.3%) and kayaks (18.3%) – whose routes are closer to the coast – were used by much less tourists. Regarding the routes, Cape Shiretoko (50.1%) was the most frequent option, while Kamuiwakka Fall (21.7%) and Rusha Bay (8.9%) also registered high number of visitors, when compared with the remaining alternatives.

Regarding the motivations of the visitors, observing the landscape (87.9%) or the wildlife (65.5%) was clearly more important than the boat experience itself (20%). Nevertheless, it was perceived that, after the trip, only 39.3% of the visitors were satisfied with wildlife observation, suggesting a reasonably high level of dissatisfaction (once 65.5% were motivated for this aspect). In fact, not seeing the elements (landscape or wildlife) that were expected was indicated as a reason for dissatisfaction by 23.0% of the visitors. Anyway, very high levels of loyalty were observed (95.7% of the travellers would recommend the destination, and 95.1% expressed their intention to return), probably because it was perceived that the elements of dissatisfaction were not under the control of the service providers.

Despite these high levels of loyalty, the analysis revealed a mismatch between the expectations of the visitors based on the information they had collected before and the satisfaction with the concrete experience. Thus, a next step in the analysis was to identify whether different sources of information could have different impacts of the satisfaction obtained. In fact, the results obtained have shown that lower levels of satisfaction were related to the utilization of the Internet and guidebooks as main sources of information, while local sources (tourist offices, hotels, and shops) did not seem to have that negative effect. This can also be related with the timing of collecting information: as the visibility largely depends on weather conditions, it is possible that information collected in the day of the trip (local sources) can be more reliable regarding the realism of the expectations.

When observing in detail the expectations and satisfaction obtained for each combination of route and type of boat (described in detail in the article), it was also possible to identify that the mismatch between expectations and motivations shows high variations. This suggests that the information provided is too much general, not establishing a clear distinction between what can be seen and enjoyed in each type of route and each type of boat. Thus, the analysis stresses the importance of providing more accurate information about the concrete experiences that can be achieved for each of services provided, instead of offering a general perspective of the site. This lack of precise information about what to expect in each route, along with the consequences of choosing different types of boats, has clearly led to some dissatisfaction that could have been avoided by offering more accurate information.

Case Study 4.2: E-Services in Urban Tourism

Romão J, Leeuwen ES van, Neuts B, Nijkamp P (2015) Tourist loyalty and urban e-services: a comparison of behavioural impacts in Leipzig and Amsterdam. Journal of Urban Technology 22(2):85–101

Recent developments in ICT deeply transformed the tourism activities, and information became a critical tool for destination attractiveness while increasing the importance of using of e-services. Information influences the expectations of the visitors and their motivations, satisfaction, and loyalty to a destination. If the behavior of tourists during the travel can be seen as a measure of the performance of a destination, the implications on satisfaction and loyalty allow to infer about its future performance (based on the intentions to revisit or to recommend the place). By using structural models (SEM), this work analyzes the role of information for this double process of performance evaluation in two urban destinations (Leipzig, in Germany, and Amsterdam, in the Netherlands). The results emphasize the heterogeneity of tourism destinations, once different results were obtained in the two cities for most of the relations under analysis.

The first model (future performance) analyzes the characteristics, motivations, perceptions, preferences, and behaviors of tourists, identifying different segments, the most relevant motives for the visit, the main factors of satisfaction, and their implications on the loyalty to the destination. The second model (current performance) focuses on the relation between the characteristics of tourists, the type of e-services used, and the expenditures in the destination.

In the first model, it was observed that satisfaction with the immaterial assets of the cities had positive implications on the loyalty of the tourists in both destinations. The economic impact of loyalty relates to the "free of charge" and reliable promotion of the destination. Nevertheless, important differences were observed when looking at the type of loyal tourists: in Amsterdam, loyalty was higher for tourists with high education levels and low-income levels (probably related to university students visiting the city), while in Leipzig loyalty was mostly identified for business travellers with high income. For the second model (analyzing the relation between the type of e-services and the expenditures at the destination), it was observed that higher expenditures in Amsterdam were made by users of virtual tours, while in Leipzig they are linked to the utilization of personalized information; probably as a tool to find affordable services, e-forums were used by tourists with lower expenditures in both cities.

The study emphasizes the heterogeneity of tourism destinations, as very few general tendencies can be identified. Both the specific assets and services provided in each destination and the particular characteristics of the visitors they attracted to each of them have different implications on the touristic performance of the city, both in terms of the current performance (expenditures during the visit) and the future performance (intention to revisit or to recommend). Nevertheless, the heterogeneity of the behaviors of tourists regarding their preferences for the utilization of diverse e-services reveals the importance of developing specific information contents and using different channels in order to address the diverse market segments visiting the destination.

Case Study 4.3: Tourism, Innovation, and Regional Specialization

Romão J, Nijkamp P (2017) A spatial econometric analysis of impacts of innovation, productivity and agglomeration on tourism competitiveness. Current Issues in Tourism. DOI: https://doi.org/10.1080/13683500.2017.1366434

This study examines whether and how the development of regional systems of innovation influences regional tourism competitiveness (measured by the gross value added by the tourism sector), including a geographical representation of the data, an exploratory analysis based on local indicators of spatial association and an econometric spatial panel data model, providing a quantified analysis of the impacts of each explanatory variable on regional tourism performance, along with the identification of spatial effects. The study covers a large number (237) of NUTS 2 regions in the European Union, which are relevant for the purposes of the study, as they generally have a specific institutional framework for regional and tourism policies while also exhibiting some territorial coherence (although, in a strict sense, they cannot exactly be considered a tourism destination, once normally, there is more than one destination in each NUTS 2 region).

The determinants of the regional tourism performance considered reflect the territorial capital of each region, and they relate to the regional specialization in tourism (share of tourism in regional employment and gross value added), tourism demand (nights spent at regional tourism accommodation establishments), production factors (human capital, measured by the level of education of the work force, and physical capital, measured by the gross fixed capital formation in the tourism sector), and immaterial regional resources (productivity and regional investment in research and development).

The results of the econometric model revealed the expected positive impacts on regional tourism performance of tourism demand, investment, and productivity in the tourism sector, along with the qualifications of the regional work force and the regional investment in research and development. Nevertheless, when the impacts of specialization in tourism are considered, a positive impact is found when this is measured through the share of the gross value added in tourism in the regional economy, but a negative impact is observed when the measure is the share of employment in tourism. This explains the lower levels of productivity where tourism services are more labor-intensive, suggesting that tourism supply in those regions is based on products with low value added.

In fact, the exploratory spatial analysis performed had revealed a large number of Southern European regions with high levels of specialization in tourism and relatively low achievements in terms of value added, suggesting high pressure on local resources, with low impact on the regional economy. Adequate policies oriented to increase the value added of these services (through the diversification of local supply, integrating other types of endogenous resources into the tourism services, and developing a strategy of product diversification) are proposed.

These problems are also reflected in the distribution of the spatial clusters relating tourism performance to education, innovation, and productivity. Despite the overall positive correlation between these factors and tourism performance observed in the econometric model, the exploratory analysis revealed the existence of a very limited number of clusters of regions where high levels of tourism performance relate to high levels observed in any of those factors. On the contrary, a large number of regions show low values for the gross value added in tourism while revealing high scores for productivity, education, and R&D. In fact, the results reveal a modest importance of research and development activities in regions where tourism specialization is high, suggesting a low contribution of the knowledge sector for the regional economy, despite the potential of tourism services to integrate knowledge and new technologies.

This result clearly shows the importance of a balanced and diversified regional economic structure, in which tourism can develop close and more intense links to other (related) sectors, along with the integration of knowledge into innovation processes, as proposed by the recent conceptual developments related to the *smart tourism* approach or to the policy guidelines related to the *smart specialization* strategies.

Case Study 4.4: Urban Attractiveness for Tourists and Residents

Romão J, Kourtit K, Neuts B, Nijkamp P (2017) The Smart City as a Common Place for Tourists and Residents: a Structural Analysis on the Determinants of Urban Attractiveness. Cities. DOI: https://doi.org/10.1016/j.cities.2017.11.007

This article analyzes the determinants of urban attractiveness, both for the resident population and international tourism demand, in 40 global cities, by using a latent growth curve model. The impacts of a diverse set of drivers of urban value creation and attractiveness are taken into account, acknowledging that the dynamics and growth processes related to these urban functions may have different impacts on different types of stakeholders (in this case, resident population and international visitors), potentially leading to the emergence of conflicts between them.

The conceptual framework of the study adopts the concept of "Sustainable Smart Cities," linking the idea of sustainability (to assess social and environmental questions), with the idea of "smartness" (or creativity), reflecting the role of knowledge, technologies, and innovation within the economic context of modern cities. By using an extensive dataset (including 70 indicators), the model assesses the impacts of factors related to both contemporary smart economies (general economic conditions, cultural interaction, and research and development) and urban sustainability (livability, accessibility, and environmental conditions), offering a comprehensive analysis of the determinants of urban attractiveness.

The results obtained suggest that cultural dynamics appears to be a major determinant for attracting new residents while supporting a strong international tourism industry. On the other hand, economic strength (in terms of the absolute growth of GDP) appears to contribute for the attractiveness of residents, while the dynamics observed in research and development activities influences the quality of their employment. The social aspects of sustainability (framed under the concept of livability) and the urban environment seem to exert high impacts on urban attractiveness both for residents and tourists, while accessibility appears mostly relevant for visitors. The results also suggest a difficult relation between livability and environment and the growth of population and volume of visitors. A detailed analysis of the results suggests that cities with a dynamic economy offer opportunities for current and new residents, contributing to increase the city size and its growth rates, without relevant impacts on tourism demand. Moreover, the dynamics in research and development environment appears as benefiting the resident population, but the model shows different relations regarding population growth rates and absolute size.

A strong effect of the aspects related to cultural interaction was also confirmed, especially in their implications for the attractiveness of visitors, as the cities with high scores on this item are also attractive destinations with above-average international tourism demand. Moreover, it is also clear that residents benefit from attraction factors such as shopping and dining opportunities, world heritage sites, museums, theatres, or concert halls, which leads to the identification of a positive effect of cultural interaction on population growth.

Finally, it was noteworthy that problems of livability can be identified in populous urban centers with strong tourism demand. Livability appears as strongly associated with a favorable environment for residents (including positive aspects related to creative industries, working environment, and living conditions). As it was observed, the cities with the highest score on livability were Paris, Vienna, Vancouver, Berlin, Barcelona, and Amsterdam, which are perceived as having a competitive attractiveness advantage. However, the results of the models also reveal a negative relationship between population growth and livability, which may create a vicious circle: livability is an important residential attractor, but when facing an excessive growth, some negative consequences can emerge, like those related to house rents or price levels. Regarding the aspects related to tourism dynamics, it was observed that higher scores on livability were related to a below-average total tourism demand, coexisting with an accelerated growth over the 5-year period. This suggests that urban functionalities can be attractive for residents and visitors while potentially causing conflicts in the long run.

References

Ahvenniemi H, Huovila A, Pinto-Seppä I, Airaksinen M (2017) What are the differences between sustainable and smart cities? Cities 60:234–245

Al Haija AA (2011) Jordan: tourism and conflict with local communities (2011). Habitat Int 35:93–100

Aldebert B, Dang R, Longhi C (2011) Innovation in the tourism industry: the case of tourism@. Tour Manag 32:1204–1213

Asheim B, Coenen L (2006) Regional innovation systems in a globalising learning economy. J Technol Transfer 31:163–173

Asheim B, Smith HL, Oughton C (2011) Regional innovation systems: theory, empirics and policy. Reg Stud 45(7):875–891

Avdikos V (2015) Processes of creation and commodification of local collective symbolic capital; a tale of gentrification from Athens. City Cult Soc 6(4):117–123

Balsas C (2004) Measuring the livability of an urban centre: an exploratory study of key performance indicators. Plan Pract Res 19(1):101–110

Barcelona City Council (2017) Barcelona tourism for 2020 a collective strategy for sustainable tourism. Ajuntament de Barcelona, Barcelona

Binkhorst E, Dekker T (2009) Towards the co-creation tourism experience? J Hosp Mark Manag 18(2–3):311–327

Boes K, Buhalis D, Inversini A (2016) Smart tourism destinations: ecosystems for tourism destination competitiveness. Intl J Tour Cities 2(2):108–124

Boschma R (2016) Smart specialisation and regional innovation policy. Welsh Econ Rev 24:17

British Council (2010) Mapping the creative industries: a toolkit, Creative and cultural economy series 2. British Council, London

Buhalis D (2000) Marketing the competitive destination of the future. Tour Manag 21:97–116

Buhalis D, Law R (2008) Progress in information technology and tourism management. Tour Manag 29:609–623

Capello R, Caragliu A, Nijkamp P (2011) Territorial capital and regional growth: increasing returns in knowledge use. Tijdschr Econ Soc Geogr 102(4):385–405

Caragliu A, Del Bo C, Nijkamp P (2011) Smart cities in Europe. J Urban Technol 18(2):65–82

Castro C, Armario E, Ruiz D (2007) The influence of market heterogeneity on the relationship between a destination's image and tourists' future behavior. Tour Manag 28:175–187

Chen C, Tsai D (2007) How destination image and evaluative factors affect behavioral intentions? Tour Manag 28:1115–1122

Colomb C, Navy J (2017) Protest and resistance in the tourist city. Routledge, London

Cooke P (2001) Regional innovation systems, clusters, and the knowledge economy. Ind Corp Chang 10(4):945–974

Currid-Halkett E, Scott AJ (2013) The geography of celebrity and glamour: reflections on economy, culture, and desire in the city. City Cult Soc 4:2–11

Daskalopoulou I, Petrou A (2009) Urban tourism competitiveness: networks and the regional Asset Base. Urban Stud 46:779–801

Davis M (2006) A planet of slums. Verso, New York

Domicelj S (1992) Recreational visitation and cultural development: push or pull? Habitat Int 16(3):79–87

Dredge D, Gyimóthy S, Birkbak A, Jensen TE, Madsen AK (2016) The impact of regulatory approaches targeting collaborative economy in the tourism accommodation sector: Barcelona, Berlin, Amsterdam and Paris, Impulse paper 9. Aalborg University, Aalborg

European Commission (2006) Innovating in tourism: how to create a tourism learning area. European Commission, Brussels

European Commission (2011) Creative Europe – a new framework programme for the cultural and creative sectors (2014–2020). European Commission, Brussels

Foray D, Goddard J, Beldarrain X, Landabaso M, McCann P, Morgan K, Ortega-Argilés R (2012) Guide to research and innovation strategies for smart specialisation. S3P – European Union, Regional Policy, Brussels

Fusco-Girard L, Nijkamp P (2009) Cultural tourism and sustainable local development. Ashgate, Aldershot

Hall CM, Williams A (2008) Tourism and innovation. Routledge, New York

Hansen T, Winther L (2011) Innovation, regional development and relations between high- and low-tech industries. Eur Urban Reg Stud 18(3):321–339

Hjalager A (2010) A review of innovation research in tourism. Tour Manag 31:1–12

ICOMOS (2016) Cultural heritage, the UN sustainable development goals and the new urban agenda. ICOMOS, Paris

Jenkins H (2006) Convergence culture: where old and new media collide. New York University Press, New York

Kashef M (2016) Urban livability across disciplinary and professional boundaries. Front Archit Res 5:239–253

Kim J, Fesenmaier DR (2017) Sharing tourism experiences: the Posttrip experience. J Travel Res 56(1):28–40

Kozak M, Rimmington M (2000) Tourist satisfaction with Mallorca, Spain, as an off-season holiday destination. J Travel Res 38:260–269

Lin Y, Huang J (2006) Internet blogs as a tourism marketing medium: a case study. J Bus Res 59:1201–1205

Liu J, Nijkamp P, Lin D (2017) Urban-rural imbalance and tourism-led growth in China. Ann Tour Res 64:24–36

Lo I, McKercher B, Cheung C, Law R (2011) Tourism and online photography. Tour Manag 32:725–731

Lundvall B (2002) National systems of production, innovation and competence building. Res Policy 31:213–231

Malakauskaite A, Navickas V (2010) Level of clusterization and tourism sector competitiveness. Eng Econ 21(1)

Mansson M (2011) Mediatized tourism. Ann Tour Res 38(4):1634–1652

Martin R (2014) Path dependence and the spatial economy. In: Fischer M, Nijkamp P (eds) Handbook of regional science. Springer, New York, pp 609–629

Martin CJ (2016) The sharing economy: a pathway to sustainability or a nightmarish form of neoliberal capitalism? Ecol Econ 121:149–159

Mazanek J (2010) Managing the heterogeneity of city tourists. In: Manzanek J, Wöber K (eds) Analysing international city tourism. Springler, Berlin, pp 81–94

Medina-Muñoz D, Medina-Muñoz R, Zuñiga-Collazos A (2013) Tourism and innovation in China and Spain: a review of innovation research on tourism. Tour Econ 19(2):319–337

Meijer A, Thaens M (2018) Urban technological innovation: developing and testing a sociotechnical framework for studying Smart City projects. Urban Aff Rev 54(2):363–387

Milio S (2014) Impact of the economic crisis on social, economic and territorial cohesion of the European Union vol. 1. Directorate-General for Internal Policies, Policy Department B: Structural and Cohesion Policies, Brussels

Millar C, Choi C (2011) The innovative future of service industries: (anti-)globalization and commensuration. Serv Ind J 31(1):21–38

Modica M, Reggiani A (2015) Spatial economic resilience: overview and perspectives. Netw Spat Econ 15(2):211–233

Neffke F, Henning M, Boschma R (2009) How do regions diversify over time? Industry relatedness and the development of new growth paths in regions. Econ Geogr 87(3):237–265

Neuts B, Romão J, van LEV, Nijkamp P (2013) Describing the relationships between tourist satisfaction and destination loyalty in a segmented and digitalized market. Tour Econ 19(5):987–1004

Neuts B, Romão J, Nijkamp P, Shikida A (2014) A quality assessment of tourist information: the case of nautical tourism at Shiretoko Peninsula. Almatourism 9:24–34

OECD (2014a) Better life index. OECD, Paris

OECD (2014b) Tourism and the creative economy. OECD Studies on Tourism, Paris

Piirainen KA, Tanner AN, Alkærsig L (2017) Regional foresight and dynamics of smart specialization: a typology of regional diversification patterns. Technol Forecast Soc Chang 115:289–300

Richards G (2013) Tourism and creativity in the city. Curr Issue Tour 17(2):119–144

Riganti P (2009) From cultural tourism to cultural e-tourism. In: Fusco Girard L, Nijkamp P (eds) Cultural tourism and sustainable local development. Ashgate, Aldershot, pp 263–288

Rihova I, Buhalis B, Gouthro MB, Moital M (2018) Customer-to-customer co-creation practices in tourism: lessons from customer-dominant logic. Tour Manag 67:362–375

Rodríguez I, Williams AM, Hall CM (2014) Tourism innovation policy: implementation and outcomes. Ann Tour Res 49:76–93

Romão J, Nijkamp P (2017) A spatial econometric analysis of impacts of innovation, productivity and agglomeration on tourism competitiveness. Curr Issues Tour. https://doi.org/10.1080/136 83500.2017.1366434

Romão J, Neuts B, Nijkamp P, van LES (2015a) Tourist loyalty and e-services: a comparison of behavioral impacts in Leipzig and Amsterdam. J Urban Technol 22(2):85–101

Romão J, Neuts B, Nijkamp P, van Leeuwen ES (2015b) Culture, product differentiation and market segmentation: a structural analysis of the motivation and satisfaction of tourists in Amsterdam. Tour Econ 21(3):455–474

Romão J, Kourtit K, Neuts B, Nijkamp P (2017) The smart city as a common place for tourists and residents: a structural analysis on the determinants of urban attractiveness. Cities. https://doi.org/10.1016/j.cities.2017.11.007

Sabiote-Ortiz CM, Frías-Jamilena DM, Castañeda-García JA (2016) Overall perceived value of a tourism service delivered via different media: a cross-cultural perspective. J Travel Res 55(1):34–51

Sassen S (2010) The city: its return as a lens for social theory. City Cult Soc 1:3–11

Scott AJ (2007) Capitalism and urbanization in a new key? The cognitive-cultural dimension. Social Forces 85(4):1465–1482

Scott AJ (2017) The constitution of the city. Palgrave Macmillan, Cham

Sigala M (2009) WEB 2.0, social marketing strategies and distribution channels for city destinations. In: Gascó-Hernandez M, Torres-Coronas T (eds) Information communication technologies and city marketing: information opportunities for cities around the world. IGI Global, Hershey, pp 221–245

Sigala M (2012) Exploiting web 2.0 for new service development: findings and implications from the Greek tourism industry. Int J Tour Res 14:551–566

Sigala M, Marinidis D (2012) E-democracy and web 2.0: a framework enabling DMOS to engage stakeholders in collaborative destination management. Tour Anal 17(2):105–120

Tödtling F, Kaufmann A (2001) The role of the region for innovation activities of SMEs. Eur Urban Reg Stud 8(3):203–215

Tussyadiah IP (2014) Toward a theoretical foundation for experience design in tourism. J Travel Res 53(5):543–564

Tussyadiah I, Fesenmaier D (2009) Mediating tourist experiences. Ann Tour Res 36(1):24–40

Úbeda-García M, Cortés EC, Marco-Lajara B, Zaragoza-Sáez P (2014) Strategy, training and performance fit. Int J Hosp Manag 42:100–116

UNCTAD (2013) Trade in creative products reached new peak in 2011, UNCTAD figures show. UNCTAD Press release

UNESCO (2003) Convention for the safeguarding of the intangible cultural heritage. UNESCO, Paris

UNESCO (2009) Understanding creative industries: cultural statistics for public policy. UNESCO, Paris

UNESCO (2016) The HUL guidebook: managing heritage in dynamic and constantly changing urban environments. UNESCO, Paris

UNWTO (2003) Study on tourism and intangible cultural heritage. UNWTO, Madrid

UNWTO (2012) Global report on city tourism. UNWTO, Madrid

Wang Y, Weaver DB, Kwek A (2016a) Beyond the mass tourism stereotype: power and empowerment in Chinese tour packages. J Travel Res 55(6):724–737

Wang D, Xiang Z, Fesenmaier DR (2016b) Smartphone use in everyday life and travel. J Travel Res 55(1):52–63

Wei Y, Huang C, Lam PTI, Yuan Z (2015) Sustainable urban development: a review on urban carrying capacity assessment. Habitat Int 46:64–71

Weidenfeld A (2013) Tourism and cross border regional innovation systems. Ann Tour Res 42:191–213

Wiliams A, Shaw G (2011) Internationalization and innovation in tourism. Ann Tour Res 38(1):27–51

Yang Z, Cai J (2015) Do regional factors matter? Determinants of hotel industry performance in China. Tour Manag 52:242–253

Zhang Y, Xu J, Zhuang P (2011) The spatial relationship of tourist distribution in Chinese cities. Tour Geogr 13(1):75–90

Chapter 5
Tourism Dynamics and Regional Sustainable Development

Contents

Abstract The concepts of competitiveness and sustainability emerged in the litera-ture during the 1980s and they were quickly adopted within tourism studies. In fact, these concepts are closely interrelated when analyzing tourism dynamics in the long run. As these are crucial aspects for the planning and management processes of any kind of tourism destination, they received broad attention, both from academic research and also from a large set of international tourism-related organizations, including different proposals and frameworks for a quantitative analysis. Nevertheless, the continuous recent growth of tourism is clearly related to air travel, as the sector contributes, at least, to 5% of the global CO_2 emissions. Despite this problem, an increasing awareness of consumers regarding environmental impacts

Case Study 5.1: Tourism Dynamics and Regional Competitiveness
Romão J, Saito H (2017) A spatial econometric analysis on the determinants of tourism. competi-tiveness in Japanese Prefectures. Asia Pacific Journal of regional Science 1(1):243–264
Case Study 5.2: Tourism and Sustainable Development
Romão J, Neuts B (2017) Smart tourism, territorial capital, and sustainable regional development: experiences from Europe. Habitat International 68:64–74
Case Study 5.3: Sustainable Wellness Tourism
Romão J, Machino K, Nijkamp P (2017) Assessment of Wellness Tourism Development in Hokkaido: A Multicriteria and Strategic Choice Analysis. Asia Pacific Journal of regional Science 1(1):265–290
Case Study 5.4: Wellness Tourism and Community Development
Romão J, Machino K, Nijkamp P (forthcoming) Integrative diversification of wellness tourism services in rural areas - An operational framework model applied to East Hokkaido (Japan)

© Springer Nature Singapore Pte Ltd. 2018   95
J. Romão, *Tourism, Territory and Sustainable Development*, New Frontiers
in Regional Science: Asian Perspectives 28,
https://doi.org/10.1007/978-981-13-0426-2_5

and the contribution of tourism for the socio-economic development of host communities at the destinations is acknowledged, leading to the emergency of different new segments of tourism activity. Considering its novelty and high potential for the implementation of innovative initiatives oriented to the sustainable development of rural areas, particular attention is given to the case of *wellness tourism*. Finally, the communal aspect of most of the resources attracting tourists to a destination is discussed, as it raises different problems related both to their utilization and also to the unequal appropriation of benefits within a community, reinforcing the need for participatory and representative decision-making processes.

Keywords Competitiveness · Sustainable development · Strategic planning · Participatory management · Wellness · Common pool resources · Collective action

5.1 Introduction

The concepts of competitiveness and sustainability emerged in the economic literature during the 1980s, and they were quickly adopted in tourism studies, mostly during and after the 1990s. While focusing on the conditions and determinants for the achievement of a competitive advantage in global markets, the concept of competitiveness was mostly oriented to the efficient organization of production systems (at different territorial levels, since the individual firm to the national economy). On the other hand, the concept of sustainability was mostly oriented to the importance of an adequate allocation of resources that ensures socio-economic benefits in the short term, without compromising the integrity of the resources in the future. Nevertheless, when applying a long-term approach to the analysis of tourism dynamics, competitiveness and sustainability are clearly interrelated concepts, as it was acknowledged in the literature.

Although the concept of competitiveness was initially linked to the development of niche forms of tourism, with high value added based on the uniqueness of territorial resources and low negative impacts on the environment of the destinations, broader analysis of the problem enlarged its scope, by systematizing the different elements determining the competitiveness of tourism destinations. Consequently, different attempts have been made in order to define indicators and methodologies for its evaluation and quantification, both in terms of academic research and also in terms of guidelines and recommendations offered by different international institutions working in tourism. Nevertheless, it is normally difficult – mostly taking into account the specific conditions of each destination and the lack of relevant data – to perform international comparisons of competitiveness at the destination level.

Similarly, also the concept of sustainability was initially linked to the idea of small-scale forms of tourism, ensuring the preservation of sensitive resources, mostly those related to the environmental aspects of the territories. Different new forms of tourism have emerged related to these concerns, like ecotourism, geotourism, responsible tourism, or cultural tourism. More recently, the concept of *wellness tourism* has also emerged, emphasizing the importance of natural and cultural resources, authentic local experiences, community engagement, and positive socio-economic contributions for the residents at the destinations. Moreover, the concept of sustainable development is also linked to the idea of empowerment of local communities, suggesting the importance of implementation of community-based participatory decision-making processes, which is particularly important for the case of tourism, taking into account its dependence on the uniqueness and authenticity of local resources, along with the interference of tourists in the daily life of residents (which can be positive, negative, or a combination of both positive and negative aspects).

Different authors and institutions also emphasized the importance of the social and economic pillars of sustainable development when analyzing the tourism sector, claiming that the concepts of sustainability and sustainable development must be applied in the research and planning of all types of tourism destinations, including those based on massive fluxes of tourists. In that sense – like it had happened regarding the measure of competitiveness – different scholars and institutions developed efforts in order to find adequate sets of indicators to evaluate the different dimensions of the potential contribution of tourism for the sustainable development of destinations. On the other hand, the definition and global acceptance of the sustainable development goals defined by the United Nations also lead tourism organizations to define the specific potential contributions of the tourism sector for those achievements. Nevertheless, it is also important to notice that tourism is a major contributor for the global CO_2 emissions and that the continuous growth of tourism is clearly linked to a significant growth of air travel.

It is also noteworthy that most of the local resources attracting tourists to a destination – both the material aspects (related to nature, landscapes, monuments, or architecture) and the immaterial aspects (local knowledge and traditions, cultural events, or lifestyles) – can be framed within the common pool resources approach, which does not necessarily fit within the private realm of commercial activities pursued by entrepreneurs nor in the public sphere of public institutions. These resources, created or used by local communities, normally play a decisive role in tourism destinations, through their commodification and integration into tourism products and services. These processes may lead to different types of problems, both related to possible overuse, degradation, and lack of incentive for their preservation and also regarding the private appropriation of benefits (by the companies operating in the tourism sector, mostly those related to transportation and accommodation), for the utilization of common resources, often collectively produced. Receiving scarce attention in the economic literature, these communal aspects of tourism resources also call for participatory processes of planning and management, based on collective decisions.

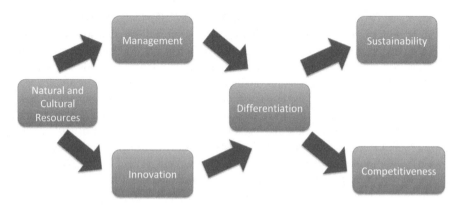

Fig. 5.1 Territorial resources, differentiation, competitiveness, and sustainability

Covering all these topics, this chapter starts with a discussion on the concept of competitiveness in tourism, including possible measures at different territorial levels (Sect. 5.2). This idea is then linked to the concept of sustainability, less focused on the sustainable use of resources (previously discussed, in Chap. 2) and more oriented to the potential impacts of tourism on sustainable development (Sect. 5.3). In both cases, the discussion includes contributions from academic research along with initiatives and guidelines proposed by international institutions with relevant work in tourism (United Nations World Tourism Organization, World Economic Forum, Organization for Economic Cooperation and Development, World Travel and Tourism Council, UNESCO, or the European Commission). Section 5.4 illustrates the case of wellness tourism as an example of a comprehensive approach to sustainable tourism, by aiming at offering positive impacts on the three pillars of sustainable development (economic, social, and environmental). Finally, Sect. 5.5 frames the analysis of the utilization of territorial resources for tourism purposes within the common pool resources approach, reinforcing the discussion on the importance of community involvement in tourism development processes. Figure 5.1 offers a synthesis of the principles for the definition of strategy of destination differentiation aiming at reaching a sustainable competitive position.

5.2   Competitiveness and Sustainability in Tourism

Introduced in the economic literature during the 1980s (Porter 1985, 2003), the concept of competitiveness, related to the achievement of a competitive advantage at the firm level, had strong implications in economic policies in the subsequent years, not only for the definition of entrepreneurial strategies but also at the regional or the national levels. In general terms, this formulation distinguishes between strategies of cost leadership (based on cost advantages) and differentiation (based on the uniqueness of the products or services supplied) in order to achieve a competitive position. This strategy depends on four major factors: firm strategy, structure, and rivalry (related to the market conditions and competition level faced by each company), support industries (related to the role of suppliers or interconnected activities, contributing to enhance the competitive position of a given company or industry – both in terms of costs or differentiation), demand conditions (the level of quality and improvements required by consumers), and factor conditions (related to the availability, quality, and cost of the inputs required for the production).

The concept has been applied to the analysis of tourism dynamics, not only when observing the performance of tourism companies but also when analyzing the competitive position of tourism destinations, regions, or countries. As an example, a short note by Poon (1994) establishes a link between the development of "niche" forms of tourism (oriented to small scale) and the concept of destination differentiation, adapting to tourism sector one of the generic strategic formulations proposed by Porter. In this case, this small-scale supply of tourism activities should be oriented to high value added in products and services, with low negative externalities related to environmental degradation or negative implications on the daily life of local residents. On the contrary, the development of forms of mass tourism related to strategies of cost leadership would lead to low value added for the local economies and high negative externalities. In fact, in a different way but with similar implications, Gilbert (1984) had proposed (one decade before) the concept of *status area* (small-scale tourism based on the prestige of a destination) against the idea of a *commodity area* (large-scale tourism destinations, based on low costs and high levels of infrastructures).

During the subsequent years, several authors adopted the concept of differentiation as a strategic process for the achievement of a competitive position within a globalized tourism markets, stressing the importance of the integration of the unique and inimitable territorial assets into the supply of tourism products and services, as it was discussed in detail in the Chap. 3. Relevant examples were offered by Kozak (1999), Buhalis (1999), or Hassan (2000), also addressing and discussing the importance of preserving sensitive local resources, as will be observed later on. This process implies a long-term perspective on the development of tourism products, services, and activities, taking into account the carrying capacity of the places and the need to protect the resources that attract tourists to a destination while integrating them into the local tourism supply.

Combining these concerns with the strategic formulations proposed by Porter (1985) for the achievement of competitive advantages in tourism, Ritchie and Crouch (2003) proposed a definition of tourism competitiveness that also includes the concerns with the sustainable use of resources and the implications of tourism dynamics on sustainable development. These authors state that what makes a destination competitive is "the ability to increase tourism expenditure, to increasingly attract visitors, while providing them with satisfying, memorable experiences, and to do so in a profitable way, while enhancing the well-being of destination residents and preserving the natural capital of the destination for future generations" (Ritchie and Crouch 2003, p 3). This definition, which has been broadly accepted within the literature on tourism, clearly integrates the ideas of growth, socio-economic impacts at the destination, benefits for the host community, consumer satisfaction, and protection of territorial resources, offering a broad and systematic overview of what is a competitive destination within a long-term perspective.

This systematic perspective includes a comprehensive model of destination competitiveness, including core resources and attractors (such as climate, culture and history, or entertainment), supported by a set of factors and resources (such as infrastructure, accessibility, or hospitality), while requiring appropriate destination management institutions and dedicated policies, plans, and development approaches, which are amplified by qualifying determinants (related to location, safety, cost, value, image, or carrying capacity). These five pillars determining tourism competitiveness are influenced by three layers of factors: an *outer layer* (more stable) comprising climate, geography, and the environment; an *intermediate layer* including sociocultural and demographic characteristics; and an *inner layer* (which can be influenced through short- or mid-term policies) related to economic, technological, and political aspects. These layers influence bot the *macro-level* (the global tourism system) and the *micro-level* (the competitive environment faced by each firm).

Although this formulation offers an interesting conceptual framework for the analysis of the complexity of tourism destination competitiveness, many of the factors proposed are difficult or impossible to quantify, mostly when looking for comparisons between different destinations. Thus, different authors have addressed this problem, proposing alternative formulations and indicators to measure competitiveness in tourism, as exemplified by Dwyer and Chulwon (2003), Enright and Newton (2004), Navickas and Malakauskaite (2009), or Tsai et al. (2009). Song et al. (2012) offer a detailed analysis and comparison between these analytical frameworks, when discussing their advantages and limitations, in particular those related to the absence of comparable data when addressing the levels of competitiveness among different destinations.

Also at the institutional level, different attempts have been made in order to analyze and to quantify competitiveness in tourism, as exemplified by the European Commission (2007). At the global level, the travel and tourism competitiveness index, developed by the World Economic Forum (2017, for the most recent edition), appears as the most common framework used in tourism studies. The index comprises a broad range of indicators, organized in four pillars: enabling environment (including aspects related to business environment, safety and security, health, human resources, or information and communication technologies), policy framework (openness of the economy, price competitiveness, environmental sustainability, and priority given to tourism), infrastructure (airports, other transports, and tourism services), and natural and cultural resources. Despite these efforts, it is important to notice that – due to the limitations in order to obtain accurate and comparable data at other territorial levels – the rankings based on this framework focus on the national (or supranational) level, with few applications to specific cities. Thus, the local level (at which destinations compete within the global markets) or the regional level (where we can observe the impacts of tourism on economic networks and structures) are not properly addressed.

Another important criticism pointed out regarding this index is that – while offering a descriptive approach to tourism competitiveness – it does not offer an explanatory framework, as observed by Mazanek et al. (2007). This observation relates to the fact that competitiveness indexes are based on the computation of scores based on input indicators, not taking into consideration the outputs generated by tourism activities. Thus, these authors propose a structural approach, by measuring the impacts of the determinants of competitiveness on output indicators, like the market share or demand growth, aiming at an explanatory analysis and the achievement of more precise managerial and policy and implications. Nevertheless, it can also be observed that the quantity of demand (expressed by number of visitors or market shares) is not necessarily an adequate measure of competitiveness, as it does not imply the achievement of high economic impacts or benefits for the local populations. With this problem in mind, other output variables used in the literature relate to the gross value added by tourism activities (as it expresses the economic impact of tourism on the local economies) or the productivity per worker in the tourism sector (expressing the local efficiency in the provision of tourism services).

A combination between the definitional and the explanatory perspectives is proposed by Medina-Muñoz et al. (2013), suggesting the adoption of indicators from the definitional approach (like those related to the ability of a destination to attract tourists) in combination with aspects from the explanatory approach (contextual factors and aspects related to the production of tourism products and services). This type of analysis would allow to link the determinants of competitiveness to output indicators, reflecting how the particular conditions of each destination affect their competitive performance. Some of the case studies presented in this book follow this type of approach: in previous chapters, Case Study 3.2. (Romão et al. 2017a) analyzes the impact of material territorial factors (nature and culture) on the gross value added by tourism in European regions, while Case Study 4.3 (Romão and Nijkamp 2017) focuses on the relation between immaterial factors (like innovation efforts or qualification of the labor force) on regional tourism competitiveness in Europe; in this chapter, Case Study 5.1 (Romão and Saito 2017) addresses the impact of diverse material and immaterial aspects on the gross value added by tourism in Japanese Prefectures.

Although most of the comparative studies on tourism competitiveness focus on the national level, several recent works address this question on the regional level, analyzing the impacts of different aspects of the regional territorial capital (Capello et al. 2011), perceived as the regional capability to incorporate knowledge into innovative products and services. Apart from the examples offered in this book, Cracolici and Nijkamp (2008) use an indicator related to tourism satisfaction as a proxy for tourism competitiveness in Southern Italian regions, while Camisón and Forés (2015) analyze the relation between regional economic competitiveness and the competitiveness of tourism companies, thus emphasizing the importance of a dynamic regional economy in order to boost regional tourism competitiveness. The authors propose the concept of *tourism districts*, stressing the potential role of agglomeration economies (related to the concentration of tourism activities) in order to increase regional innovation capabilities in the tourism sector.

As discussed in Chap. 3, tourism destinations are multi-product and multi-service areas (Buhalis 2000; Romão et al. 2015), whose supply is characterized by *co-creation* processes, *co-terminality* (direct interaction between producer and consumer), *spatiality*, and *temporality* (consumption and production of tourism services occur in the same place at the same time), with high potential for the implementation of place-based innovation strategies based on local networks (European Commission 2006; Hall and Williams 2008; Brouder and Eriksson 2013). As it was discussed in Chap. 4, this is enhanced by the developments in information and communication technologies (ICT) and their applications in tourism (Buhalis and Law 2008; Hjalager 2010). The importance of these localized networks is reinforced by the dependence of tourism supply on the uniqueness of territorial resources for the achievement of a differentiated competitive position, implying the integration of cultural and natural assets into the tourism supply while preserving their characteristics, both in terms of their ecological values (Kozak 1999; Buhalis 1999; Hassan 2000; Page and Dowling 2002) or their cultural features (Domicelj 1992; Zhang et al. 2015), in particular for the historical districts of cities (Al Haija 2011).

The concept of *smart tourism* recently proposed by Boes et al. (2016) emphasizes the potential role of digital technologies for the reinforcement of local networks, the development of collaborative processes, the co-creation of destinations and experiences, and the importance of participatory processes of governance at the destination level, with important implications for the territorial planning of spaces, infrastructure, and services (Binkhorst and Den Dekker 2009; Kim and Fesenmaier 2015). The close relation between the multiple tourism products and services and other related economic sectors can also contribute to reinforce local and regional innovation networks based on local knowledge, resources, and capabilities, as suggested by the *smart specialization* approaches to regional development (Foray et al. 2012; Boschma 2016). In this context, the competitiveness of tourism can contribute and can also benefit from the overall competitiveness of the regional economies where the destinations are integrated.

5.3   Tourism for Community Sustainable Development

The concepts of sustainability and sustainable development were globally accepted both in the academic literature and within institutional guidelines for development strategies after the publication of *Our Common Future* (World Commission on Environment and Development 1987) and the Rio Summit on Sustainable Development (organized by the United Nations in 1992), based on the central idea that sustainable development "meets the needs of the present without compromising the ability of future generations to meet their own needs." Sharpley (2009) describes in detail the early efforts to apply these concepts into tourism studies and practices, pointing out examples such as the "Strategy for Sustainable Tourism Development" (arising from a conference in Vancouver in March 1990), the "Sustainable Tourism Development Conference" held in Edinburgh in November 1990, the publication of

The Green Light: A Guide to Sustainable Tourism by the English Tourist Board (1991), the foundation of the *Journal of Sustainable Tourism* in 1992, or the publication of *Sustainable Tourism Development: A Guide for Local Planners* by the World Tourism Organization, in 1993. Another example is the publication of *Tourism Policy and International Tourism in OECD Countries* (OECD 1994), identifying six axes for sustainable tourism development in rural areas, including the scenic values of natural landscapes, wildlife, cultural assets, facilities for sports, accessibilities, and managerial skills.

Nevertheless, different types of concerns had been previously expressed regarding the negative implications of tourism development, mostly after observing the large processes of urbanization and construction of infrastructures in coastal areas during the 1960s, related to massive seasonal flows of tourists for the enjoyment of *sun-and-sea* destinations around the world (as discussed in Chap. 3). Broader concerns regarding the limits of the resources for the development of the world economy were also clearly expressed by Meadows et al. (1972), pointing for the need for different approaches and policies for economic development, and also in the "United Nations Conference on the Human Environment," held in Stockholm in 1972. For the specific case of tourism, David (2016) describes the early case of Charles Lindbergh, who became world famous for his contributions to aviation (and, in particular, for the first flight between the United States and Paris, in 1927) and would later regret his own efforts for the development of air travels. Lindbergh would become member of different organizations for the protection of the environment and a strong voice against the development of massive forms of tourism.

In fact, the intense growth of tourism activities over the last decades seems to be closely related to a significant growth in air travel. UNWTO (2013) estimated that tourism activities represented 9% of the world's GDG in 2012 (10% in 2015, according to UNWTO 2016b), more than 200 million jobs and almost 30% of the global exports of services. International arrivals have experienced a continuous growth, reaching more than 1000 million, for the first time, in 2013, and 1.322 million in 2017 (UNWTO 2018). At the same time, UNWTO (2013) acknowledges that, along with local problems related to land use and degradation, waste management and water consumption, tourism is increasingly contributing for climate change, being responsible for 5% of the CO_2 emissions at the global level. Thus, even if the awareness regarding environmental problems seems to increase, along with the development of new and more *environmental-friendly* forms of travel and leisure, this continuous growth of international air travels does not seem in accordance with the basic principles of environmental sustainability. This question has not been properly addressed by any tourism-related international organization, even when tourism is seen as driver of sustainable development (UNWTO 2013) or when this organization has declared the year of 2017 as the "International Year of Sustainable Tourism for Development," as observed by Mullis (2017).

As discussed in Chap. 3, the analysis of the problems related to the scale of tourism activities and the need to preserve sensitive resources, often implying the definition of limits and restrictions for their utilization within the tourism context, has gained rising importance during the 1990s, after the popularization of the concept of sustainable development. Different authors advocated the creation of a solid link between the differentiation of destinations based on the unique features of their territories and the need to preserve them in the long run. Williams and Ponsford (2009) would define as *environmental paradox* this double process: the supply of tourism services relies on the exploitation of resources that must be, at the same time, preserved. With a different perspective, Douglas (2014) pointed out that environmental resources or cultural practices and values only become part of the tourism experience when commoditized, increasing the potential problems of degradation and overuse. Jovicic (2014) offers a systematic overview of these contributions.

Nevertheless, questions related to sustainability in tourism cannot be addressed only in terms of the impact of tourism activities on environmental resources. In fact the concepts of sustainable development and sustainability in tourism should be analyzed in a broader perspective, as pointed out by Butler (1999), when distinguishing the impacts of tourism on sensitive resources (as discussed in Chap. 3) from its impacts on sustainable development (as discussed in the current chapter). Thus, this author claims that the principles of sustainability must be applied to all types of destination, including mass tourism areas or small-scale ecological sites. Later on, when analyzing the conceptual evolution of research in tourism, Jafari (2001) would confirm this idea, proposing that the concept of sustainable development should underlie tourism policies and plans independently of the characteristics of the destinations. Rather than an *advocacy platform* (promoting tourism development, dominant during the 1960s), a *cautionary platform* (imposing limits for the development of tourism development, prevailing during the 1970s), or an *adaptancy platform* (proposing different strategic options for the development of tourism, as was generally suggested during the 1980s), the author states that a *knowledge platform* is required for the analysis of tourism dynamics, by applying the principles of sustainability independently of the destinations, scale of tourism supply, or the mix of products and services being offered. Both authors (Butler and Jafari) stress the need to achieve relevant socio-economic benefits for the residents in tourism destinations while pointing out the human dimension of sustainability.

Different authors addressed the relations between tourism dynamics and sustainable development in the subsequent years, keeping in mind both the need to preserve sensitive territorial resources and the importance of the contribution of tourism for sustainable development. Miller et al. (2005) or Weaver (2006) offer interesting examples, complementing their systematic analyses with measurement tools based on quantitative indicators. Sharpley (2009) defines a set of "principles of sustainable tourism," comprising different elements, like environmental protection (minimal impacts and relevant conservation measures), territorial characteristics as the core elements for the differentiation of the supply of tourism services (exploring uniqueness through authenticity, reflecting community values, and using design in order to enhance the sense of place), and appropriate products and services (addressing and targeting adequate market segments, improving the quality of the experience by adding value through relevant contents), while contributing for the empowerment of the host communities (ensuring mutual benefits both for visitors and hosts). Questions related to climate change and their potential impacts on coastal areas would later on reinforce the importance of the analysis of the relation between tourism, environment, and sustainable development, as witnessed, among others, by Weaver (2011). Torres-Delgado and Saarinen (2014) offer a review and synthesis of these contributions, including a systematic comparison of possible indicators.

In a broader sense, the relation between the utilization of natural resources and the processes of sustainable development has also received significant attention in the last years, focusing on different perspectives. Redclift and Woodgate (2013) or Maes and Jacobs (2017) establish a link between natural resources, economic growth, and social benefits (thus, combining the three pillars of sustainable development), emphasizing the role of territorial design and management. Differently, Halme and Korpela (2014) or França et al. (2017) focus on the potential impacts of innovation dynamics on these three pillars. More oriented to the specific case of tourism, Bertacchini and Segre (2016) or Wu et al. (2016) address the integration of cultural heritage into sustainable development strategies. On the other hand, as it was discussed in detail in Chap. 2, the economic impacts of tourism have been broadly analyzed during the last decades (Pablo-Romero and Molina 2013), including a first stage in which an optimistic perspective – based on the *tourism-led growth hypothesis* – has prevailed (for an overview, see Shubert and Brida 2011), apparently confirmed in different territories (Chen and Chiou-Wei 2009; Cortes-Jimenez and Pulina 2010; Nowak et al. 2007; Dritsakis 2004, 2012). Nevertheless, when considering longer series of data, Chou (2013), Lee and Chang (2008), or Tang and Jang (2009) reached ambiguous results, while long-term negative impacts of tourism on regional economic structures and growth processes – related to the transformations that occurred within regional economic structures – were found by Capó et al. (2007), Sheng and Tsui (2009), Adamou and Clerides (2010), or Romão et al. (2016).

The social dimension of sustainable development has also received particular attention within tourism studies, with a particular focus on the potential contribution of the sector for poverty alleviation in less developed countries or regions, as Zhao and Ritchie (2007) point out. Nevertheless, the impacts of tourism dynamics on social structures in more advanced economies have received much less attention. An exception is the work presented as Case Study 5.1 (Romão and Neuts 2017), pointing out that the contribution of tourism for the sustainable development of European regions is relatively poor, when the three pillars defining sustainability are considered. In fact, the results reveal that regions highly specialized in tourism are generally less dynamic from an overall economic point of view while registering higher levels of unemployment within the European context. The good results achieved in the environmental pillar (measured by CO_2 emission) are also related to the low industrial development generally observed in these areas.

Moreover, Case Studies 3.2 (Romão et al. 2017a) and 4.3 (Romão and Nijkamp 2017) – presented in previous chapters – had already suggested important problems within the current tourism performance of these regions (mostly located in the South of the continent), related to massive forms of tourism in areas with high ecological value coexisting with low value added and low productivity of the tourism sector, scarce innovation capabilities, and, in general terms, low economic benefits, in comparison with the economic dynamics of other European areas, as observed in Case Study 2.3 (Romão and Nijkamp, forthcoming). In fact, as observed by Mullis (2017), the contribution of tourism for wealth distribution is extremely limited, and, often, less than 10% of tourism expenditures remains at the destination, while large transnational companies related to transport and accommodation take most of the benefits of tourism dynamics.

Although the contribution of tourism for the three pillars of sustainable development does not often appear as significantly positive, the intense growth of tourism during the last decades and the prominent role of the sector within local and regional economies and job markets justify the reinforcement of the focus of different international institutions in order to explore the full potential of tourism for the achievement of higher levels or economic development, social cohesion, and environmental protection. An early systematic approach was undertaken by the World Travel and Tourism Council, the United Nations World Tourism Organization, and the Earth Council (1996). Along with the proposal of methodologies for the implementation and development of participatory decision-making processes and planning strategies, this document addresses a broad set of questions related to sustainable development, including the conservation, protection and restoration of ecosystems, sustainable patterns of production and consumption, or impacts on employment.

Over the following years, different organizations offered guidelines and developed principles for sustainable tourism development (UNESCO 2000, 2005; European Commission 2007; World Economic Forum 2017; UNWTO 2007, 2013). In particular, a joint document produced by the United Nations Environment Programme and UNWTO (2005) offers a set of guidelines for tourism policy making, in order to address issues related to climate change, conservation of natural resources and health, safety and security, or poverty alleviation, along with the promotion of sustainable consumption behaviors, while taking into consideration the life cycle of tourism products and services and the importance of monitoring methods based on specific indicators related to sustainability goals. UNWTO (2013) would update this framework, by defining five pillars for policy making (tourism policy and governance; economic performance, investment, and competitiveness; employment, decent work, and human capital; poverty reduction and social inclusion; sustainability of the natural and cultural environment), along with 12 major objectives for tourism sustainable development (economic viability, local prosperity, employment quality, social equity, visitor fulfillment, local control, community well-being, cultural richness, physical integrity, biological diversity, resource efficiency, and environmental purity).

After the publication of the "2030 Agenda for Sustainable Development" (United Nations 2015), offering a systematic framework structure for the implementation of sustainable development strategies, by defining 17 goals and 169 targets, the analysis of the impacts of tourism dynamics on sustainable processes of development has been more clearly specified. In particular, UNWTO (2015) states that the tourism sector should contribute for the achievement of the goals numbered 8 (inclusive and sustainable economic growth), 12 (sustainable consumption and production), and 14 (sustainable use of oceans and marine resources), clarifying that tourism activities have a responsibility on the protection and preservation of sensitive territorial resources, along with the promotion of socio-economic development processes benefiting the host communities in each destination.

After this general proposition, UNWTO (2016a) has triggered a new discussion aiming at improving the coordination between tourism policies and sustainable development processes, pointing out that "sustainable tourism development guidelines and management practices are applicable to all forms of tourism in all types of destinations, including mass tourism and the various niche tourism segments." The document emphasizes that the principles of sustainability must address the economic, sociocultural, and environmental dimensions of tourism dynamics while mobilizing local communities for participatory planning processes and continuous monitoring of impacts. Within this frame, the document defines three major axes, aiming at long-term sustainable development: optimal use and conservation of environmental resources and biodiversity; contribution for intercultural interchanges while conserving cultural heritage, community values, and authenticity; and viable economic activities offering socio-economic benefits for the host communities, including income, employment, and services.

In order to support the implementation and evaluation of this type of policies, UNWTO (2017) has recently launched the "Measuring Sustainable Tourism" initiative, aiming at developing an international statistical framework, combining traditional economic indicators with environmental and social aspects, at the global, national, and subnational territorial levels. This approach takes into consideration five measurement pillars previously identified (UNWTO 2016c): tourism businesses and their key characteristics; tourism activity and visitor expenditure; environmental flows; environmental assets and other infrastructure; and accounting for ecosystems. Similarly, the European Commission (2016) also developed a *toolkit* for the evaluation of sustainable destination management, comprising four major sections: destination management (public policy and customer satisfaction), economic value (tourism flows, enterprise performance, employment, supply chain), social and cultural impact (community impact, health and safety, gender equality, inclusion, cultural heritage, and local identity and assets), and environmental impact (transport impact, climate change, waste management, sewage treatment, water management, energy usage, landscape, and biodiversity protection).

In the context of the management of cultural heritage (in this case, the sites classified as *World Heritage*), with important implications for tourism dynamics, UNESCO (2013) also provided a set of orientations regarding its integration into broad policies for sustainable development. The purpose of the document is to define a framework for the integration of cultural heritage into processes of transformation of contemporary societies, through its linkages to the economic system. This approach is in accordance with the characteristics of contemporary economies discussed in Chap. 4, where a convergence between the economic and the cultural spheres can be observed, with the integration of cultural values into products and services, the commodification of cultural production, and the emergence of the *experience economy*, with a strong component of emotional and immaterial aspects. In this sense, heritage is seen as a *living site*, rather than a set of monuments, and its intrinsic value must be protected and transmitted to future generations while exploring its instrumental potential contribution for the three pillars of sustainable development (including the integration into tourism dynamics).

With a more specific focus on the urban context, ICOMOS (2016) has also recently addressed the relations between cultural heritage and the sustainable development goals (UN 2015), taking into consideration the specific Target 11.4, which appeals for "making cities and human settlements inclusive, safe, resilient and sustainable by strengthening efforts to protect and safeguard the world's cultural and natural heritage." Also assuming the immaterial aspects of cultural heritage, the document takes into consideration major trends influencing and raising new challenges for contemporary cities, including intense and accelerated urbanization, globalization and loss of identity, expansion of tourism, importance of local communities, new ecological perspectives on urban settlements, and human rights-based approaches to heritage, along with the identification of inadequate urban planning processes. In this context, cultural heritage is seen as a factor to create value in urban settings by driving economic development through creativity (cultural facilities, urban regeneration, events, or tourism), enabling social cohesion (through employment, valorization of local traditions, and knowledge or reinforcement of community values), and improving the livability and environmental sustainability of urban areas.

Apart from the definition of aims, axis, and actions, a strategic plan of sustainable tourism development also requires adequate methodologies, normally implying a high level of institutional coordination and involvement of a wide range of stakeholders. The example proposed by David (2016) offers a relevant overview of the main issues to address, stressing that such a plan must be based on a common vision for the future of tourism in a destination (accepted and shared among stakeholders), along with a mission statement, explaining the ways to achieve that vision. From that vision, goals (driving forces of the strategic plan) and objectives (specific-oriented targets to reach the goals) can be defined. In this framework, strategies are seen as long-term operations to meet the objectives, while tactics relate to short-term actions for immediate achievements. Although these principles seem to be consensual and generally applicable to any kind of strategic development process, their integration into the context of tourism and sustainable development is generally rather complex, once it implies a strong coordination between stakeholders with very different objectives and interests (entrepreneurs, public institutions, managers of ecological and cultural sites and facilities, residents, NGOs with different types of intervention, or residents). In fact, such a participatory process of planning for sustainable tourism development is normally difficult – if not impossible – to find in contemporary tourism destinations.

5.4   Wellness and Sustainable Tourism Development

The generalized awareness with environmental problems, the need to preserve natural sensitive resources, and the recognition of the importance of cultural diversity and authenticity, along with the easy access to information through digital technologies, have contributed to significant changes in lifestyles over the last decades, with important implications on leisure and travel behaviors. Different new types of tourism emerged related to these concerns: ecotourism or geotourism (related to recreational or educational activities based on the ecological and geological features of the sites, often including physical exercise, sports, or adventures), cultural or heritage tourism (related to educational purposes or self-enrichment through the contact with different cultural values or historical elements), or responsible tourism (related to increasing awareness with consumption behaviors or with the relations with host communities and the contribution to their socio-economic development). There are abundant examples in the literature related to all these new market segments within the global tourism markets.

More recently, a new form of tourism emerged, combining much of these concerns with the environment, different cultural values, and positive impacts on the host communities, with a search for self-development, well-being, and promotion of healthy lifestyles. Designated in the literature as *wellness tourism*, this new form of travel seems to show very high growth rates (above the overall growth of tourism, even in a context of very intense global dynamics of this sector). Also, wellness tourism appears as a good example of a sustainable form of tourism (considering the previously mentioned three pillars of sustainability), at least from the point of view of the impacts on the destination (but not necessarily when considering the global impacts of air travel and the related CO_2 emissions and contribution for climate change, which appears as one of the crucial challenges for the sustainability of the overall development of the tourism sector).

The impressive dynamics of wellness tourism in contemporary societies (494 billion dollars worldwide in 2013, according to Yeung and Johnston 2015) is related to the emergence of new health-care behaviors, based on proactive, preventive, and holistic practices, rather than a reactive behavior in search of medical treatments when suffering from a disease. This formulation follows the definition of wellness proposed by Corbin and Pangrazi (2001), as "a multi dimensional state of being describing the existence of positive health in an individual as exemplified by quality of life and a sense of well-being." These new approaches to health care – aiming at improving the overall feeling of physical, emotional, and spiritual well-being – contributed to the emergence of a new tourism market segment, related to the travels motivated by this type of purpose (Cohen 2008).

In this sense, this segment of the global tourism market appears as clearly related to place-based authentic experiences, depending on the natural and cultural features of the destinations and offering new opportunities for the development of sustainable tourism practices, especially in rural areas, where natural landscapes can offer the adequate setting for this type of experience. Distinguishing this tourism segment from other health-related segments (like medical tourism, related to travels implying medical interventions for the treatment of diseases), Johnston et al. (2011) define wellness tourism as related to "people who travel to a different place to proactively pursue activities that maintain or enhance their personal health and wellbeing, and who are seeking unique, authentic or location-based experiences and therapies not available at home." Similarly, wellness tourists are defined as "seeking integrated wellness and prevention approaches to improve their health and quality of life." Taking into account the pyramid of hierarchy of needs conceptualized by Maslow (1943), this motivation for travelling can be classified within the self-actualization level, by considering the search for physical and spiritual health as an effort to accomplish the highest standards a human being can achieve.

It is documented in recent literature that tourists engaging in this emergent type of travel tend to pursue and to combine diverse activities while using different services. Nevertheless, the utilization of water (in particular thermal water) complemented with diverse spa-related services, and different features related to the ecological and cultural characteristics of the places appear as common aspects of the contemporary dynamics of wellness tourism. Along with the utilization of different spa-related services or therapies based on the properties of the water, these tourists normally also look for healthy and high-quality food, sports, hiking or other forms of physical exercise, cultural and educational activities, or relaxation and meditation practices (Cohen 2008). Smith and Diekmann (2017) propose a systematic synthesis of these motivations, by identifying three major motivational factors: pleasure and hedonism (related to the physical and emotional well-being), meaningful experiences (related to the authenticity and significance of the contact with different cultural values), and altruistic activities (related to sustainable consumption practices and the positive impacts on the host communities). Case Study 5.4 (Romão et al. Forthcoming) adopts this classification in order to define a framework model for wellness tourism development in rural areas.

Even if the supply of some of these services is independent of their location, others require specific features related to landscape, geography, or ecological characteristics (Johnston et al. 2011). Thus, the properties of thermal waters, the natural parks or other interesting ecological sites, non-urban scenic routes, authentic and unique local cultural heritage, or local healthy food can be pointed out among the territorial resources required for the supply of a differentiated wellness travel experience. Other requirements for the implementation and development of wellness tourism services relate to technologies, training and qualification of human resources, definition of quality standards, or the design of adequate facilities well integrated into the characteristics of landscapes, as observed by Erfurt-Cooper and Cooper (2009) or Smith and Puczkó (2013).

Thus, the creation and development of wellness products and services requires the mobilization of a broad set of stakeholders, including private companies (hotels, spa services, recreational activities) and often also public institutions (health services, natural parks, museums, cultural facilities, transports, or safety and security, which are, in many cases, provided or regulated by public organizations). The importance of the involvement and coordination of a wide range of stakeholders is clearly identified by Page et al. (2017). In this context, the development of wellness tourism in non-urban areas (which are normally the most suitable for the supply of this mix of activities and services) often faces important obstacles related to the lack of innovation and entrepreneurial capabilities, as discussed in Case Studies 5.3 (Romão et al. 2017b) and 5.4 (Romão et al. Forthcoming).

Although the emergence and global quick growth of wellness tourism is relatively recent (mostly since the end of the twentieth century), travels related to wellness practices based on the benefits of water properties have a very long history. A very ancient example is the traditional Japanese *onsen* bath, whose practice in the hot springs of the country is documented for almost 3000 years while still constituting an important element of daily life in some rural areas of Japan (and also an important motive for travel for the residents in contemporary Japanese urban areas). In Europe, at least since the Roman Empire (second century BC), the public bath was a central element in most of the cities, not only for hygienic reasons but also as a social center of daily life. The expansion of the Roman Empire to the West, East, South, and North, reaching places like the Iberian Peninsula, Constantinople (the contemporary Istanbul, in Turkey, in the border between Europe and Asia), Cartage (in the contemporary Tunisia, North of Africa) or Germany, and the United Kingdom, has clearly contributed to the implementation of different types of bath in different parts of the world, adapted to the specific cultural values and natural characteristics of each place.

The baths inherited from Romans – and also the central role of the public bath for social life – would be adopted later on by the Arabs, after the expansion of the Arabic civilization from the Middle East to Europe, started in the eighth century. With the same denomination (*Hammam*) but different processes and practices (based on the steam of water, instead of soaping, and complemented by a massage), the Turkish bath is still today present in most of the cities of the country. Other historical types of bath, whose forms depend on natural and cultural features of the places, were registered all over the world, like those related to the Maori tradition (in contemporary New Zealand) or the indigenous communities of the American continent. Steward (2012), Smith and Puczkó (2013), or Walton (2013) offer historical and geographical analyses of the utilization of water for the promotion of health, often related to travel motivations.

After the sixteenth century, mostly in European countries (including Germany, the United Kingdom, France, or Portugal), the utilization of water properties for medical treatments would gain particular importance, with the implementation of hospitals using (and sometimes exclusively oriented for) water therapies for the treatment of different diseases. As these hospitals were normally located in quiet rural areas with good natural conditions and beautiful landscapes, some of these places would gradually emerge as travel destinations for the wealthiest part of the population. In fact, during and after the eighteenth century, thermal establishments would gain importance, often complementing the water treatments with recreational facilities, like casinos. Some remarkable examples of these places for leisure and social activities are Spa (Belgium), Vichy (France), Bath (the United Kingdom), or Baden-Baden (Germany). Although the development of transport networks during the nineteenth century has contributed for a shift in tourism flows towards coastal destinations, many of these locations would keep their activity as medical facilities, also due to the development of the welfare state during the twentieth century, including subsidies for treatment of diseases in thermal establishments, as observed by Tabbachi (2008). Thus, this transformation implied that thermal establishments were no longer a privilege of the wealthier population, as they started to be used by people with different social status.

Nevertheless, the intense scientific developments observed in medicine (in particular, the discovery and generalized application of penicillin) have led to the development of different treatments, clearly much more efficient than those based on thermal waters. As a consequence, a serious decline was observed in most of the thermal establishments, leading, in many cases, to their closure. However, mostly since the end of the twentieth century and with increasing importance since the beginning of the twenty-first century, the new approaches to health care and holistic lifestyles, along with the concerns with environmental aspects, sustainability issues, and the quest for unique and authentic experiences, contributed for the redevelopment of thermal establishments, currently oriented to wellness tourism practices, often taking advantage of the historical characteristics of the buildings and facilities, as testified by Ellis (2008), Cohen (2008), or Johnston et al. (2011). Benefiting from the multipurpose motivations of these travellers (previously discussed), these establishments tend to combine the water-based services (including a variety of spa services, massage, or beauty treatments), with ecological activities, sports, hiking, cycling, healthy food, or cultural and educational facilities (museums, art galleries, or congress centers).

Thus, it seems clear that wellness tourism in contemporary societies has a high potential to continue its growth path, potentially contributing for the sustainable development of rural areas, based on their endogenous territorial resources, both related to natural assets and cultural values, while offering authentic and unique tourism experiences. In this context, four major challenges – implying the mobilization of a large set of diverse stakeholders, as discussed before – emerge, as pointed out in Case Study 5.4 (Romão et al. Forthcoming): territorial management (related to the utilization of natural and cultural resources and also transportation networks); entrepreneurship and human resources (for the provision of innovative and high-quality services, in a context which is normally characterized by low levels of entrepreneurship and innovation capabilities); *coopetition* (involving collaboration processes and coordination between organizations with different interests and motivations); and marketing, positioning, and branding strategies (in order to match the possible mix of services with the characteristics and motivations of specific groups of tourists, through adequate communication processes and channels).

5.5 The *Commons* in Tourism

It is noteworthy that most of the territorial aspects defining the attractiveness of a tourism destination can be framed within the *common pool resources* approach, as defined by Ostrom (2008). Although the focus of tourism studies based on this approach was initially on the utilization of environmental resources for tourism purposes, gradually, this focus has been enlarged, also comprising other types of territorial assets, including material and immaterial cultural heritage, landscapes, lifestyles, or even digital resources. Thus, although most of the expenses related to tourism activities are concentrated on travel and accommodation costs (with private appropriation of benefits), the motivations of tourists are generally related to other aspects of the destinations, often commonly produced by a community and potentially subject to overuse, degradation, or destruction, whose utilization for tourism purposes implies a process of commodification through integration into products and services.

Common pool resources have two major characteristics: *subtractability* (existence of rivalry among potential users, implying that the utilization by one user may exclude the possibility of utilization by others) and *nonexcludability* (generally it is difficult – or impossible – to limit the access). As these resources are generally indivisible and their boundaries are often difficult to define, it is difficult to define legitimate users or to exclude others. These resources can be subject to different property regimes (private, public, or communal), eventually changing over time, and the same type of resource may have different property regimes in different locations (Holden 2005). Examples commonly mentioned in the literature include natural resources (air, atmosphere, water, ecosystems, fisheries, forests, or wildlife), along with build infrastructures (irrigation systems, water distribution and treatment, streets, transportation systems, ports, urban areas) or immaterial assets (cyberspace, electromagnetic spectrum, genetic data, traditions, language, knowledge, or other creative assets).

Despite the difficulties to measure their economic value, it is also clear that common pool resources are generally a source of externalities, contributing for the creation and appropriation of value through different activities. Common resources related to natural landscapes often support different recreational or educational activities, including for tourism purposes, while monuments or architectural landmarks may perform similar tasks. Moreover, as observed by Scott (2017) when observing contemporary urban dynamics, also immaterial common resources constitute a source of externalities. The author mostly focuses on the agglomeration economies related to the concentration of knowledge and creative activities in specific locations, contributing to reinforce the attractiveness of the places for financial investments, co-localization of economic activities or qualified human resources, while also reinforcing the real estate value of the properties.

As it was discussed in the previous chapter, urban areas can benefit from a branding process (*place-in-brand*) related to the concentration of a specific type of knowledge applied to creative activities (design, arts, movies, cuisine, etc.). Such a process can be easily extended to the tourism sector, as the local attractiveness based on a perceived image of creativity and modernity may also exert an attractive effect on tourists, contributing for the location of accommodation establishments, both in a traditional form (hotels) or within the sphere of the so-called shared economy, with residential houses being used for tourism purposes. Moreover, other type of externalities can result from the daily life of local communities, such as their contribution for a safe environment, the cleanliness of public places, the friendly relations with visitors, etc. These communal behaviors can be also considered as common resources, potentially contributing for tourism development.

Despite the obvious importance of the commons for the economies, these resources did not receive particular attention from economic science. As Scott (2017) observes, economic analysis clearly distinguishes the private realm (firms and households regulated by markets, whose actions are based on individualized motivations and behaviors, implying private property) from the public governance (formal and informal coordination institutions, legitimized by means of democratic collective action). Nevertheless, little attention has been given to the communal aspects that do not entirely fit in any of these two cases, often being classified as *market failures*, with the implicit assumption that market regulation should be the norm for any kind of resource or economic activity. Clearly, this does not fully apply to the common pool resources, requiring the development of different analytical tools.

Different types of problems can be identified regarding the common pool resources, including both the demand and the supply side. On the demand side, a common issue identified in the literature is the *free-ride* problem, related to the overutilization and appropriation of the resources by a limited number of users, eventually leading to the exclusion of other users, degradation, or even elimination. This type of problem has been identified in very different sectors and activities, like fisheries, the utilization of specific water resources, or the appropriation of public spaces (Dietz et al. 2003). On the supply side, a common problem identified is the lack of protection of the resources, once none of the users has an individual responsibility to ensure its preservation.

Moreover, a resource can be perceived and valuated in different ways by different users, depending on their cultural background, education, or the importance they assign to it (Holden 2005). This is especially important in the case of tourism, as tourists normally do not share the same system of values and cultural values as the local residents, potentially leading to a conflictual perception about the value, norms of utilization, and importance of preserving resources that must be commonly used by tourists and the local community. The same applies to the companies involved in tourism activities, once each destination normally comprises local and nonlocal companies, with different valuations of the resources available in the territory.

In a similar way, the appropriation of potential benefits may also vary (and largely) among different users (or companies exploring the resources), once they are integrated into the tourism system through a process of commodification. In this context, although the resources are available for all the community – or even collectively produced, in the case of immaterial assets – the appropriation of benefits is a private process within market economics, potentially leading to significant imbalances. In the particular case of tourism, it is clear that transport and accommodation companies take large benefits of the common pool resources attracting tourists to a destination (like natural and cultural features of the place, local knowledge, daily life behaviors of the local residents, safety and security, etc.), not necessarily contributing for their improvement or preservation. On the other hand, large parts of the local population are often excluded from the benefits of tourism (or negatively affected by the massive presence of tourists in public areas, with potential negative externalities related to congestion, inflation of loss of cultural identities), even if their daily life behavior contributes for the attractiveness of a destination.

It is also noteworthy that the utilization of most of these common resources (like transport infrastructures, water services, public spaces, public services, monuments, or cultural heritage) is relatively stable and predictable for the local residents. Nevertheless, tourism flows are much less regular and unstable, often with high seasonal variations, implying that the utilization of common resources by tourists is much more irregular, spontaneous, and unpredictable (Briassoulis 2002). Thus, the effects of the cumulative impact on the utilization of common resources by the local community and the visitors are expressed, not only in the larger amount of users but also in the different perceptions and values they assign to them and also through the increasing complexity to predict their utilization and, consequently, to guarantee an appropriate management, potentially leading to inefficiencies, both related to excessive usage (and degradation) and very low utilization (high maintenance costs and low economic benefits).

Dietz et al. (2003) or Olstrom (2011) propose a set of general principles for the management of common pool resources, which can be applied for different resources and communities. These principles include a precise definition of boundaries, the equivalence between utilization benefits and preservation costs, collective-choice arrangements implying the mobilization of the relevant members of local communities using the resources, recognition of rights to organize, monitoring processes, creation of mechanisms for resolution of conflicts, or definition of sanctions for inappropriate use. These principles should take into consideration the complexity of the systems where the common resources are integrated, in order to achieve an effective form of adaptive governance, able to deal with changing processes, both in terms of the quantity and quality of the resources, their property regimes, and the types of users and utilizations, including a variety of institutions and stakeholders.

For the particular case of tourism, as pointed out by Briassoulis (2002), differences in perception about the preservation costs, value, and benefits of common resources between a wide and very heterogeneous set of stakeholders, often with conflicting perspectives and motivations, require a high level of coordination based on participatory management processes. Through the achievement of a common view based on a collective interest, it seems possible to achieve the benefits of utilization common resources, while preventing the problems of overuse and degradation, along with fair mechanisms for the appropriation of benefits. Such a governance model should take into account the spatial and temporal cumulative impacts on resources arising from their utilization by local residents and tourists, the volatile and less predictable tourism flows, different property regimes for the resources, diverse structures and cultures for planning and decision-making processes, and other contextual factors, including socio-economic characteristics, technology, or dynamic processes of cultural change.

It must be also noticed that, in the case of tourism, the management of common resources must be coordinated with other forms of tourism management, including product and service development, creation of routes, implementation of infrastructures and facilities, or promotional and branding strategies, which implies the involvement of a wide range of stakeholders, both related to public governance and regulation and also to private companies involved in different types of tourism activities (accommodation, food, transports, entertainment, guided tours, etc.). On the other hand, the management of common resources must also imply an active involvement of local residents, NGO, or other relevant organizations. The complexity of such a process is probably one of the reasons for the difficulties to implement this type of governance institutions in contemporary tourism destinations. Nevertheless, this aspect appears as a major challenge for the future of tourism, as it seems a necessary condition for an effective contribution of tourism for the sustainable development of the destinations, taking into consideration its three major pillars – environmental protection, economic prosperity, and social benefits for the host communities.

5.6   Concluding Remarks

Starting with a discussion on the concept of competitiveness in tourism studies at different territorial levels (firm, destination, region, and country), this chapter has been mostly focused on the relation between tourism dynamics and sustainable development, stressing that, in the long term, the concepts of competitiveness and sustainability must be closely interrelated for an adequate process of tourism development. It was also clarified that the study of sustainability in tourism requires a much broader perspective than the analysis of the sustainable use of sensitive territorial resources, implying the consideration of the socio-economic impacts of tourism on the destination and the achievement of relevant benefits for the host communities, which suggests the importance (as recommended by different international institutions) of participatory processes of tourism planning and management, taking into consideration the complexity of stakeholders, motivations, and interests involved. Despite the importance of applying the principles of sustainability to any kind of tourism destinations, some examples of recently emerged tourism segments, more oriented to the concept of sustainable development are discussed, with a particular focus on the case of wellness tourism. Finally, the chapter concludes with a discussion on the communal aspect of most of the resources (both material and immaterial) that attract tourists to a destination, raising different problems related both to the utilization of those resources and the unequal appropriation of benefits within a community, reinforcing the importance of the implementation of collective and representative decision-making processes, which is far from being accomplished in most of the destinations. In particular, this chapter has addressed the following questions:

- The concept of competitiveness has been originally applied to the firm level, but other territorial levels would be considered later on; similarly, in tourism studies the concept has been used to address the competitiveness of firms, destinations, regions, or countries.
- Due to the limitation of data available, international comparisons of tourism competitiveness are mostly focused on the national level or, more recently, at the regional level; the comparison between destinations in different countries is still difficult.
- Most of the competitiveness rankings and indexes follow a descriptive approach, based on the computation of indexes; explanatory approaches, linking input indicators to output measures of tourism performance (demand, gross value added, or productivity), can provide more interesting results in terms of policy and managerial implications.
- In the long run, the tourism competitiveness has a strong connection with sustainability in tourism, as it implies the preservation of the resources that make a destination attractive and also the achievement of relevant socio-economic benefits for the host communities.
- The principles of sustainable development in the tourism sector should be applied to the processes of planning of any kind of tourism destination.
- Sustainability in tourism development implies the creation of participatory management structures, involving all the relevant institutions and stakeholders in a destination; this is far from being a general practice.
- A sustainable process of tourism development implies the definition of a common vision and the statement of a mission the future of a destination, shared by the different stakeholders involved; from this point, it is possible to define common objectives, goals, strategies, and tactics.
- Different forms of tourism (ecotourism, geotourism, responsible tourism, etc.) have emerged with a focus on the concept of sustainability; more recently, the concept of wellness tourism seems to address all the relevant issues related to the three pillars of sustainable development.
- Despite the systematic approaches to the role of tourism within the international guidelines for sustainable tourism development, air travelling is a major contributor for CO_2 emissions and climate change, while most of the expenses related to tourism activities do not stay at the destination, offering limited benefits for the host communities.
- Although the economic benefits of tourism are subject to private appropriation, most of the resources determining the attractiveness of a destination are commonly produced or used by a local community, which imposes problems of degradation, overuse, and unequal share of benefits.
- Despite the limitations that still can be observed in contemporary tourism, this sector has a high potential to contribute for the sustainable development of destinations and regions, as it relies on local resources and opens the opportunity to establish fruitful connections with other economic sectors, including creative activities and ICT.

Case Study 5.1: Tourism Dynamics and Regional Competitiveness

Romão J, Saito H (2017) A spatial econometric analysis on the determinants of tourism. Competitiveness in Japanese Prefectures. Asia Pacific Journal of regional Science 1(1):243–264

By using spatial econometric methodologies and techniques, this work analyzes the determinants of tourism performance in Japanese Prefectures, taking into consideration different aspects of tourism demand (volume, length of stay, and share of foreigners) and also diverse territorial characteristics with potential impact on tourism dynamics (level of specialization in tourism and qualifications of the work force), along with the spatial effects and regional interactions eventually occurring between them. While local and global indicators of spatial autocorrelation are used in a first stage in order to identify and to explain different patterns of regional tourism dynamics and their determinants, a spatial econometric model is applied in a second stage, offering an overall explanation for the relations under analysis. The combination of these methodologies allows to identify different agglomeration processes and spatial heterogeneity among Japanese Prefectures, leading to some policy and managerial recommendations.

The results reveal the importance of the central regions of Japan (especially those around Tokyo Metropolitan area) in terms of the GDP produced by the tourism sector, with clusters of regions with high levels for the GDP in tourism around Ibaraki, Chiba, and Yamanashi. These are also the regions where foreigners tend to assume greater importance within the total number of visitors, suggesting the importance of inbound tourism for the higher achievements in terms of tourism performance. Moreover, the high levels of GDP per habitant in tourism registered in Tokyo do not have a correspondence in terms of tourism demand per capita (relatively lower), suggesting that tourism products and services supplied in this area have higher value added than in other parts of Japan (which also reveals an higher productivity). Being a leader among the Japanese Prefectures regarding the GDP produced by the tourism sector, Tokyo does not rank among the first positions when looking at the specialization in tourism. Tokyo and the central areas of Japan also have higher levels of education for the work force, an important resource for regional performance on innovation.

On the other hand, the Northern regions of Japan show much lower levels of GDP produced by the tourism sector, even when tourism has particular importance for regional employment. Hokkaido ranks in the first positions in terms of the share of the active population employed in tourism but reveals a weaker position in terms of the contribution of tourism for the regional GDP, suggesting that the region provides services with relatively low value added, achieving less economic benefits for the regional economy. Also, Hokkaido has a relatively low qualification of the work force win the national context.

A regression model including spatial effects offers an overall explanation for the relations under analysis, identifying a positive correlation between the gross value added by tourism activities and the education levels, tourism demand, and share of international visitors within the nights spent in accommodation establishments, which was seen as major determinant of tourism performance. Additionally, relevant spatial effects were identified, both for the dependent variable (revealing that tourism dynamics in one region has a positive impact on the performance of its neighbors) and for the error term (revealing the existence of negative unmodelled spillover effects). It was also possible to conclude that a high specialization in tourism does not necessarily lead to a high performance of this sector, once this parameter was not statistically significant. Similarly, the length of stay was not identified as a major determinant of regional tourism performance either.

Considering that the central areas of Japan are those with better tourism performance, the results reveal the importance of implementing interregional cooperation processes, mostly in the areas where tourism is less developed. According to the results, this cooperation can be focused on the reinforcement of work force qualifications and promotional activities oriented to the attraction of foreign tourists. As many tourists currently perform multi-destination travels, this type of collaboration between regions with less resources and weaker tourism dynamics can help to achieve results that would be more difficult to obtain in isolation. This aspect is reinforced by the detection of negative regional spillover effects, which should be mitigated or reverted.

Case Study 5.2. Tourism and Sustainable Development

Romão J, Neuts B (2017) Smart tourism, territorial capital, and sustainable regional development: experiences from Europe. Habitat International 68: 64–74

By using a structural equations model, this study focuses on the impacts of territorial resources related to nature and culture (environmental dimension), innovation capabilities, and specialization patterns (smart specialization) on regional sustainable development (spatial sustainability). The main purpose is to identify if and how territorial resources, innovation dynamics, and tourism performance and specialization contribute for processes of sustainable regional development goals in 252 European NUTS 2 regions (which is the territorial scale at which regional development policies are implemented at European level, including smart specialization strategies, aiming at the mobilization of existing knowledge, technology, and human resources). This analysis takes into account the Millennium Goals defined by the United Nations, and it is one of the very few attempts to evaluate the impacts of tourism on the three main pillars of sustainable development (economic, social, and environmental).

The regions under analysis are characterized in terms of different dimensions, assuming that the formation of territorial capital depends on material and immaterial assets. Material resources include natural assets (percentage of the regional territory protected under the Natura 2000 network), cultural assets (number of cultural heritage sites classified by UNESCO), and investment in the tourism sector (gross fixed capital formation in the sector). Immaterial aspects include human resources (share of employment with tertiary education) or innovation efforts (investment in research and development). Regional tourism specialization is measured taking into account the share of gross value added or employment in tourism, in relation to the total regional gross value added and total employment. Tourism performance is estimated through tourism demand (number of nights in commercial tourism establishments) and total gross value added by the sector. Finally, sustainable development indicators follow the generally accepted idea of the three pillars of sustainability: economic growth (measured by the regional gross domestic product per inhabitant), social cohesion (measured by the level of unemployment), and environmental conditions (measured according to the CO_2 emissions).

As a general conclusion, it was possible to conclude from the results of the model that different patterns of tourism dynamics coexist in European regions. In particular, it was observed that the contribution of tourism specialization for the achievement of sustainable development goals is relatively poor in the regions where this sector plays a more relevant socio-economic role, expressed through its importance in the regional specialization patterns. On the other hand, a weak socio-economic performance – along with high specialization in tourism – is observed in regions where natural resources are more abundant. These results suggest that tourism supply is based on large-scale and low value-added products and services, with high impacts on natural sensitive resources (as it was previously observed in Case Study 3.2). Similarly, the most tourism-dependent European regions are also those revealing highest levels of unemployment.

Although these regions present good results for CO_2 emissions (which can be related to low levels of industrial development), increasing the value added of tourism activities (through the reinforcement of the linkages with other economic sectors) appears as a crucial aspect to increase the contribution of tourism for a sustainable process of development. Creative industries or information and communication technologies can contribute to such a process of integration of knowledge and innovations into the tourism products and services.

The results also show that regions with higher employment in tourism are those with lower levels of education, while regions with higher value added by the tourism sector are those where the workforce is more educated. In general terms, the regional gross domestic product per capita is clearly linked to the level of education of the workforce. These results also suggest that these problems are more important in the South of Europe, where the regions with lower levels of education are located, confirming their difficulties for the integration of knowledge and technology into their economic systems.

Case Study 5.3: Sustainable Wellness Tourism

Romão J, Machino K, Nijkamp P (2017) Assessment of Wellness Tourism Development in Hokkaido: A Multicriteria and Strategic Choice Analysis. Asia Pacific Journal of regional Science 1(1):265–290

New tendencies in health care have contributed for a fast and intense growth of wellness tourism in contemporary societies. As observed in several studies, these travellers normally combine different activities by using different services, including a variety of spa services based on water properties or therapies, physical exercise, hiking, or cultural and educational activities. Some of these services can be offered independently of their location, but other crucial services for this type of tourism depend on local territorial characteristics related to landscape, geography, or ecological assets, which include specific properties of water, existence of natural parks, healthy food, or the opportunity to interact with local communities and to experience significant new forms of cultural interaction.

Japan has a long tradition in this type of water-based wellness services (related to the traditional onsen bath), along with abundant natural resources related to health and wellness services. Nevertheless, the data available for the global dynamics of wellness tourism reveals that the benefits obtained by Japanese establishments are relatively low, when compared with other countries (including neighbor Asian countries, with much less thermal resources). According to international data about this sector, the diversification of spa services and wellness activities appears as a crucial element to increase the economic benefits arising from this type of tourism, while the services offered in Japan are mostly exclusively focused on the traditional bath itself. In this context, the country seems to have the appropriate resources to offer a differentiated and unique place-based wellness experience, whose economic impact could be significantly higher if the traditional bath could be complemented by other services, enlarging the value chain of the sector.

The island of Hokkaido (North of Japan), with low population density and abundant geothermal and natural resources, appears as a potentially appropriate destination for this kind of tourism, by developing a diverse set of wellness tourism services, in combination with the traditional onsen experience. The exploration of opportunities within this emergent and fast-growing tourism segment could contribute for the sustainable development of a region that is geographically and economically distant from the most central and developed areas of Japan. Thus, despite the existence of similar resources and opportunities in other parts of Japan, this study focuses the specific case of Hokkaido.

Interviews and questionnaires to experts and relevant stakeholders in this field, supported by a systematic literature review, were the basis for the assessment of potential development and foreseeable impact of wellness services in Hokkaido performed in this work, by combining different decision-making techniques, aiming at identifying the conditions for an integrative diversification of wellness tourism services in the region, assuming the traditional onsen experience as the central aspect. A foresight analysis is undertaken considering four future scenarios while identifying the main factors influencing such a process of development. Also, the experts were asked to measure the estimated impact of the assessment factors on the future scenarios, allowing the identification of the most preferable views for the future of wellness tourism in the region, by using a multicriteria analysis. The results at this stage are then complemented by a strategic choice analysis, through the reorganization of the assessment factors into a SWOT matrix, allowing the identification of the elements playing the most crucial role in this process.

Regarding the most preferable scenarios for the future, the results indicate "traditional services for the Japanese market" (which corresponds to the current situation) and "diversification of services for external markets" (implying a process of wellness service diversification and internationalization). This result also suggests that the main motivation of Japanese visitors relates to the traditional onsen experience, while foreign tourists expect a diversified set of wellness services. It was possible to observe that the scenario related to traditional services without internationalization is mostly driven by the characteristics of territorial resources and the limitations related to the competitive environment. On the other hand, the scenario related to internationalization and diversification of services appears as driven by innovation dynamics and the opportunities opened by the global dynamics in wellness tourism.

As the scenario of internationalization seems to have higher potential economic impact on the region, a strategic choice analysis was used in order to identify which factors may have the most important contribution for its achievement. This was done by reorganizing the assessment factors considered in the previous step according to the traditional format of a SWOT matrix, being classified (and quantitatively evaluated by the expert panel) as "strengths," "weaknesses," opportunities," or "threats." The cost-efficiency relation of tourism services (perceived as very high against the rival destinations in Asia) appears as a major problem, which can be addressed by enlarging the value chain of the tourism sector (through a process of diversification), contributing to increase the efficiency of the supply of tourism services. In order to achieve this purpose, the characteristics of the landscape and the regional natural resources appear as crucial elements for the implementation of diverse nature-based services.

On the other hand, the qualifications of human resources for the tourism sector and the limited knowledge capabilities for innovation in wellness services are perceived as significant barriers for such a process of diversification oriented to external markets. Thus, entrepreneurial initiatives already promoted by major accommodation companies may contribute for the development of local knowledge and innovation capabilities.

Case Study 5.4: Wellness Tourism and Community Development

Romão J, Machino K, Nijkamp P (forthcoming) Integrative diversification of wellness tourism services in rural areas – An operational framework model applied to East Hokkaido (Japan)

This work develops a systematization of the main elements for a strategy of wellness tourism development in rural areas, assumed as a new tourism segment that should coexist with other travel motivations already implemented, by following a process of integrative diversification. The framework model takes into account three spatial levels – establishment, destination, and region – and explores the roles and interrelations among stakeholders needed to support such a strategic process. This process aims at creating a unique and differentiated supply of services for this new and emergent tourism market segment, promoting a sustainable integration of natural and cultural territorial resources into tourism dynamics, and contributing for the achievement of relevant benefits for the host communities. As this kind of tourism services depends on local natural and cultural resources and it is expected to generate positive socio-economic impacts, the analysis takes into account the idea of sustainable tourism development.

The model results from the combination of three concepts: integrative diversification (a process of thematic differentiation at the establishment and the destination levels to be integrated into the broader tourism dynamics of the region), product development (a long-term process molding the assets of a destination to meet the needs of tourists), and an endogenous growth-based approach to innovation dynamics (focused on knowledge spillovers arising from local entrepreneurship capabilities). As a result of this systematization, four major challenges are identified: territorial management (natural and cultural resources, transportation networks, or land use); entrepreneurship and human resources (for the development of innovative services); "coopetition" (collaboration and coordination between different organizations, eventually with conflictive interests); and marketing, positioning, and branding strategies (for a correct identification of priority segments and the definition of communication strategies).

After the presentation of the conceptual model, the work develops an exploratory application to East Hokkaido (North of Japan), taking into account the existence of traditional services related to the typical Japanese bath practices (onsen), abundant hot springs, and natural and cultural resources that seem in accordance with the motivations identified for this type of tourists. Moreover, recent policy orientations from the Japanese Government acknowledge the underutilization (from an economic point of view) of onsen resources in Japan while proposing the integration of endogenous resources in the core of the strategies for the development of rural areas. In this context, tourism and health are considered priority sectors, which makes this case particularly attractive. On the other hand, East Hokkaido seems to have relevant resources for the development of a set of services supporting the creation of a differentiated and unique wellness tourism destination, by fulfilling the needs and motivations of this type of travellers.

Tourism dynamics in East Hokkaido has been relatively low until now, but the region has seven onsen areas (Onneyu, Nukabira, Shikaribetsu, Tokachigawa, Utoro, Kawayu, and Akanko), all of them with accommodation services, including both the traditional Japanese hotels (Ryokan) and more "conventional" hotels. Moreover, the area has four national natural parks (Daisetsuzan, Kushiro Shitsugen, Akan, and Shiretoko, which is also a World Heritage Site), other 44 relevant natural and scenic spots, 11 botanical gardens, 33 museums, 2 aquariums, 1 zoo, and also facilities for sports like ski or golf. Also, the contact with the indigenous Ainu communities still living in this territory – with their lifestyles and cultural values clearly in line with the principles of sustainable development – could enrich, from a cultural point of view, the uniqueness of such a tourism experience. In fact, personal enrichment through education and new cultural encounters also appears as one of the main motivations of these travellers, along with the search for spiritual and physical well-being and the contribution for socio-economic development of the destinations.

It was also seen that several central elements which are essential for the diversification of wellness-related services (the onsen bath, natural resources, and local food) are among the main motivations of foreigners visiting Hokkaido, which seems to reveal an important opportunity for the development of this type of tourism. In this context, the mobilization of local knowledge and entrepreneurial initiatives to develop innovative products and services appears as the major challenge for the region, considering the establishment spatial level of analysis. At the destination level, the creation of routes integrating the onsen and other spa-related services with different natural and cultural resources into coherent and attractive programs appears as the most important challenge. Finally, these routes should be consistently integrated in the overall tourism dynamics of the regions, including transport networks, accessibility to urban centers and transportation nodes, or aspects related to security, safety, health care, or ICT.

Moreover, it is also noteworthy that many of these innovative initiatives to develop an adequate mix of wellness-related services depend on public institutions in charge of museums, cultural facilities, or natural parks. Thus, entrepreneurship for such a development process must have a broader focus than the realm of the private initiative, also comprising public institutions and the coordination between them. Finally, it seems also clear that the development of wellness tourism in areas like East Hokkaido depends much more on the creation of new services and the qualification of human resources than on the construction of new buildings, facilities, or infrastructures.

References

Adamou A, Clerides S (2010) Prospects and limits of tourism-led growth: the international evidence. Rev Econ Anal 3:287–303

Al Haija AA (2011) Jordan: tourism and conflict with local communities (2011). Habitat Int 35:93–100

Bertacchini E, Segre G (2016) Culture, sustainable development and social quality: a paradigm shift in the economic analysis of cultural production and heritage conservation. City Cult Soc 7:69–70

Binkhorst E, Den Dekker T (2009) Agenda for co-creation tourism experience research. J Hosp Market Manag 18(2–3):311–327

Boes K, Buhalis D, Inversini A (2016) Smart tourism destinations: Ecosystems for tourism destination competitiveness. Int J Tour Cities 2(2):108–124

Boschma R (2016) Smart specialisation and regional innovation policy. Welsh Econ Rev 24:17

Briassoulis H (2002) Sustainable tourism and the question of commons. Ann Tour Res 29(4):1065–1085

Brouder P, Eriksson R (2013) Tourism evolution: on the synergies of tourism studies and evolutionary economic geography. Ann Tour Res 43:370–389

Buhalis D (1999) Limits of tourism development in peripheral destinations: problems and challenges. Tour Manag 20:183–185

Buhalis D (2000) Marketing the competitive destination of the future. Tour Manag 21:97–116

Buhalis D, Law R (2008) Progress in information technology and tourism management: 20 years on and 10 years after the internet – the state of eTourism research. Tour Manag 29:609–623

Butler RW (1999) Sustainable tourism: a state-of-the-art review. Tour Geogr 1(1):7–25

Camisón C, Forés B (2015) Is tourism firm competitiveness driven by different internal or external specific factors? New empirical evidence from Spain. Tour Manag 48:477–499

Capello R, Caragliu A, Nijkamp P (2011) Territorial capital and regional growth: increasing returns in knowledge use. Tijdschr Econ Soc Geogr 102(4):385–405

Capó J, Font A, Nadal J (2007) Dutch disease in tourism economies: evidence from the Balearics and the Canary Islands. J Sustain Tour 15(6):615–627

Chen C, Chiou-Wei S (2009) Tourism expansion, tourism uncertainty and economic growth: new evidence from Taiwan and Korea. Tour Manag 30(6):812–818

Chou M (2013) Does tourism development promote economic growth in transition countries? A panel data analysis. Econ Model 33:226–232

Cohen M (2008) Spas, wellness and human evolution. In: Cohen M, Bodeker G (eds) Understanding the global spa industry: spa management. Elsevier, London, pp 3–25

Corbin CB, Pangrazi RP (2001) Toward a uniform definition of wellness: a commentary. Research Digest 3:1–8

Cortes-Jimenez I, Pulina M (2010) Inbound tourism and long-run economic growth. Curr Issue Tour 13(1):61–74

Cracolici M, Nijkamp P (2008) The attractiveness and competitiveness of tourist destinations: a study of southern Italian regions. Tour Manag 30:336–344

David LE (2016) Managing sustainable tourism, 2nd edn. Routledge, New York

Dietz T, Ostrom E, Stern PC (2003) The struggle to govern the commons. In: Marzluff et al (eds) Urban ecology – an international perspective on the interaction between humans and nature. Springer, Berlin, pp 611–622

Domicelj S (1992) Recreational visitation and cultural development: push or pull? Habitat Int 16(3):79–87

Douglas JA (2014) What's political ecology got to do with tourism? Tour Geogr 16(1):8–13

Dritsakis N (2004) Tourism as a long-run economic growth factor: an empirical investigation for Greece using causality analysis. Tour Econ 10(3):305–316

Dritsakis N (2012) Tourism development and economic growth in seven Mediterranean countries: a panel data approach. Tour Econ 18(4):801–816

Dwyer L, Chulwon K (2003) Destination competitiveness: determinants and indicators. Curr Issue Tour 6(5):369–414

Ellis S (2008) Trends in the global spa industry. In: Cohen M, Bodeker G (eds) Understanding the global spa industry: spa management. Elsevier, London, pp 66–83

Enright M, Newton J (2004) Tourism destination competitiveness: a quantitative approach. Tour Manag 25:777–788

Erfurt-Cooper P, Cooper M (2009) Health and wellness tourism. Spas and hot springs. Channel View Publications, Bristol

European Commission (2006) Innovation in tourism – how to create a tourism learning area. European Commission, Brussels

European Commission (2007) Agenda for a sustainable and competitive European tourism. European Commission, Luxembourg

European Commission (2016) The European tourism Indicator system: ETIS toolkit for sustainable destination management. European Commission, Brussels

Foray D, Goddard J, Beldarrain X, Landabaso M, McCann P, Morgan K, Ortega-Argilés R (2012) Guide to research and innovation strategies for smart specialisation. S3P – European Union, Regional Policy, Brussels

França CS, Broman G, Robert K, Basile G, Trygg L (2017) An approach to business model innovation and design for strategic sustainable development. J Clean Prod 140:155–166

Gilbert D (1984) The need for countries to differentiate their tourist product and how to do so. Seminar papers: Tourism managing for results. University of Surrey, Surrey

Hall CM, Williams AM (2008) Tourism and innovation. Routledge, London

Halme M, Korpela M (2014) Responsible innovation toward sustainable development in small and medium-sized enterprises: a resource perspective. Bus Strateg Environ 23:547–566

Hassan S (2000) Determinants of market competitiveness in an environmentally sustainable tourism industry. J Travel Res 38(3):239–245

Hjalager A (2010) A review of innovation research in tourism. Tour Manag 31:1–12

Holden A (2005) Achieving a sustainable relationship between common pool resources and tourism: the role of environmental ethics. J Sustain Tour 13(4):339–352

ICOMOS (2016) Cultural heritage, the UN sustainable development goals, and the new urban agenda. ICOMOS, Paris

Jafari J (2001) The scientification of tourism. In: Smith V, Brent M (eds) Hosts and guests revisited: tourism issues of the 21st century. Cognizant Communication Corporation, New York, pp 28–41

Johnston K, Puczkó L, Smith M, Elis S (2011) Wellness tourism and medical tourism: where do spas fit? Global Spa and Wellness Summit, Miami

Jovicic DZ (2014) Key issues in the implementation of sustainable tourism. Curr Issues Tour 17(4):297–302

Kim J, Fesenmaier DR (2015) Measuring emotions in real time: implications for tourism experience design. J Travel Res 54(4):419–429

Kozak M (1999) Destination competitiveness measurement: analysis of effective factors and indicators. European Regional Science Association Conference Papers, Dublin

Lee C, Chang C (2008) Tourism development and economic growth: a closer look at panels. Tour Manag 29(1):180–192

Maes J, Jacobs S (2017) Nature-based solutions for Europe's sustainable development. Conserv Lett 10(1):121–124

Maslow AH (1943) A theory of human motivation. Psychol Rev 50:370–396

Mazanek J, Wober K, Zins A (2007) Tourism destination competitiveness: from definition to explanation? J Travel Res 46:86–95

Meadows DH, Meadows DL, Randers J, Behrens WW III (1972) The limits to growth. Universe Books, New York

Medina-Muñoz D, Medina-Muñoz R, Chim-Miki A (2013) Tourism competitiveness assessment: the current status of research in Spain and China. Tour Econ 19(2):297–318

Miller G, Twining-Ward L, Bakker M, Carbone G, Duka T, Farrell B, Font X, Jack E, Tapper R (2005) Monitoring for a sustainable tourism transition: the challenge of developing and using indicators. Cabi Publishing, London

Mullis B (2017) The growth paradox: can tourism ever be sustainable?. World Economic Forum. Available online at https://www.weforum.org/agenda/2017/08/the-growth-paradox-can-tourism-ever-be-sustainable/

Navickas V, Malakauskaite A (2009) The possibilities for the identification and evaluation of tourism sector competitiveness factors. Eng Econ 1(61):37–44

Nowak J, Sahli M, Cortés-Jiménez I (2007) Tourism, capital good imports and economic growth: theory and evidence for Spain. Tour Econ 13(4):515–536

OECD (1994) Tourism policy and international tourism in OECD countries. OECD, Paris

Olstrom E (2011) Background on the institutional analysis and development framework. Policy Stud J 39(1):7–27

Ostrom E (2008) The challenge of common-pool resources. Environment 50(4):8–20

Pablo-Romero M, Molina JA (2013) Tourism and economic growth: a review of empirical literature. Tour Manag Perspect 8:28–41

Page SJ, Dowling RK (2002) Ecotourism. Prentice Hall, Harlow

Page SJ, Hartwell H, Johns N, Fyall A, Ladkin A, Hemingway A (2017) Case study: wellness, tourism and small business development in a UK coastal resort: public engagement in practice. Tour Manag 60:466–477

Poon A (1994) The 'new tourism' revolution. Tour Manag 15(2):91–92

Porter M (1985) Competitive advantage – creating and sustaining superior performance. The Free Press, New York

Porter M (2003) The economic performance of regions. Reg Stud 37(6/7):549–578

Redclift M, Woodgate G (2013) Sustainable development and nature: the social and the material. Sustain Dev 21(2):92–100

Ritchie J, Crouch G (2003) The competitive destination: a sustainable tourism perspective. CABI International, Oxfordshire

Romão J, Neuts B (2017) Smart tourism, territorial capital, and sustainable regional development: experiences from Europe. Habitat Int 68:64–74

Romão J, Nijkamp P (2017) A spatial econometric analysis of impacts of innovation, productivity and agglomeration on tourism competitiveness. Curr Issue Tour. https://doi.org/10.1080/1368 3500.2017.1366434

Romão J, Nijkamp P (forthcoming) Spatial impacts assessment of tourism and territorial capital: a modelling study on regional development in Europe

Romão J, Saito H (2017) A spatial econometric analysis on the determinants of tourism. Competitiveness in Japanese Prefectures. Asia Pacific J Reg Sci 1(1):243–264

Romão J, Neuts B, Nijkamp P, van LES (2015) Culture, product differentiation and market segmentation: a structural analysis of the motivation and satisfaction of tourists in Amsterdam. Tour Econ 21(3):455–474

Romão J, Guerreiro J, Rodrigues PMM (2016) Tourism growth and regional resilience: the 'beach disease' and the consequences of the global crisis of 2007. Tour Econ 22(4):699–714

Romão J, Guerreiro J, Rodrigues P (2017a) Territory and sustainable tourism development: a space-time analysis on European regions. Region 4(3):1–17

Romão J, Machino K, Nijkamp P (2017b) Assessment of wellness tourism development in Hokkaido: a multicriteria and strategic choice analysis. Asia Pacific J Reg Sci 1(1):265–290

Romão J, Machino K, Nijkamp P (Forthcoming) Integrative diversification of wellness tourism services in rural areas – an operational framework model applied to East Hokkaido (Japan)

Scott AJ (2017) The constitution of the city. Springer, Cham

Sharpley R (2009) Tourism development and the environment: beyond sustainability? Earthscan, London

Sheng L, Tsui Y (2009) A general equilibrium approach to tourism and welfare: the case of Macao. Habitat Int 33:419–424

Shubert S, Brida J (2011) Dynamic model of economic growth in a small tourism driven economy. In: Matias A, Nijkamp P, Sarmento M (eds) Tourism economics – impact analysis. Springer, Berlin, pp 149–168

Smith MK, Diekmann A (2017) Tourism and wellbeing. Ann Tour Res 66:1–13

Smith MK, Puczkó L (2013) A geographical and historical analysis. In: Smith M, Puczkó L (eds) Health, tourism and hospitality. Routledge, London, pp 49–78

Song H, Dwyer L, Cao Z (2012) Tourism economics research: a review and assessment. Ann Tour Res 39(3):1653–1682

Steward JR (2012) Moral economies and commercial imperatives: food, diets and spas in Central Europe: 1800–1914. J Tour Hist 4(2):181–203

Tabbachi M (2008) American and European spa. In: Cohen M, Bodeker G (eds) Understanding the global spa industry: spa management. Elsevier, London, pp 26–40

Tang C, Jang S (2009) The tourism-economy causality in the United States: a sub-industry level examination. Tour Manag 30(4):553–558

Torres-Delgado A, Saarinen J (2014) Using indicators to assess sustainable tourism development: a review. Tour Geogr 16(1):31–47

Tsai H, Song H, Wong K (2009) Tourism and hotel competitiveness. J Travel Tour Market 26(5):522–546

UNESCO (2000) Sustainable tourism and the environment. UNESCO, Paris

UNESCO (2005) World heritage Centre – sustainable tourism Programme. UNESCO, Paris

UNESCO (2013) Managing cultural world heritage. UNESCO, Paris

United Nations (2015) Transforming our world: the 2030 agenda for sustainable development. A/RES/70/1, resolution adopted by the general assembly on 25 September 2015 (New York)

United Nations Environment Programme and UNWTO (2005) Making tourism more sustainable – a guide for policy makers. UNWTO, Madrid

UNWTO (2007) Practical guide to tourism destination management. UNWTO, Madrid

UNWTO (2013) Sustainable tourism for development guidebook. UNWTO, Madrid

UNWTO (2015) Tourism and the sustainable development goals. UNWTO, Madrid

UNWTO (2016a) Measuring sustainable tourism at sub-national and destination level. Meeting of the working group of experts on 20–21 October 2016 – Discussion Paper #1. UNWTO, Madrid

UNWTO (2016b) Tourism highlights, 2016 edn. UNWTO, Madrid

UNWTO (2016c) Measuring sustainable tourism at sub-national and destination level. Meeting of the working group of experts on 20–21 October 2016 – Discussion Paper #1. UNWTO, Madrid

UNWTO (2017) Measuring sustainable tourism. UNWTO, Madrid

UNWTO (2018) World tourism barometer. UNWTO, Madrid

Walton JK (2013) Health, sociability, politics and culture—spas in history, spas and history: an overview. In: Walton JK (ed) Mineral springs resorts in global perspective. Routledge, London, pp 1–14

Weaver D (2006) Sustainable tourism: theory and practice. Elsevier, Oxford

Weaver D (2011) Can sustainable tourism survive climate change? J Sustain Tour 19(1):5–15

Williams P, Ponsford I (2009) Confronting tourism's environmental paradox: transitioning for sustainable tourism. Futures 41:396–404

World Commission on Environment and Development (1987) Our common future. Oxford University Press, New York

World Economic Forum (2017) The travel & tourism competitiveness report 2017. World Economic Forum, Geneva

World Travel and Tourism Council, United Nations World Tourism Organization, Earth Council (1996) Agenda 21 for the travel and tourism industry: towards environmentally sustainable development. UNWTO, Madrid

Wu SR, Fan P, Chen J (2016) Incorporating culture into sustainable development: a cultural sustainability index framework for green buildings. Sustain Dev 24(1):64–76

Yeung O, Johnston K (2015) The global wellness tourism economy report 2013 and 2014. Global Wellness Institute, Miami

Zhang X, Zhou L, Wu Y, Skitmore M, Deng Z (2015) Resolving the conflicts of sustainable world heritage landscapes in cities: fully open or limited access for visitors? Habitat Int 46:91–100

Zhao W, Ritchie J (2007) Tourism and poverty alleviation: an integrative research framework. Curr Issue Tour 10(2–3):119–143

Chapter 6
Spatial-Economic Impacts of Tourism on Regional Development: Contemporary Challenges

Contents

Abstract This concluding chapter proposes a conceptual framework for the analysis of some relevant problems observed in contemporary tourism dynamics, by combining the theoretical formulations discussed along this book with the results obtained in a series of studies comprising a large number of European regions. As this sample includes regions with very different characteristics (high and low levels of economic development, different patterns of specialization and tourism dynamics, diverse cultural and natural endowments, or different innovation and technological capabilities), the conclusions and recommendations can be generalized to a broader geographical perspective. This conceptual framework is centered on the concepts of *authenticity*, *significance*, the *environmental paradox*, *smart tourism*, *co-creation* of destinations and experiences, the role of information for the segmen-

J. Romão, *Tourism, Territory and Sustainable Development*, New Frontiers in Regional Science: Asian Perspectives 28, https://doi.org/10.1007/978-981-13-0426-2_6

tation of markets and differentiation of supply, the *life cycle of tourism destinations*, *path dependence* processes, and the importance of history, variety, specialization, or *integrative diversification* of tourism products. As a result, a set of challenges for the future of tourism – to be addressed at the policy and managerial levels – is discussed. These challenges relate to the provision of memorable trips oriented to personalized and significant experiences based on a sustainable use of territorial resources, the promotion of diverse and balanced regional economies by reinforcing the interrelations between the tourism sector and the overall creative economy, and the implementation of effective processes of participatory governance for the definition of sustainable development strategies.

Keywords Significance · Co-creation · Innovation · Integrative diversification · Sustainability · Participatory governance

6.1   Introduction

Over the past seven decades, a continued expansion could be observed in the tourism sector, which has become one of the largest and fastest-growing economic activities in the world. From 25 million international arrivals registered in 1950, more than 1 billion were observed for the first time in 2013. This number has continued to grow, reaching 1.322 million in 2017, while 1.8 billion are projected for 2030 (UNWTO 2018). The contribution of tourism for global employment is estimated in 10% of the working places (200 million jobs), while the sector represents 30% of the overall exports of services. Nevertheless, as also observed by UNWTO (2013), air travel and other impacts of tourism activities contribute – at least – for 5% of the global CO_2 emissions, revealing the unsustainability of this growth path, which may contribute to irreversible environmental damages on the planet.

This is not the only important problem related to tourism dynamics in contemporary societies, as it was discussed, at the conceptual level, along all the previous chapters of this book. Potential long-term implications and distortions of regional economic structures during the phases of quick development of tourism destinations may contribute to a loss of welfare for the local population, as discussed in Chap. 2. The commodified utilization of sensitive natural and cultural resources, through their integration into tourism products and services, may contribute to overuse, degradation, or destruction (for natural assets) or a loss of authenticity and significance (for material and immaterial cultural heritage), as observed in Chap. 3. Despite the high potential of tourism for the creation and reinforcement of interrelations with the most creative sectors of the economy, tourism activities are still far from achieving their full potential in terms of incorporation of knowledge and technology while potentially contributing for processes of congestion, inflation, and gentrification of lack of affordable housing solutions and contemporary cities, as discussed in Chap. 4. Moreover, the contributions of tourism for sustainable processes of local and regional development supported by participatory governance systems are also far from being achieved, as observed in Chap. 5.

At the empirical level, five of the studies presented along this book offer a systematic overview of different aspects of contemporary tourism dynamics in the European continent, comprising a large number of regions (237, at least), with different levels of economic development, innovation capabilities, natural endowment, or tourism specialization patterns. These studies have led to the empirical verification of several important problems related to the role of tourism within contemporary societies, which can be generalized to other parts of the world. Case Study 2.1 (Romão and Nijkamp Forthcoming) problematizes the impacts of territorial characteristics and tourism dynamics on the regional economic performance, while Case Study 5.2 (Romão and Neuts 2017) enlarges the scope of the analysis by focusing on the impacts of those aspects on the three pillars of sustainable development. Questions related to the material aspects of the regional territorial capital (nature and culture) are discussed in Case Studies 3.1 (Romão 2015) and 3.2 (Romão et al. 2017), while the impacts of immaterial aspects (like qualifications of innovation dynamics) on tourism competitiveness are addressed in Case Study 4.3 (Romão and Nijkamp 2017).

Combining the conceptual approach presented along the book with the empirical analysis undertaken in these five case studies, a set of problems related to contemporary tourism dynamics will be presented in Sect. 6.2, including questions related to the sustainable use of natural and cultural resources, innovation dynamics and specialization patterns, impacts of tourism on regional economic growth, and the relations between tourism performance and regional sustainable development. In Sect. 6.3, a systematic set of relevant concepts that were theoretically developed over the last decades is presented, aiming at framing and discussing the problems previously raised. These concepts include the ideas of authenticity, significance, the environmental paradox, the importance of place, smart tourism, co-creation of destinations and experiences, the crucial role of information for the segmentation of markets and differentiation of supply, the life cycle of tourism destinations, path dependence processes, and the importance of history, variety, specialization, or integrative diversification of tourism products.

Considering the problems identified and the conceptual framework proposed, a set of challenges for the future of tourism in the twenty-first century is proposed in Sect. 6.4, with a view to policy and managerial implications. As the purpose of this analysis is to frame these challenges in a broad context of regional development processes, the territorial unit considered is that of the NUTS 2 regions (according to the Eurostat classification), which are the appropriate geographical and institutional levels for the definition of innovation and regional development policies, including the smart specialization strategies (Foray et al. 2012; Boschma 2016) under implementation in Europe. Also in other parts of the world, similar territorial levels are used in order to define and to implement regional economic, innovation, or tourism plans and strategies. Thus, this chapter offers a systematic and conclusive overview of all the aspects discussed in the previous chapters of this book, aiming at offering a policy-oriented strategic perspective for the future of tourism.

6.2 Problematizing Contemporary Tourism

Taking into consideration the conceptual framework discussed in the previous chapters and the results of the empirical analysis related to the previously mentioned case studies, this chapter problematizes some crucial aspects of contemporary tourism dynamics. Taking the European case as a departure point, the analysis can be extended to other parts of the world where tourism plays a prominent role.

6.2.1 Nature and Tourism

The relationship between tourism and nature is, from a spatial perspective, complex, as discussed in Chap. 3. By using spatial econometric techniques (panel data models with spatial effects and local indicators of spatial autocorrelation), two studies (Case Studies 3.1 and 3.2, presented in Chap. 3), including 237 European NUTS 2 regions and focused on the relation between natural resources, tourism demand, and gross value added by tourism activities, lead to the identification of relevant problems related to the sustainable use of those resources, at least in South European regions. These are regions where tourism demand is generally relatively high in the European context, while large parts of their territories are included on the Natura 2000 network (a European standard applied with the same criteria in all regions, which has been used as a proxy for their biodiversity and the value of the existing natural assets).

In a first study (Romão 2015), local spatial autocorrelation indicators revealed a positive spatial correlation between tourism demand, bed places available, and natural resources in the Western Mediterranean area, with the identification of clusters of regions with high tourism demand and a high level of protected natural resources in some regions of Portugal, Spain, France, Italy, or Austria, while low values for both cases were identified mostly in Northern European regions. In the regression (spatial panel data) model computed, it was confirmed that the abundance of natural resources was positively correlated with high levels of tourism demand. Nevertheless, a second study (Romão et al. 2017) revealed different results when the dependent variable of the model was replaced – instead of tourism demand (measured by the number of nights spent in accommodation establishments) – by the gross value added by tourism activities. In this case, the expected positive impacts of natural resources on regional tourism dynamics were not observed, leading, on the contrary, to a negative correlation between these two variables.

Although it could be argued that this type of negative correlation could be linked to the type of data used in the model (protective measures implemented in Natura 2000 areas could prompt a reduction in tourism dynamics), it was observed in the first study that these regions with more protected natural areas are also those where tourism demand is higher. This was confirmed by indicators of spatial autocorrelation revealing the existence of a large number of regions from Southern Europe, where abundant natural resources coexist with high levels of tourism demand and a low value added by tourism activities. Globally, these results confirm that massive forms of tourism generate low positive impacts on regional economies, despite the potential negative impacts on ecosystems and landscapes, which is a problem that must be addressed in any destination in the world. In that sense, segmentation approaches like those presented for the natural heritage site of Shiretoko (Japan) in Case Studies 2.1 (Neuts et al. 2016) and 3.3 (Romão et al. 2014) have particular relevance for their contribution for the identification of the most suitable market segments to be targeted.

6.2.2 Innovation and Tourism

Tourism is increasingly considered as a knowledge-based activity in the context of intense technological and social innovation, as discussed in detail in Chap. 4. Case Study 4.3 (Romão and Nijkamp 2017) focused on the impact of immaterial elements of the territorial capital of each region (as a precondition for innovation dynamics, as defined by Capello et al. 2011) on the gross value added by the tourism sector, as a proxy for its competitiveness. Following a similar methodology based on spatial econometric techniques and analyzing the same large set of European regions as it was done for the previously mentioned case studies (3.1 and 3.2), the purpose of the analysis was to discuss how and if these preconditions (like the qualifications of human resources or the investment in research and development activities) could exert a significant impact on regional tourism competitiveness.

Although the results of the model confirmed some expected positive impacts on tourism competitiveness (level of tourism demand, investment in the tourism sector, or the level of specialization in tourism, when measured by the share of the gross value added by the sector within the regional gross value added), when specialization was measured taking into consideration the share of the work force employed in tourism, a negative correlation with tourism competitiveness could be found. This result suggests that regions where the tourism sector is more labor-intensive register lower levels of productivity, with lower levels of gross value added and lower impacts on the regional economies.

Similarly to the previous case studies, the analysis of local indicators of spatial autocorrelation revealed that Southern European regions are those where these problems appear to be more pronounced. Although the tourism demand or the investment in tourism is generally very high for these regions, a clear lack of connection was observed between tourism, education of the work force, investments in research and development activities, and productivity in the tourism sector, suggesting important difficulties for the integration of knowledge into innovation processes. It was also clear that regions where education, innovation, and productivity achieve a higher importance (mostly in Northern Europe) are also those where gross value added in tourism is less relevant in the context of the regional economies.

It is noteworthy that European regions are among those with the highest levels of labor qualifications or innovation capabilities at the global level. Thus, if the relation between tourism and regional innovation dynamics is remarkably weak in the European context, it is possible to expect even more problematic situations in other parts of the world. Moreover, the negative impacts of some aspects of the integration of tourism into the contemporary creative patterns of consumption and production in contemporary societies may contribute to exacerbate problems of gentrification, inflation, or housing shortage in urban areas, as discussed in detail in Chap. 4.

6.2.3   Tourism and Regional Growth

The role of tourism as a determinant of economic growth was discussed in Chap. 2 and also analyzed within this series of studies on the contemporary dynamics of European tourism. A third level of analysis was presented in Case Study 2.3 (Romão and Nijkamp Forthcoming), considering the same group of regions and using similar spatial econometric techniques in order to analyze the relation between territorial capital, tourism dynamics, and economic growth, measured by the regional gross domestic product per capita. In this case, it was observed that regions more specialized in tourism and regions where natural resources are more abundant tend to show lower levels of revenue per capita, suggesting low impacts and benefits for the local economies arising from these territorial assets and economic activities. This analysis confirmed the results previously obtained by Milio (2014), concluding that regions more specialized in tourism and construction revealed lower levels of resilience when facing the international economic crisis started in 2007.

These results also suggest a process of divergence between Southern (where tourism demand and specialization are more important) and Northern European regions, showing that those regions where tourism has a greater importance for the creation of value added are also among the less-developed ones within the European context. At the same time, high levels of investment in the tourism sector were observed in Southern Europe, potentially contributing to high sunk costs in terms of equipment and infrastructures, which are not necessarily useful for other economic activities. On the other hand, regional specialization patterns concentrated around tourism activities tend to generate new opportunities for complementary services, new business, or start-up companies, reinforcing the importance of the tourism sector, while focusing the regional knowledge, labor skills, and innovation capabilities in these activities. This can be seen as a process of *path dependence lock-in* (Martin 2014), also revealing that tourism is far from reaching its potential leading role as a driver of regional innovation dynamics, by reinforcing its linkages with other – and more advanced – potentially related sectors (Neffke et al. 2009), as discussed in Chap. 4.

These results also confirm the concerns expressed by Capó et al. (2007), concluding that the positive impacts of tourism on regional economies tend to decrease over time, potentially becoming negative in the long run. This is related to the processes of high investments of tourism products and services during the process of quick development of a tourist destination, potentially contributing to the reduction of importance of other economic sectors, including agriculture and manufacturing. In fact, a similar process has also been identified for the region of Algarve, located in the South of Portugal, where tourism reveals a high socio-economic importance (Romão et al. 2016). This example (presented in Case Study 2.2) may be seen as illustrative of the vulnerability of regional economies depending on tourism, independently of their location.

6.2.4 Tourism and Sustainable Development

The relationship between tourism, environmental quality, and sustainable development is an uneasy one, as discussed in Chap. 5. The final study concerning this analysis of European tourism dynamics (Romão and Neuts 2017, presented in Case Study 5.2) analyzes the impacts of different aspects of territorial capital (both material and immaterial assets) of European regions, along with their tourism dynamics, on the three pillars of sustainable development (economic, social, and environmental) and, in particular, on the specific goals where tourism is expected to exert a positive influence (UNWTO 2015) within the Millennium Goals defined by the United Nations Organization (United Nations 2015). This analysis comprises a larger set or NUTS 2 regions (252) than the previously mentioned studies. Here, a structural equation model has been used, in order to deal with three dependent variables, used to assess the different dimensions of sustainability (GDP per habitant for the economic dimension, unemployment rate for the social issues, and CO_2 emissions for the environmental factor).

Despite the different regional patterns of tourism dynamics coexisting in contemporary European regions, it could be observed that, for those where tourism assumes a larger socio-economic importance, the contribution of this sector to the achievement of the Millennium Goals is relatively poor. Confirming the results of the previous studies, this analysis also revealed that regions particularly endowed with natural resources are generally highly specialized in tourism, with a high tourism demand but reduced socio-economic impacts, generating a relatively low value added and leading to high levels of unemployment. As a positive note, these regions show a relatively good performance in terms of CO_2 emissions, which can also be related to the low development of manufacturing activities.

On the other hand, the level of education seems to exert a very high impact on regional growth at the European Level, but regions where specialization in tourism is higher (when measured by the share of this sector within regional employment) seem to be those where the work force is less educated. Nevertheless, high levels of education appear to be correlated with high levels of value added by tourism services, which suggests that the incorporation of knowledge into tourism products can contribute to the achievement of higher value added and higher socio-economic impacts in the regions. These different types of relations clearly reveal the heterogeneity of European regions regarding tourism dynamics and its socio-economic impacts, which seem to depend on a broader set of variables.

Again, it is noteworthy that if a weak impact of tourism dynamics on the processes of regional sustainable development is observed within the European context, this relation can be much more problematic in less-developed parts of the world. With less-developed technological capabilities and more vulnerable socio-economic structures and specialization patterns, these regions may tend to exacerbate the importance of tourism and the pressure for an overutilization of sensitive territorial resources, without generating a high value added for the local economies.

6.3   Conceptual Framework for a New Agenda

Taking into consideration the main problems identified in the previous chapter and the overall conceptualization presented along this book, this chapter offers a synthesis of the main ideas underlying a conceptual framework to analyze and to address those problems.

6.3.1   Authenticity, Significance, the Environmental Paradox, and the Importance of Place

As a place-based activity, the consumption of tourism services implies the physical presence of the consumers in the place where products and services are provided. Thus, this production relies on the utilization of territorial resources, which, at the same time, must be preserved for the future. This *environmental paradox*, as defined by Williams and Ponsford (2009), emphasizes the importance of the sustainable use of resources, which are essential for the supply of a broad set of tourism services comprising a unique experience that can differentiate among each destination. Thus, these unique territorial resources are essential for the provision of an *authentic* tourism experience (Cohen 1988; Wait 2000), which cannot be replicated elsewhere. On the other hand, these particular features are experienced differently according to the characteristics, background, and motivations of different tourists, for whom these resources may be related to different types of *significance* (Chambers 2009), as discussed in Chap. 3. In this context, the preservation of local cultural values is a crucial aspect in the context of commoditization of culture and nature for tourism purposes and the generalization of processes of *co-creation* of experiences and destinations, where the supply of services tends to be adapted to the specific demands of each type of tourist.

In this sense, the concepts of competitiveness (linked to the provision of unique services with high valued for the visitors) and sustainability (linked to the preservation of resources for the future and the socio-economic impacts on local communities) are clearly linked, as pointed out by Ritchie and Crouch (2003) and discussed in detail in Chap. 5. Although, in a first stage (Poon 1994), the ideas of differentiation and sustainability were clearly connected to the concept of niche tourism (as opposite to mass tourism), as proposed in early attempts to adopt the strategic formulations for the achievement of competitive advantages proposed by Porter (1985), other authors (Butler 1999; Jafari 2001) have later on stressed the importance of this approach for all types of tourism destinations, with the necessary strategic adaptations depending on the position of each of them within its evolutionary life cycle (Butler 1980). In fact, since the late 1990s, a large number of authors have discussed the ideas of uniqueness and differentiation within the context of the need to preserve territorial resources and to control their utilization.

It seems also clear that the creation of a unique tourism experience based on local territorial resources enhances the possible connections with other related economic sectors, reinforcing the potential impacts on regional economies, as analyzed in Chap. 4. In this context, it is not surprising that most international organizations with competences on tourism regulation and policies have defined principles and guidelines for tourism development taking into consideration the long-term relations between the ideas of competitiveness and sustainability in tourism, as can be witnessed in documents published by UNESCO (2000, 2005), the European Commission (2007), the World Economic Forum (2008), or UNWTO (2007, 2013, 2015).

6.3.2 Smart Tourism, Co-creation of Destinations and Experiences, and the Importance of Information

As a place-based activity, tourism services also present the particular characteristic of co-terminality (direct interaction between producer and consumer), along with spatiality and temporality (consumption and production of tourism services occur in the same place at the same time). With the recent and ongoing progress in the development of information and communication technologies, this potential circulation of information and interaction between tourism service providers and users has clearly increased, enhancing the potential for the development of practice and place-based innovation strategies, as analyzed in detail in Chap. 4. Moreover, contemporary societal dynamics leading to a convergence between the economic and cultural spheres, through the commodification of culture and the integration of cultural values and symbols into products and services (Scott 2017), also contributes to emphasize the importance of the tourism experiences, as a dynamic part of the contemporary creative economies (OECD 2014), with potential positive impacts on regional innovation dynamics.

Keeping in mind that innovation is essentially a localized learning process (European Commission 2007; Hjalager 2010), tourism destinations can be seen as cooperative innovative networks, where the coordination of a large set of products and services being offered – often by small or very small companies – must meet the particular needs, motivations, and perceptions of a largely segmented market, with different types of consumers. In particular, the increased interoperability offered by the developments related to the emergence of the so-called social networks (*Web 2.0*), with their mobile applications (*Web 3.0*), creates better conditions for the development of processes of *co-creation* of services (Liburd and Christensen 2013) or to become *tools of mass collaboration* (Sigala 2009). These collaborative processes can offer relevant impacts on the development of new, personalized, and innovative services (Sigala 2009) but also on the implementation of collaborative governance models (Sigala and Marinidis 2012) or education and training processes (Liburd and Christensen 2013).

In this context, the concept of *smart tourism* has recently also emerged (Boes et al. 2016), following a tendency to conceptualize processes of spatial or socio-economic development in contemporary societies (smart cities, smart specialization, smart development), by incorporating the potential contributions of new digital technologies to planning processes related to various aspects of life (environmental control, resource management, spatial planning, social balance, governance models, etc.). In the case of *smart tourism*, these aspects can be addressed at the destination level within processes of *coopetition* developed among companies, institutions, and communities which do not necessarily share the same objectives (in fact, companies tend to be rivals) but need to cooperate in order to ensure the preservation of resources, authenticity of the local experiences, benefits for the local communities, shared use of resources, services and public spaces between tourists and residents, or other business-oriented activities like the promotion of the destination.

6.3.3   Tourism Life Cycle, Path Dependence, and the Importance of History

The importance of the analysis of the evolution of a tourism destination over time – and its policy and managerial implications – was early systematized by Butler (1980) in his conceptualization of the *tourism area life cycle*, by applying to tourism the product life cycle approaches developed in marketing and management studies. In the context of tourism, this analysis points out the differences over time of the type of visitors, influence on daily life of hosting communities, socio-economic impacts, investments in services, amenities and infrastructures, promotional efforts, or resource management, implying different strategic responses and initiatives in different historical moments. These aspects were discussed in detail in Chap. 2.

Emphasizing the spatial and historical dimensions of development processes, the conceptual framework proposed by the evolutionary economic geography (EEG) approach (Boschma and Martin 2010) seems particularly relevant for the analysis of place-based economic activities, as is the case for tourism. In particular, Ma and Hassink (2013) or Sanz-Ibáñez and Clavé (2014) linked this theoretical framework to the evolving character of tourism destinations proposed by Butler. Brouder and Eriksson (2013) offered a synthesis of the potential contributions of EEG to tourism studies, including the concepts of related variety (how different sectors are structurally interconnected) or regional branching (how the recombination of existing economic conditions, infrastructures, and knowledge can lead to the emergence of new types of business).

Central to this approach is the concept of *path dependence* (discussed in detail in Chap. 2 and described in Sect. 6.3.3), a set of territorial characteristics, which define the initial conditions for regional development, by influencing and constraining the possible future outcome. The synthesis proposed by Martin (2014) for the main sources of path dependence can be clearly applied to the analysis of tourism destinations: natural resources (which are, in many cases, central aspects of tourism attractiveness); sunk costs of local productive, physical, and infrastructural assets (with particular importance for the cases of transport infrastructures or large entertainment facilities); agglomeration economies, local external economies of specialization, or localized spin-off firm births (interaction dynamics and agglomeration process within related economic activities); interregional linkages and dependencies (frequently occurring in the tourism sector, as travellers often visit more than one destination, not necessarily within the same administrative territorial unit); or local technological lock-in (as a result of the concentration of knowledge production in a prominent economic sector, which, in the case of tourism, does not seem particularly advanced). It seems clear that the dynamics of the tourism sector and the processes of regional development are strongly dependent on the initial conditions each region has to face.

6.3.4   Integrative Diversification, Specialization, and the Importance of Variety

Assuming the evolution of a regional economic system as a historical and place-dependent process of mutation, where knowledge spillovers arising from the interaction between different agents (and sectors) potentially generate innovative solutions, the strategy of tourism product development and destination differentiation proposed by Benur and Bramwell (2015) – *integrative diversification*, by integrating secondary products and services into the core elements of the regional tourism supply – is particularly relevant. This strategic approach, aiming at the diversification and increasing value added of tourism supply, seems to be compatible with the EEG conceptual framework, which focus on the internal processes and mechanisms by which an economy self-transforms itself, assuming a spatially uneven distribution of economic activities evolving along time.

In this sense, the concepts of path dependence (how past decisions, development processes, or traditions act as preconditions for the present actions and outcomes) and related variety (interconnections between related economic sectors) appear as particularly useful when analyzing not only the diversification of tourism services and destination management but also their connection to other economic activities, in the broader context of regional innovation or development policies. In particular, the incorporation of knowledge and new technological developments related to information and communication technologies, multimedia production, transportation solutions, or energy production and consumption appears to have a high potential to develop more close and strong connections with innovation dynamics in tourism.

As observed in Case Study 2.3 (Romão and Nijkamp Forthcoming), regions where tourism achieves a higher importance within the regional economy are also those where investment in the tourism sector is higher (and also correlated with low levels of economic growth), which can be related to sunk costs, agglomeration processes, and interdependencies, as sources of path dependence. On the other hand, regions with high specialization in tourism show, in general, low levels of qualification of the work force, along with low investments in research and development activities, as shown in Case Study 4.3 (Romão and Nijkamp 2017). Although this disadvantage in terms of knowledge production and innovation capabilities appears as an obstacle, a structural transformation and diversification of these regional economies (mostly in Southern Europe), reducing the dependence of tourism activities, seems to be needed in order to achieve higher levels of value added for the local economies and well-being for the resident population.

6.4   Outlook: Challenges for Tourism in the Twenty-First Century

Assuming the questions problematized in Sect. 6.2 as a departure point and the conceptual systematization presented in Sect. 6.3 as an analytical framework, this chapter identifies three major challenges for the future of tourism, implying a continuous effort on academic research and on the integration of new knowledge into planning processes, governance practices, and entrepreneurial initiatives, necessarily adapted to the characteristics of each destination.

6.4.1   Memorable Trips: Sustainable Use of Resources for Personalized Significant Experiences

Tourism is mostly about providing memorable experiences, which offer value to the visitors, according to different motivations, perceptions, and needs. In the context of a globalized competition, this segmentation of demand requires an accurate and precise differentiation of supply, in order to meet the needs and desires of different consumers, taking advantage of the interoperability based on large fluxes of information arising from the utilization of information and communication technologies within the tourism sector. This communication between producers, consumers, and institutional managers emerges as a powerful tool to enhance the processes of *co-creation* of experiences, potentially contributing to innovation services and practices. Taking into account that the uniqueness of these experiences relies on the *commodified* utilization of sensitive resources, adequate management processes are required in order to guarantee their preservation, along with the provision of a *significant* experience for different types of tourists, as discussed in Chap. 3.

To do so, this process of differentiation must be rooted in the *authenticity* and uniqueness of the local territorial resources, the local cultural values, and the carrying capacity of sensitive resources, both at natural and cultural levels, and also including the utilization of public spaces, local services, or transportation networks. This question has prompted important problems during the 1960s and 1970s, when a very strong and massive development of tourism in coastal areas was observed, with important negative impacts on ecosystems and landscapes. Today, with the new tourism trends and the massification of urban tourism, new challenges can be observed in the context of cities, with new problems related to inflationary processes (at least in some urban centers), house shortage or inflation in rents, congestion in transportation networks, or commodification of local cultures.

Along with the preservation of local sensitive resources, both related to the natural and cultural aspects of the destination, which seem to require the involvement of diverse representative stakeholders within participatory management processes based on collective decisions, also more global changes – including in lifestyles – seem to be needed in order to ensure the sustainability of tourism development. The impressive dynamics of tourism in contemporary societies appears as closely linked to a significant increase in air travelling, which is a major contributor for the global CO_2 emissions. Thus, new travelling patterns oriented to short trips (using public transports, like trains, and complemented at the destination by soft modes of transportation, like cycling or walking) appear as a plausible alternative to long-distance travels (using planes).

6.4.2   Diverse Economies: Tourism in the Context of a Creative Innovative Economy

As observed, digital technologies – not only related to information and communication but also related to multimedia production or geo-representation and visualization – with an increasing number of possible applications in mobile devices have a high potential for development within the tourism sector, potentially contributing for the match between destination differentiation and consumer segmentation, to the achievement of higher value added, for the integration of knowledge into products and services, or for the improvement of the qualifications of the labor force involved in the sector. Moreover, the rising importance of the integration of cultural and symbolic values into products and services – and, in particular, in the tourism experiences – can contribute to benefit a large number of creative activities, as observed in Chap. 4.

Nevertheless, the relatively poor achievements – in terms of economic growth, sustainable development, or socio-economic resilience – observed in the regions most dependent on tourism, suggest the importance of a reorganization of their regional economic structures. It is also important to notice that a regional process of specialization focused on a small number of related sectors tends to increase the potential spin-offs between them, but it also increases the vulnerability of the regional economic structure to negative impacts on those sectors. Keeping in mind the relative volatility of tourism demand, which is extremely sensitive to factors that are not easily controllable (weather conditions, fashion and trends, emergence of new destinations, variations on available income, or security threats), it seems advisable to develop a balanced economic structure that is not strictly dependent on tourism activities.

Moreover, as it has been observed, tourism services do not always generate high levels of value added to the regional economy and do often not incorporate advanced knowledge and technology. Thus, mostly when regions are in the development stage of tourism development, with a high growth of tourism demand and the consequent expectations for high returns on investment in the short run, it seems important, in the context of regional policies, to ensure that the development of tourism-related activities is followed by the development of other economic sectors, which can contribute to a higher integration of knowledge, innovation, qualified human resources, and value added in the regional economies.

6.4.3 Shared Spaces: Communities, Participatory Governance, and Sustainable Development

There is no tourism without tourists and there is no destination without communities of residents. Thus, public spaces, public and private services, natural and cultural resources, or transportation and mobility services and infrastructures, which are used for the daily life of residents, must be shared with an increasing number of visitors, in the context of a continuous and relatively high growth of tourism activities, as observed in Chaps. 4 and 5. This implies new problems and requires coordination and regulation policies, both in rural areas (where the implications on sensitive natural resources are more relevant) and urban centers (where congestion, inflation, or gentrification processes are more important). Although the general principles for sustainable or smart development call for the implementation of participatory processes of governance at local level, this aspect is far from being implemented in most places. The (sometimes massive) presence of tourists temporarily living within a local community creates new problems and challenges regarding the shared use of resources. Keeping in mind that tourism, like any other economic activity, should contribute to the well-being of the communities, the potential problems and benefits related to their presence should be adequately addressed.

On the other hand, it also noted that most of the economic benefits of contemporary tourism tend to be concentrated within the transportation and accommodation sectors, with low impacts on the social and economic pillars of sustainable development of tourism destinations (and eventually with high negative impacts on the environmental pillar). Thus, the integration of tourism development plans within broader regional development strategies, reinforcing the linkage between tourism, creative activities or other economic sectors, aiming at reinforcing the value added of tourism services, incorporation of knowledge, and regional innovation dynamics appear as crucial in order to fulfill the high potential of tourism to generate positive spillovers on the local economies, along with higher impacts on social cohesion.

In this context, the effective implementation of participatory processes of decision, planning, management, and monitoring of tourism destinations appears as a crucial aspect of future development, assuming that tourism will continue to increase in the future. The awareness to this problem already assumed at international level, the potential role of information and communication technologies enhancing the processes of collective decision-making, and the increasing levels of education and social awareness of the populations seem to create adequate conditions for the implementation of such processes. Tourism is on a rising edge all over the world, but economic and political cycles cause quite some fragility for this sector, so that a broad-based and well-anchored tourism sector seems to be a wise strategy for all stakeholders involved.

6.5 Concluding Remarks

By using the results previously obtained in a series of studies about the regional dynamics of contemporary European tourism, this concluding chapter aimed at proposing and discussing a conceptual framework for the analysis of some relevant problems observed, mostly in regions where tourism achieves higher importance within the regional economic structures (as it is the case of most of the Southern European regions). Although this analysis was focused on European destinations, the fact that very diverse types of regions were considered (with high and low economic development, different patterns of specialization and tourism dynamics, diverse cultural and natural endowments, or different innovation and technological capabilities) allows to generalize the conclusions and recommendations to a broader geographical perspective, considering the global challenges faced by contemporary tourism.

From this conceptual framework, three major challenges for tourism development were proposed, aiming at overcoming the problems identified and raising some questions to be addressed at policy and managerial level, not only in the strict sense of tourism dynamics but mostly focusing on the relation between tourism, territorial resource management, innovation policies, specialization patterns, or living conditions of the host communities. Aspects related to the incorporation of information and knowledge into the tourism sector and to different levels of territorial governance appear as crucial elements, as they can impact the three challenges previously identified.

The development and increasing interoperability related to information and communication technologies have led to a deep transformation in the tourism sector in the last 20 years. Concepts like the *co-creation* of tourism destinations or smart tourism emerged in the literature, reflecting new business and managerial practices, increasing incorporation of information and knowledge, while contributing for a more transparent, informed, and fruitful experience. This process can lead to the development of new services, with higher value added and requiring more skilled human resources. On the other hand, new and more precise processes of monitoring tourism flows and resource management by policy institution can benefit from these technological developments, while participatory processes of analysis and decision-making can potentially be implemented, involving the different stakeholders involved in the complex tourism system, including the communities of residents in tourism destinations.

The incorporation of information, knowledge, and technology into tourism products and services calls for their integration into broader innovation and human resource plans, requiring policies that can frame the tourism sector within the regional socio-economic strategies. This framework is also necessary in order to guarantee a balanced economic structure, where the connections between tourism and other sectors can be maximized, while preventing the dependency on the fluctuations of tourism demand. On the other hand, the utilization of sensitive territorial resources related to nature or culture, along with the management of public spaces and infrastructures, requires the implementation of processes of participatory decision, involving the local population in planning and monitoring tourism development and its impacts.

The general problems and challenges proposed can have different characteristics and importance in different regions. Aspects like the position of each destination within the tourism life cycle, the importance of tourism for the regional economy, the level of qualifications and type of skills of the working force, the innovation capabilities, or the investments already made in tourism-related equipment and infrastructures clearly impose different conditions and constrains for the implementation of new policies. At the institutional level, the maturity and coordination between different regulatory and planning organisms or the tradition on community-based participatory decisions can also vary according to local social and historical conditions. In that sense, specific research is required in each region in order to identify which are the crucial problems and challenges to be addressed.

References

Benur A, Bramwell B (2015) Tourism product development and product diversification in destinations. Tour Manag 50:213–224

Boes K, Buhalis D, Inversini A (2016) Smart tourism destinations: ecosystems for tourism destination competitiveness. Int J Tour Cities 2(2):108–124

Boschma R (2016) Smart specialisation and regional innovation policy. Welsh Econ Rev 24:17

Boschma R, Martin R (2010) The aims and scope of evolutionary economic geography. In: Boschma R, Martin R (eds) The handbook of evolutionary economic geography. Edward Elgar, Cheltenham, pp 3–39

Brouder P, Eriksson R (2013) Tourism evolution: on the synergies of tourism studies and evolutionary economic geography. Ann Tour Res 43:370–389

Butler R (1980) The concept of the tourist area life-cycle of evolution: implications for management of resources. Can Geogr 24(1):5–12

Butler R (1999) Sustainable tourism: a state-of-the-art review. Tour Geogr 1(1):7–25

Capello R, Caragliu A, Nijkamp P (2011) Territorial capital and regional growth: increasing returns in knowledge use. Tijdschr Econ Soc Geogr 102(4):385–405

Capó J, Font A, Nadal J (2007) Dutch disease in tourism economies: evidence from the Balearics and the Canary Islands. J Sustain Tour 15(6):615–627

Chambers E (2009) From authenticity to significance: tourism on the frontier of culture and place. Futures 41:353–359

Cohen E (1988) Authenticity and commoditization in tourism. Ann Tour Res 15:371–386

European Commission (2007) Agenda for a sustainable and competitive European tourism. European Commission, Luxembourg

Foray D, Goddard J, Beldarrain M, Landabaso M, McCann P, Morgan K, Nauwelaers C, Ortega-Argilés R (2012) Guide to research and innovation strategies for smart specialisation. S3P-European Union, Brussels

Hjalager A (2010) A review of innovation research in tourism. Tour Manag 31:1–12

Jafari J (2001) The scientification of tourism. In: Smith V, Brent M (eds) Hosts and guests revisited: tourism issues of the 21st century. Cognizant Communication Corporation, New York, pp 28–41

Liburd J, Christensen I (2013) Using web 2.0 in higher tourism education. J Hosp Leisure Sport Tour 12(1):99–108

Ma M, Hassink R (2013) An evolutionary perspective on tourism area development. Ann Tour Res 41:89–109

Martin R (2014) Path dependence and the spatial economy. In: Fischer M, Nijkamp P (eds) Handbook of regional science. Springer, New York, pp 609–629

Milio S (2014) Impact of the economic crisis on social, economic and territorial cohesion of the European Union, Vol. 1. Directorate-General for Internal Policies, Policy Department B (Structural and Cohesion Policies), Brussels

Neffke F, Henning M, Boschma R (2009) How do regions diversify over time? Industry relatedness and the development of new growth paths in regions. Econ Geogr 87(3):237–265

Neuts B, Romão J, Nijkamp P, Shikida A (2016) Market segmentation and their economic impacts in an ecotourism destination: an applied modelling study on Hokkaido, Japan. Tour Econ 22(4):793–808

OECD (2014) Tourism and the creative economy. OECD Studies on Tourism, Paris

Poon A (1994) The 'new tourism' revolution. Tour Manag 15(2):91–92

Porter M (1985) Competitive advantage – creating and sustaining superior performance. The Free Press, New York

Ritchie J, Crouch G (2003) The competitive destination: a sustainable tourism perspective. CABI International, Oxfordshire

Romão J (2015) Culture or nature: a space-time analysis on the determinants of tourism demand in European regions. Discussion Papers Spatial and Organizational Dynamics 14

Romão J, Neuts B (2017) Smart tourism, territorial capital, and sustainable regional development: experiences from Europe. Habitat Int 68:64–74

Romão J, Nijkamp P (2017) Impacts of innovation, productivity and agglomeration on tourism competitiveness – a spatial econometric analysis of European regions. Curr Issue Tour. https://doi.org/10.1080/13683500.2017.1366434

Romão J, Nijkamp P (Forthcoming) Impacts of tourism and territorial capital on regional development in Europe: a spatial econometric investigation

Romão J, Neuts B, Nijkamp P, Shikida A (2014) Determinants of trip choice, satisfaction and loyalty in an eco-tourism destination: a modeling study on the Shiretoko Peninsula, Japan. Ecol Econ 107:195–205

Romão J, Guerreiro J, Rodrigues PMM (2016) Tourism growth and regional resilience: the "beach disease" and the consequences of the global crisis of 2007. Tour Econ 22(4):699–714

Romão J, Guerreiro J, Rodrigues PMM (2017) Territory and sustainable tourism development: a space-time analysis on European regions. Region 4(3):1–17

Sanz-Ibáñez C, Clavé S (2014) The evolution of destinations: towards an evolutionary and relational economic geography approach. Tour Geogr 16(4):563–579

Scott AJ (2017) The constitution of the city. Palgrave Macmillan, Cham

Sigala M (2009) Web 2.0, social marketing strategies and distribution channels for City destinations. In: Gascó-Hernandez M, Torres-Coronas T (eds) Information communication technologies and City marketing. IGI Global, Hershey, pp 221–245

Sigala M, Marinidis D (2012) E-democracy and web 2.0. Tour Anal 17(2):105–120

UNESCO (2000) Sustainable tourism and the environment. UNESCO, Paris

UNESCO (2005) World heritage Centre – sustainable tourism Programme. UNESCO, Paris

United Nations (2015) Transforming our world: the 2030 agenda for sustainable development. In: A/RES/70/1, resolution adopted by the general assembly on 25 September 2015. York, New

UNWTO (2007) Practical guide to tourism destination management. UNWTO, Madrid

UNWTO (2013) Sustainable tourism for development guidebook. UNWTO, Madrid

UNWTO (2015) Tourism and the sustainable development goals. UNWTO, Madrid

UNWTO (2018) Tourism highlights. UNWTO, Madrid

Wait G (2000) Consuming heritage – perceived historical authenticity. Ann Tour Res 27(4):835–862

Williams P, Ponsford I (2009) Confronting tourism's environmental paradox: transitioning for sustainable tourism. Futures 41:396–404

World Economic Forum (2008) The travel & tourism competitiveness report 2008. WEF, Geneva

Printed by Printforce, the Netherlands